this Constitution

this Constitution
From Ratification to the Bill of Rights

American Political Science Association
American Historical Association

Congressional Quarterly Inc.

Library of Congress Cataloging-in-Publication Data

American Political Science Association.
    This Constitution: from ratification to the Bill of Rights/
American Political Science Association, American Historical
Association.
        p. cm.
    Includes index.
    Summary: Surveys the history of the Constitution, its origins,
ratification, adaptation, and possible future.
ISBN 0-87187-464-4
    1. United States--Constitutional history.
[1. United States--Constitutional history.] I. American Historical
Association. II. Title.
KF4541.Z9A54   1988
342.73'029--dc19
[347.30229]   88-412
                         CIP
                         AC

Illustration Acknowledgments appear on p. 299.

Contents

Preface

In 1982, Project '87, a joint effort of the American Historical Association and the American Political Science Association, began publication of a quarterly magazine entitled *this Constitution: A Bicentennial Chronicle.* Conceived and developed by Sheilah Mann, the director of Project '87, and supported by the National Endowment for the Humanities as part of its special initiative on the Bicentennial of the United States Constitution, *this Constitution* provided a link between the scholars of constitutional history, politics, and theory and a public audience engaged in thinking about constitutional questions. Its final issue, number 18, appeared in the spring of 1988.

This volume is the second of two collections of essays from *this Constitution.* The first took articles from issues 1 through 12; this volume contains selections from issues 13 through 18.[1] The first collection highlighted constitutional principles and theory. This volume focuses on the founding period, beginning with the deliberations of the Constitutional Convention, proceeding to the public response to the document and its design for a government, then the initiation of the government under the new charter and the adoption of the Bill of Rights. The book concludes with essays devoted to questions of contemporary rights and constitutional adaptation.

The magazine benefited from the direction of its editorial board, chaired first by Harry Scheiber, University of California at Berkeley, then by Frank Sorauf, University of Minnesota, and finally by Milton Klein, University of Tennessee. Other members included Patricia Bonomi, New York University; Frances K. Burke, Suffolk University; Bonnie Cochran, Bethesda-Chevy Chase (Md.) High School; Milton C. Cummings, Johns Hopkins University; Charles Eldredge, National Museum of American Art; Margaret Horsnell, American International College; James O. Horton, George Washington University; Gary Puckrein, National Museum of American History; Dot Ridings, League

---

[1] The article by Paul J. Weber, "Call a Second Convention?", appears for the first time in this volume.

of Women Voters; and Richard Wilson, Montgomery County (Md.) Public Schools. Charles S. Snyder created the original design for the magazine and laid out each issue; Rebecca Hirsh found the photographs that accompany the articles.

Support for *this Constitution* came also from the founders of Project '87—James MacGregor Burns and Richard B. Morris—and the members of the joint committee of scholars, which has governed Project '87 over the last decade.

The ultimate contribution came from the authors who responded to Project '87's invitation to share their expertise with a wider national and international audience. Through their efforts, the magazine, like all of Project '87's materials and programs, has rested upon a solid foundation of scholarship, tailored to the specific needs of readers and users in public and educational settings.

Project '87 is grateful to the staff of Congressional Quarterly, especially David R. Tarr, Colleen McGuiness, Carolyn McGovern, and Kathryn C. Suárez, for making the articles from *this Constitution* available to a still larger readership.

Cynthia Harrison
Managing Editor, *this Constitution*
Deputy Director, Project '87

I. The Constitutional Convention: The Setting, the Players, and the Outcome

The Origins of the Constitution

Gordon S. Wood

When did the story of the Constitution begin? Some might say it began more than twenty-five hundred years ago in the city-states of ancient Greece. Others might place its beginnings nearly three-quarters of a millennium back in the fields of Runnymede. Still others might say the Constitution had its origins three centuries or so ago during the tumultuous years of the seventeenth-century English revolutions. Or others, more patriotic perhaps, might date the beginnings of the Constitution from events in the Western Hemisphere, from the Mayflower Compact, the Massachusetts Charter of 1629, or from any number of charters and constitutional documents that the colonists resorted to during the first century and a half of American history. More likely, the story of the Constitution might begin with the imperial crisis and debate of the 1760s. It is just possible that the forty years between 1763 and 1803 in America were the greatest era in constitutionalism in modern Western history. Not only did Americans establish the modern conception of a constitution as a written document defining and delimiting the powers of government, but they also made a number of other significant constitutional contributions to the world, including the device of a convention for creating and amending constitutions, the process of popular ratification of constitutions, and the practice of judicial review by which judges measure ordinary legislation against the fundamental law of the constitution. During these brief forty years of great constitutional achievements between 1763 and 1803 the story of the Constitution of 1787 is only a chapter. But it is a crucial and significant chapter.

It is hard for us today to appreciate what an extraordinary, unforeseen achievement the Constitution of 1787 was. We take a strong national government so much for granted that we can scarcely understand why the American Revolution-

3

aries of 1776 did not create the Constitution at once. But in 1776 virtually no American contemplated something like the Constitution of 1787. No one in 1776 even imagined for Americans a powerful continental-wide national government operating directly on individuals. The colonists in the British empire had experienced enough abuses from far-removed governmental power to make them leery of creating another distant government. And besides, the best minds of the eighteenth century, including Montesquieu, said that a large continental-sized republic was a theortetical impossibility. In 1776 it was obvious to all Americans that their central government would have to be a confederation of some sort, some sort of league or alliance of the thirteen independent states. The Articles of Confederation created such a central government.

Confederation

    The Articles of Confederation were our first national constitution. Proposed by the Continental Congress in 1777, they were not ratified by all the states until 1781. Although we today pay very little attention to the Articles and can hardly take them seriously, at the time they were a remarkable achievement. The Articles created a much stronger federal government than many Americans expected; it was in fact as strong as any similar republican confederation in history. Not only were substantial powers concerning diplomacy, the requisitioning of soldiers, and the borrowing of money granted to the Confederation Congress, but the Articles specifically forbade the separate states to conduct foreign affairs, make treaties, and declare war. All travel restrictions and discriminatory trade barriers between the states were eliminated, and the citizens of each state were entitled to the "privileges and immunities" of the citizens of all states. When we compare these achievements with what the present-day European nations are struggling to attain in their own continental union, we can better appreciate what an extraordinary accomplishment the Articles represented.

    Despite the notable strength of this Confederation, however, it was clear that it was something less than a unitary national government. Under the Articles the crucial powers of commercial regulation and taxation—indeed, all final lawmaking authority—remained with the states. Congressional resolutions were only recommendations to be left to the states to enforce. And should there be any doubts of the decentralized nature of the Confederation, Article 2 stated bluntly that "each

Fort Oswego on Lake Ontario, one of the outposts where the British maintained troops in violation of the 1783 Treaty of Paris

State retains its sovereignty, freedom and independence, and every power, jurisdiction, and right, which is not by this confederation expressly delegated to the United States, in Congress assembled." The "United States of America" had a literal meaning that is unfamiliar to us today. The Confederation was based on the equal representation of each state in the Congress. It was less a single government than it was a treaty among sovereign states. It was intended to be and remained, as Article 3 declared, "a firm league of friendship" among states jealous of their individuality. Not only ratification of the Articles of Confederation but any subsequent amendment of them required the consent of all the states.

As a confederation the United States achieved a good deal, including the winning of the war and independence from Great Britain. But scarcely a half dozen years after the final ratification of the Articles in 1781, the Confederation was virtually moribund and nearly every American was calling for its reform. The Confederation government was not adequate to the demands of the 1780s; a more powerful central government was needed. The calling of the Philadelphia Convention in 1787 and the new Constitution were the results.

It seems to be a simple story, but it is not. For despite a general dissatisfaction with the Articles by 1786-1787 and a general willingness to add to the powers of Congress, the

Constitution that was created in 1787 was not what most people expected. The new federal government was not simply a stronger league of friendship with some additional powers granted to the Congress. It was a radically new government altogether—one that utterly transformed the structure of central authority and greatly weakened the power of the states. The Constitution of 1787 created an overarching national republic that operated on individuals directly; its creation was inconceivable a decade earlier. What had happened? What could have changed American thinking so dramatically? Given the Americans' loyalty to their states and their deep-rooted fears of centralized governmental authority, explaining the Constitution of 1787 is not as easy as it looks.

Some Americans in the 1780s talked about a crisis in the United States, and historians have seized upon this talk and labeled the 1780s "the Critical Period of American History." Yet documenting a real crisis in the society, a crisis sufficient to justify the radical change of government in 1787, is not a simple matter. To be sure, there was an economic depression in 1784-1785 caused by the buying spree and the overextensions of credit following the war, but by 1786 the country was coming out of it and people were aware of returning prosperity. Commerce was confused and disrupted, but the commercial outlook was far from bleak. American merchants were pushing out in every direction in search of markets and were sailing even as far away as China. The 1780s do not seem to be a time of crisis; they were in fact a time of unprecedented exuberance and expansion. The American population grew as never before (or since), and more Americans than ever were off in pursuit of happiness and prosperity. "There is not upon the face of the earth a body of people more happy or rising into consequence with more rapid stride, than the inhabitants of the United States of America," the secretary of the Continental Congress Charles Thomson wrote Thomas Jefferson in 1786. "Population is increasing, new houses building, new lands clearing, new settlements forming, and new manufacturers establishing with a rapidity beyond conception." The general mood was optimistic and expectant.

No wonder then that many historians have doubted that there was anything really critical happening in the society. Perhaps the critical period, wrote Charles Beard in his *An Economic Interpretation of the Constitution* published in 1913, was not really critical after all, "but a phantom of the imagination produced by some undoubted evils which could have been remedied without a political revolution." Perhaps the crisis, said Jackson Turner Main in his 1961 study, *Antifederalists*, was only "conjured up" by a few leaders since "actually the country faced no such emergency." Was the movement for the Constitution something of a fraud without justification in the social and economic reality of the day?

But then we have all those despairing statements by Americans in the 1780s declaring that America was in the midst of a crisis more serious than anything experienced during the darkest days of the war. Many believed that America's great experiment in republicanism was in danger and that America's "vices" were plunging the nation into "ruin." The enlightened Philadelphia physician Benjamin Rush went so far as to say that Americans were on the verge of "degenerating into savages or devouring each other like beasts of prey." Even the sober and restrained George Washington was astonished at the changes the few years since 1776 had produced: "From the high ground we stood upon, from the plain path which invited our footsteps, to be so fallen! so lost! it is really mortifying."

How can we explain such excited and despondent statements—statements that can be multiplied over and over? What had happened? Could Americans, so confident in 1776, have lost their nerve so quickly? Could any problems with the Articles of Confederation, with the weaknesses of the union, have brought forth such fearful handwringing? Explaining the sense of crisis in the 1780s and hence the movement for the Constitution requires something more than just detailing the defects of the Confederation Congress. Such defects, however serious, could hardly account for the pervasive sense of crisis.

There are in fact two levels of explanation for the Constitution, two different sets of problems, two distinct reform movements in the 1780s that eventually came together to form the Convention of 1787. One operated at the national level and involved problems of the Articles of Confederation. The other operated at the state level and involved problems in the state legislatures. The national problems account for the ready willingness of people in 1786-1787 to accede to the convening of delegates at Philadelphia. But the state problems, problems that went to the heart of America's experiment in republicanism, account for the radical and unprecedented nature of the federal government created in Philadelphia.

National Problems

The weaknesses of the Articles of Confederation were apparent early, even before the Articles were formally ratified in 1781. By 1780 the war was dragging on longer than anyone had expected, and the skyrocketing inflation of the paper money that was being used to finance it was unsettling commerce and business. The Articles barred congressional delegates from serving more than three years in any six-year period, and leadership in the Confederation was changeable and confused. The states were ignoring congressional resolutions and were refusing to supply their allotted contributions to the central government. The Congress stopped paying interest on the public debt. The Continental army was smoldering with resentment at the lack of pay and was falling apart through desertions and even outbreaks of mutiny. All these circumstances were forcing various groups, including the army and merchant and creditor interests centered in the mid-Atlantic states, to seek to add to the powers of the Congress. They tried to strengthen the Congress by broadly interpreting its enumerated powers, by directly amending the Articles, and even by threatening military force against those states that did not fulfill their obligations to Congress.

A shift in congressional leadership in the early 1780s demonstrated the increasing influence of these concerned groups. Older popular radicals such as Richard Henry Lee of Virginia and Samuel Adams of Massachusetts were replaced by such younger men as James Madison of Virginia and Alexander Hamilton of New York. These new leaders were more interested in authority and stability than in popular liberty. Disillusioned by the Confederation's ineffectiveness, these nationalists in the Congress set about reversing the localist and centrifugal thrust of the Revolution. They strengthened the regular army at the expense of the militia and promised pensions to the Continental army officers. They reorganized the departments of war, foreign affairs, and finance in the Congress and replaced the committees that had been running these department with individuals.

The key man in the nationalists' program was Robert Morris, a wealthy Philadelphia merchant who was made superintendent of finance and virtual head of the Confederation in 1781. Morris undertook to stabilize the economy and to involve financial and commercial groups with the central government. He persuaded the Congress to recommend to the states that paper-money laws be repealed and to require that the states' contributions to the general expenses be paid in specie (gold or silver coin), and he sought to establish a bank to make the federal government's bonds more secure for investors.

Carrying out this nationalist program depended on amending the Articles so as to grant the Confederation the power to levy a 5 percent duty on imports. Once the Congress had revenues independent of the states, the Confederation could pay its debts and would become more attractive to prospective buyers of its bonds. Although Morris was able to get the Congress to charter the Bank of North America, the rest of the nationalists' economic proposals failed to get the consent of all the states. In 1782 congressional efforts to get the states to approve the 5 percent import amendment foundered first on Rhode Island's refusal and then on Virginia's. When a compromise attempt in 1783 to get a revenue for Congress also came to nothing, those who hoped to reform the Articles became increasingly discouraged.

Samuel Adams

After the victory at Yorktown in October 1781 and the opening of peace negotiations with Great Britain, the States rapidly lost interest in the Congress. Some nationalists even sought to use the unrest in the army to further their cause. The prospect of the Congress's demobilizing the army without fulfilling its promises of back pay and pensions created a crisis that brought the United States as close to a military coup d'état as it has ever been. In March 1783 the officers of Washington's army, encamped at Newburgh on the Hudson River, issued an address to the Congress concerning their pay and actually considered some sort of military action against the Confederation. Only when Washington personally intervened and refused to support a movement that he said was designed "to open the floodgates of civil discord, and deluge our rising empire in blood" was the crisis averted.

Before resigning his commission as commander in chief, Washington in June 1783 wrote a circular letter to the states, which he called his "legacy" to the American people. In it he recommended the creation of "a supreme power to regulate and govern the general concerns of the confederated republic." This was the moment, said Washington, "to give such a tone to our federal government as will enable it to answer the ends of its institution." It was a time of testing for the American people, "the eyes of the whole world are turned upon them." Upon the willingness of the states to grant sufficient power to Congress to fulfill its needs and preserve its credit depended whether the United States would "be respectable and prosperous, or contemptible and miserable, as a nation . . . whether the revolution must ultimately be considered as a blessing or a curse ... not to the present age alone" but also to "unborn millions."

Yet news of the peace treaty with Great Britain shattered much of this wartime unionist sentiment, and Washington's pleas for strengthening the central government were smothered by the reassertion of traditional state loyalties and jealousies. By December 1783 the Congress, in Thomas Jefferson's opinion, had lost most of its usefulness. "The constant session of Congress," he said, "can not be necessary in time of peace." After clearing up the most urgent business, the delegates should "separate and return to our respective states, leaving only a Committee of the states," and thus "destroy the strange idea of their being a permanent body, which has unaccountably taken possession of the heads of their constituents."

Congressional power, which had been substantial during the war years, now began to disintegrate. The congressional delegates increasingly complained of how difficult it was just to gather a quorum. The Congress could not even agree on a permanent home for itself: it wandered from Philadelphia to Princeton, to Annapolis, to Trenton, and finally to New York City. The states reclaimed their authority and began taking over the payment of the federal debt that many individuals had earlier hoped to make the cement of union. By 1786 nearly one-third of the Confederation's securities had been converted into state bonds, thus creating a vested interest among public creditors in the sovereignty of the individual states. Under these circumstances the influence of those, in Alexander Hamilton's terms, "who think continentally" rapidly declined, and the chances of amending the Confederation piecemeal declined with them.

The Confederation's inability to regulate its international commerce led to even more confusion and frustration. Both northern merchants and southern planters needed to penetrate the markets of the European empires with American produce. Southern agrarian leaders such as Jefferson and James Madison feared that if the European mercantilist states prohibited American farmers from selling their surplus crops freely in their empires, American society would be decisively affected. Not only would the industrious character of the American farmers be undermined, but if Americans could not sell abroad the United States would be unable to pay for the manufactured goods imported from Europe, and therefore would have to develop large-scale manufacturing for itself. This industrialization would in turn create in America the same mob-ridden manufacturing cities and the same corrupt, rank-conscious, and dependent societies that existed in Europe. Under these conditions the independent farmer-citizenry that sustained American republicanism could not long endure.

Yet the mercantilist empires of the major European nations remained generally closed to the new republic in the 1780s. John Adams in Britain and Jefferson in France made strong diplomatic efforts to develop new international commercial relationships based on the free exchange of goods, but these efforts failed. The French refused to take as much American produce as had been expected, and Britain effectively closed its markets to competitive American goods while recapturing American consumer markets for its own products. The Confederation lacked the authority to retaliate with its own trade regulations, and state and sectional jealousies blocked several attempts to grant the Congress a restricted power over commerce. The Confederation Congress watched helplessly as the separate states attempted to pass conflicting navigation acts of their own. By the mid-1780s Connecticut was laying even heavier duties on goods from Massachusetts than on those from Great Britain.

The Confederation felt its lack of power internationally as much as it did domestically. Abroad the reputation of the United States dwindled as rapidly as did its credit. The Dutch and French would lend money only at extraordinary rates of interest. Since American ships now lacked the protection of the British flag, many of them were seized by corsairs from the Muslim states of North Africa, and their crews sold as slaves. The Congress had no money to pay the necessary tribute and ransoms to these Barbary pirates.

In the late-eighteenth century world of hostile empires, it was even difficult for the new republican confederacy to maintain its territorial integrity. Britain refused to send a diplomatic minister to the United States and ignored its treaty obligations to evacuate its military posts in the Northwest, claiming that the United States had not honored its own commitments. The treaty of peace had specified that the Confederation would recommend to the states that loyalist property that had been confiscated during the Revolution be restored, and that neither side would make laws obstructing the recovery of prewar debts. When the states flouted these treaty obligations, the impotent Confederation could do nothing; and therefore British troops remained in Detroit, Niagra, Oswego, and other posts within American territory.

Britain was known to be plotting with the Indians and encouraging separatist movements in the Northwest and in the Vermont borderlands, and Spain was doing the same in the Southwest. Spain in fact refused to recognize American claims to the territory between the Ohio River and Florida. In 1784, in an effort to influence American settlers moving into Kentucky and Tennessee, Spain closed the Mississippi River to American trade. Many of the Westerners were ready to deal with any government that could ensure access to the sea for their agricultural produce. As Washington noted in 1784, they were

George Washington

"on a pivot. The touch of a feather would turn them any way."

In 1785-1786, John Jay, a New Yorker and the secretary of foreign affairs, negotiated a treaty with the Spanish minister to the United States, Diego de Gardoqui. By the terms of this agreement, Spain was opened to American trade in return for America's renunciation of its right to navigate the Mississippi for several decades. Out of fear of being denied an outlet to the sea in the West, the southern states prevented the necessary nine-state majority in the Congress from agreeing to the treaty. But the willingness of a majority of seven states to sacrifice western interests for the sake of northern merchants aroused long-existing sectional jealousies and threatened to shatter the Union. In an address to the Congress in August 1786 Jay defended his treaty on the grounds that it was the best the United States could get from Spain, at least until it "shall become more really and truly a nation than it at present is."

By 1786 these problems made revision of the Articles of Confederation inevitable. Even those who later opposed the Constitution acknowledged that the Confederation Congress needed additional powers. Reform of the Articles by piecemeal amendment had run afoul of the jealousies of one state or another, and many were now looking toward some sort of convention of all the states as a solution.

Although some like Hamilton had suggested the calling of a national convention as early as 1780, the events in the mid-eighties that led to the Philadelphia Convention actually began as continuations of earlier attempts to strengthen the union within the framework of the Articles. The desire to grant Congress the power to regulate foreign trade was the stimulus. In 1785, at a conference at Mount Vernon, Virginia and Maryland resolved a number of disputes concerning the navigation of Chesapeake Bay and the Potomac River. This conference suggested the advantages of independent state action and led to Virginia's invitation to the states to meet at Annapolis in 1786 "to consider and recommend a federal plan for regulating commerce." Some hoped to make this Annapolis meeting a prelude to a full convention for amending the Articles. Madison was one of these, "yet," as he told Jefferson in August 1786, "I despair so much of its accomplishment at the present crisis that I do not extend my views beyond a Commercial Reform. To speak the truth *I almost despair even of this.*" But with only delegates from five states in attendance, the Annapolis meeting had little choice but to risk calling another convention. The stakes now were higher and this convention would have to be concerned with more than matters of commercial regulation. After only two days of discussion, the Annapolis delegates issued a report drafted by Hamilton requesting the states to elect delegates to a second convention to be held in Philadelphia on the second Monday in May of the following year "to devise such further provisions as shall appear to them necessary to render the constitution of the federal government adequate to the exigencies of the Union." After seven states agreed to send delegates to Philadelphia, the Confederation Congress belatedly recognized this independent state action and in February 1787 authorized the approaching convention to meet "for the sole and express purpose of revising the Articles of Confederation."

Although by 1787 nearly all of America's political leaders agreed that some reform of the Articles was necessary, few expected what the Philadelphia Convention eventually created. For the new national government framed in 1787 went way beyond what the weaknesses of the Articles demanded. Granting the Congress the authority to raise revenue, to regulate trade, to pay off its debts, and to deal effectively in international affairs did not require the total scrapping of the Articles and the formation of an extraordinary powerful and distant national government the like of which was beyond anyone's imagination a decade earlier. The new Constitution of 1787 therefore cannot be explained by the obvious and generally acknowledged defects of the Articles of Confederation. Something more serious lay behind the proposals, deliberations, and resultant Constitution of the Philadelphia Convention.

State Politics   By the mid-1780s a number of American leaders were alarmed by politics within the states. The Revolutionaries in 1776 had placed great faith in the ability of the state legislatures to promote the public good. The new Revolutionary state constitutions had made the state legislatures more representative, had greatly increased their size, and had granted enormous power to them. But in the years after 1776 the state legislatures did not fulfill the Revolutionaries' initial expectations. The Revolution unleashed acquisitive and commercial interests that no one had quite realized existed in American society, and these factional interests were demanding and getting protection and satisfaction from state legislatures that were elected annually (an innovation in most states) by the broadest electorates in the world. Everywhere in the state electioneering and the open competition for office increased, and new petty uneducated entrepreneurs like Abraham Yates, a part-time lawyer and shoemaker of Albany, and William Findley, a Scotch-Irish ex-weaver of western Pennsylvania, used popular electoral appeals to vault into political leadership in the state legislatures.

The rapid turnover of seats and the scrambling among different interests made lawmaking seem chaotic. Laws, as the Vermont Council of Censors said in 1786, were "altered—realtered—made better—made worse; and kept in such a fluctuating position that persons in civil commission scarce know what is law." In fact, noted James Madison, more laws were enacted by the states in the decade following independence than in the entire colonial period—all in response to pressures from shifting factions. Madison could only conclude sadly that "a spirit of *locality*" in the state legislatures was destroying "the aggregate interests of the community." In all the states the representatives, said Ezra Stiles, president of Yale College, were concerned only with the special interests of their electors. Whenever a bill was read in the legislature, "every one instantly thinks how it will affect his constituents." Appealing to the people therefore had none of the beneficial effects that good republicans had expected. A bill in Virginia having to do with court reform was "to be printed for consideration of the public," said Madison; but "instead of calling forth the sanction of the wise & virtuous," this appeal to the public, Madison feared, would only "be a signal to interested men to redouble their efforts to get into the Legislature." Democracy, in other words, was no solution to the problem; it was the problem. Pandering to voters and horse-trading politics were not what many Americans had expected from the Revolution.

By the mid-1780s many American leaders were convinced that the state legislatures and majority factions within those legislatures had become the greatest source of tyranny in America. The legislatures were swallowing up the powers of the other branches of government and were passing stay laws, paper money bills, and other debtor relief legislation in violation of the rights of creditors and other minorities. Such tyranny struck at the heart of America's experiment in republicanism, for, said Madison, it brought "into question the fundamental principle of republican Government, that the majority who rule in such governments are the safest Guardians both of public Good and private rights."

These abuses of power by the state legislatures, more than

the defects of the Articles of Confederation, were the real source of the crisis of the 1780s; and ultimately it was these abuses that lay behind the radical reform of the central government. The confusing and unjust laws coming out of the state legislatures, Madison informed Jefferson in Paris in October 1787, had become "so frequent and so flagrant as to alarm the most stedfast friends of Republicanism," and these abuses "contributed more to that uneasiness which produced the Convention, and prepared the public mind for a general reform, than those which accured to our national character and interest from the inadequacy of the Confederation to its

John Adams

immediate objects."

In 1786 a rebellion of nearly two thousand debtor farmers who were threatened with foreclosure of their mortgaged property broke out in western Massachusetts. This rebellion, led by a former militia captain, Daniel Shays, confirmed many of these anxieties about state politics. The insurrection, which temporarily closed the courts and threatened a federal arsenal, occurred in the very state that was considered to have the best-balanced constitution. Although Shays's rebels were defeated by militia troops, his sympathizers were victorious at the polls early in 1787. The newly chosen state representatives soon enacted debtor relief legislation that added to the growing fears of legislative tyranny.

By 1787 many expected the Philadelphia Convention to solve not only the problems of the Articles of Confederation but also the problems of state politics. Two different and hitherto separate reform movements now came together to save both the Congress from the states and the states from themselves. At the national level, various groups—public creditors, merchants, diplomatic officials—had long been trying to amend the Articles. Now they were joined by others: urban artisans who hoped that a stronger national government would prevent competition from British imports; and southerners who wanted to gain representation in the national government proportional to their growing numbers. But reinforcing these groups clamoring for changes in the Articles were also those deeply concerned with the problems of state politics. It was these state problems that ultimately forced Americans to redefine the crisis they faced in the most momentous terms. Since majoritarian tyranny and the legislative abuses of the states flowed from the Revolutionary aim of increasing the participation of the people in government, the very success of the Revolutionary experiment in popular government was at stake. Thus creating a new central government was no longer simply a matter of cementing the Union or standing firm in foreign affairs or satisfying the demands of particular creditor, merchant, and artisan interests. It was now a matter, as Madison declared, that would "decide for ever the fate of Republican Government."

Gordon S. Wood is professor of history at Brown University, and the author of *The Creation of the American Republic, 1776-1787* (University of North Carolina Press, 1969).

Society and Republicanism: America in 1787

James A. Henretta

"In all times," John Winthrop told the first Puritan migrants to the Massachusetts Bay colony in 1630, "some must be rich, some poor, some high and eminent in power and dignity, others mean and in subjection." A century and a half later his descendant James Winthrop likewise pointed to the power of the rich and well-born. "Every society naturally divides itself into classes," he wrote in 1788, and men who compose "the *natural aristocracy* . . . will command a superior degree of respect." John Winthrop praised rule by the privileged few, but his descendant condemned it. In 1788 James Winthrop emerged as a leading Massachusetts Anti-Federalist. He opposed ratification of the Philadelphia Convention because its system of "government is so constituted as to admit but few to exercise the powers of it." In his eyes, it did not provide "for a genuine and fair representation of the people."

This dialogue between the Winthrops underlines the radical nature of the American Revolution. The repudiation of British rule ended the traditional colonial social and political order. The Declaration of Independence spoke of human equality, of the right of all people to enjoy "life, liberty, and the pursuit of happiness." Ordinary Americans quickly used their new-found freedom. In 1778 voters in James Winthrop's Massachusetts rejected a state constitution proposed by the Assembly. "Said Constitution and Form of Government," the residents of the small western town of Greenwich explained,

> Entirely Divests the good People of this State of Many of the Privileges which God and Nature has Given them . . . and [gives] away that Power to a few Individuals, which ought forever to remain with the People. . . .

The republican doctrine of popular sovereignty placed ultimate authority in the hands of "the People." But who were "the People"? Did "the People" include women as well as men? Black slaves as well as free whites? Did the republican doctrines of political liberty and legal equality imply social equality as well?

Between 1776 and 1789 Americans passionately debated these questions. The fate of the revolution—and the republican experiment—seemed to hang in the balance. This extraordinary intellectual and political ferment stemmed in part from the contradictions within republican ideology. Some Americans gave an "aristocratic" definition to republicanism; they championed rule by the "natural aristocracy." Other citizens argued for a "democratic" republic characterized by greater legal and political equality. The harsh economic conditions of the 1780s increased social tensions and raised the stakes of this debate. The resulting political factionalism led to the writing of the Philadelphia Constitution. These ideological and economic conflicts likewise shaped the debates over ratification. In particular, they explain Madison's astute analysis of social and political factions in *Federalist* No. 10.

Republicanism   Europeans were especially conscious of the relationship between the social order and republicanism. In his famous *Letters from an American Farmer* (1782), the French essayist Hector St. John de Crevecoeur explained that Europe was ruled by "great lords who possess everything, and a herd of people who have nothing." In America, historical development had eroded the foundations of tradition hierarchical society; here, there "are no aristocratical families, no courts, no kings, no bishops. . . ." Europeans also pointed out that the American Revolution had instituted legal equality, further undermining social privilege and hierarchical authority. "The law is the same for everyone both as it protects and as it punishes," one visitor noted. "In the course of daily life everyone is on the most perfect footing of equality."

Like James Winthrop, Europeans were well aware that legal equality had not prevented the formation of social classes in the United States. "Wealth, power and higher education rule over need and ignorance," one visitor declared bluntly. Yet class divisions in America differed from those in Europe. The colonies had lacked—and the republican state constitutions prohibited—a legally privileged class of nobles. The absence of an aristocracy of birth encouraged many Americans to seek upward mobility and to create class divisions based on achievement. "In Europe to say of someone that he rose from nothing is a disgrace and a reproach," an aristocratic Polish visitor explained in 1798. "It is the opposite here. To be the architect of your own fortune is honorable. It is the highest recommendation."

Some Americans disagreed. Many Patriot leaders held "aristocratic-republican" values. These men and women preferred a society based on inherited wealth and family status. They questioned the wisdom of a social order based on equality of opportunity and financial competition. During the war many small-scale traders had reaped windfall profits from military supply contracts and sharp dealing in scarce commodities. "Fellows who would have cleaned my shoes five years ago, have amassed fortunes, and are riding in chariots," complained Boston's James Warren in 1779. Such envious sentiments were echoed by established families who wished to preserve their social and political dominance. Many American political leaders likewise lamented the demands for political equality generated by the Revolution. "Depend upon it, Sir," the aristocratic-republican John Adams declared in a private letter, "it is dangerous . . . to alter the qualifications of voters." If property qualifications for voting were lowered, he warned,

> there will be no end to it. New claims will arise; women will demand a vote; lads from twelve to twenty-one will think their rights not enough attended to; and every man who has not a farthing, will demand an equal voice with any other, in all the acts of state.

The result would be "to confound and destroy all distinctions and prostrate all ranks to one common level." Like John Winthrop, John Adams still believed that some men were high and eminent, while others were lowly and should be in subjection.

Women and the Family

Nonetheless, republican ideology challenged all social privilege, even the patriarchal relations of power within the family. Previously, religious writers had accorded preeminent authority to the male head. "The Husband is to rule his Family and Wife. . . ," Boston minister Benjamin Wadsworth had declared in *The Well-Ordered Family* (1712). "Wives submit your selves to your own Husbands, be in subjection to them." In 1776, Abigail Adams questioned this system of patriarchal authority. She urged her husband, John, and the other men in the Continental Congress to "remember the ladies, and be more generous and favorable to them than your ancestors

Judith Sargent Murray

[were]." "We know better than to repeal our Masculine system," the future president replied with jocular condescension, "in Practice you know we are the subjects. We have only the name of Masters."

In fact, legal rules ensured male dominance in the new republican family. Statutes enacted by state legislatures perpetuated traditional English common law restrictions on married women. William Blackstone, the famous English jurist, had pointed out that under common law, "the very being or legal existence of the woman ... during marriage is incorporated and consolidated into that of the husband." This legal condition of "coverture" limited the rights of married women to own property, to sue, or to make contracts and wills. These common law rules deprived American women of most legal rights until the 1840s, when many state legislatures passed Married Women's Property Acts. Even then, less severe forms of legal inferiority restricted women's lives through most of the twentieth century.

Yet "democratic-republican" ideology encouraged demands for the legal emancipation of women even as republican practice denied them. In 1779, Judith Sargent Murray of Gloucester, Massachusetts, composed an essay "On the Equality of the Sexes" and published it in 1790. Murray stressed the importance of mutuality in marriage: "Mutual esteem, mutual friendship, mutual confidence, *begirt about by mutual forbearance.*" Similar sentiments were widespread among young, well-educated, upper-class women. They tried to reconcile the republican doctrine of equality with the cultural reality of female subordination. "I was never of opinion that the pursuits of the sexes ought to be the same," seventeen-year old Eliza Southgate of Maine wrote to a male cousin, "each [sex] ought to have a separate sphere of action." "Yet to cultivate the qualities with which we are endowed [she continued] can never be called infringing the prerogatives of man." "The men say we have no business" with politics, Eliza Wilkinson of South Carolina complained, "but I won't have it thought that because we are the weaker sex as to bodily strength we are capable of nothing more than domestic concerns. They won't even allow us liberty of thought, and that is all I want."

A few American public leaders responded positively to female demands for greater equality, but usually with male needs in mind. In his *Thoughts on Female Education* (1787), the Philadelphia physician Benjamin Rush advocated the intellectual training of women, so they would "be an agreeable companion for a sensible man." Rush and other men of affairs likewise praised "republican mothers" who instructed "their sons in the principles of liberty and government."

Ultimately, the concept of "republican motherhood" altered the character of the family and of American society. The main impetus came from religion. Beginning in the 1790s, Christian ministers celebrated women's role as moral educators. "Preserving virtue and instructing the young are not the fancied, but the real 'Rights of Women,'" the Reverend Thomas Bernard told the Female Charitable Society of Salem, Massachusetts. "Give me a host of educated pious mothers and sisters," echoed Thomas Grimké, a South Carolina minister,

> and I will do more to revolutionize a country, in moral and
> religious taste, in manners and in intellectual cultivation than
> I can possibly do in double or triple the time, with a similar
> host of men.

Grinké did not exaggerate. Women played a central role
in the Second Great Awakening (1790-1830), the evangelical
revivals that made Christianity an important part of the
emerging American national character. Many married women
now used their moral position as "guardians of virtue" to
achieve a position of near-equality within the home. Women
trained in religious academies entered the paid work force as
teachers, while other women actively campaigned for social
reform and for women's rights. Republican ideology and
religious idealism had transformed the traditional cultural
rules governing the status of women in American society.

Slavery and Property   Democratic-republicanism and Christian idealism also
threatened the institution of slavery, a prime feature of the
American legal order. In 1787, no fewer than 750,000 blacks
(20 percent of the entire population of the United States) were
held in hereditary bondage. But now their servile status was the
subject of political debate. In 1784, Virginia Methodists
condemned slavery, using both religious and republican arguments. They declared that slavery was "contrary to the Golden
Law of God on which hang all the Law and Prophets, and the
unalienable Rights of Mankind, as well as every Principle of
Revolution."

These arguments laid the intellectual basis for black
emancipation in the northern states, where there were relatively few slaves. By 1784, Massachusetts, Pennsylvania,
Connecticut, and Rhode Island had either abolished slavery or
provided for its gradual end. Two decades later, all states north
of Delaware had adopted similar legislation.

The abolition of slavery in the North exposed additional
contradictions within republican ideology. American patriots
had fought the British not only for their lives and liberty, but
also for the rights of private property. Indeed, the three values
were closely linked in republican theory. The Massachusetts
Constitution of 1780 protected every citizen "in the enjoyment
of his life, liberty, and property, according to the standing
laws." The Virginia Bill of Rights went further; it asserted that
the "means of acquiring and possessing property" was an

inherent right. Like John Adams, the authors of most state constitutions believed that only property owners could act independently and restricted voting rights to those with free-hold estates. For them, republicanism was synonymous with property rights.

There was the rub. For slaves were property. The abolition of slavery in Massachusetts in 1784, James Winthrop pointed out, meant that "a number of citizens have been deprived of property formerly acquired under the protection of law." To protect white property rights, the Pennsylvania Emancipation Act of 1780 did not free slaves already in bondage. The Act awarded freedom only to slaves born after 1780—and then only after they had served their mothers' masters for twenty-eight years. In fact, American republican ideology was ultimately derived from ancient Greece and Rome and was fully compatible with slavery. "As free men," the poet Euripedes had written of his fellow citizens in the ancient Greek republics, "we live off slaves."

This aristocratic-republican ideology combined with economic self-interest to prevent the emancipation of slaves in the South. Slaves accounted for 30 to 60 percent of the southern population and represented a huge financial investment. Most southern political leaders were slaveowners, and they actively

Black soldiers at the Battle of New Orleans, 1815

resisted emancipation. In 1776, the North Carolina legislature condemned the actions of Quakers who freed their slaves as "highly criminal and reprehensible."

Understandably, southern blacks sought freedom on their own. Two white neighbors of Richard Henry Lee, a signer of the Declaration of Independence, lost "every slave they had in the world," as did nearly "all of those who were near the enemy." More than five thousand blacks left Charleston, South Carolina, with the departing British army. Other American slaves bargained wartime loyalty to their patriot masters for a promise of liberty. Using a Manumission Act passed in 1782, Virginia planters granted freedom to more than ten thousand slaves.

Yet black emancipation in the South was doomed even before the expansion of cotton production gave slavery a new economic rationale. The rice planters of Georgia and South Carolina strongly opposed emancipation throughout the revolutionary era. Their demands at the Philadelphia Convention resulted in a clause (Article I, Section 9) that prevented Congress from prohibiting the transatlantic slave trade until 1808. By that time, southern whites had imported an additional 250,000 Africans—as many slaves as had been brought into all the mainland colonies between 1619 and 1776.

Nonetheless, republican ideology and evangical Christianity profoundly affected the lives of many black Americans. By 1787, thousands of blacks in the Chesapeake states had joined Baptist and Methodist churches. The Christian message promoted spiritual endurance among some blacks and prompted others to resist slavery by force. In 1800, Martin and Gabriel Prosser plotted a slave uprising in Richmond, Virginia. They hoped to capture the governor and to seize the arms stored in the state capital. Their "cause was similar to the Israelites'," Martin Prosser told his followers.

> I have read in my Bible where God says, if we worship him, we should have peace in all our land and five of you shall conquer a hundred, and a hundred of you a hundred-thousand of our enemies.

White Virginians nipped the insurrection in the bud, but it renewed their fears about the democratic implications of republicanism. During the war, slaves had "fought [for] freedom merely as a good," St. George Tucker suggested, but now they "claim it as a right." "Liberty and equality have brought this evil upon us," a letter to Virginia *Herald* argued following

Gabriel's Rebellion, for such doctrines are "dangerous and extremely wicked in this country, where every white man is a master, and every black man is a slave."

Democratic-republicanism appealed not only to women and blacks but also to artisans and yeomen farmers. These men formed the vast majority of the voting population. Prior to independence, they usually elected leading landowners or merchants to political office and deferred to their superior social status. Religious conflicts during the First Great Awakening (1740-1765) partially undermined these deferential attitudes. As Baptist leader Isaac Backus explained in 1768, "the common people [now] claim as good a right to judge and act for themselves in matter of religion as civil rulers or the learned clergy."

Artisans and Farmers

Political revolution translated these anti-elitist sentiments into ringing affirmations of popular power. In 1776, the voters of Mecklenberg County told their delegates to the North Carolina Constitutional Convention to "oppose everything that leans to aristocracy, of power in the hands of the rich and chief men exercised to the oppression of the poor." The new state constitutions dramatically increased the political influence of ordinary citizens. Lower property qualifications for voting gave urban artisans greater power; and reappointment of the state legislatures on the basis of population gave greater representation to ordinary western farmers.

The results were dramatic. Before 1776, only 17 percent of northern assemblymen were "middling" farmers and artisans, those with tax assessments of less than £2,000; by the 1780s these social groups constituted no less than 62 percent of the representatives. The democratic-republican thrust of the American revolution had undermined the hierarchical social order of John Winthrop and had created state governments in which, as James Winthrop put it, there could be "a genuine and fair representation of the people."

Democratic-republican demands for greater equality contributed to the intense political and constitutional struggles of the 1780s, as did an overcrowded agricultural economy. Thousands of white tenant farmers yearned to escape the hierarchical rural society of the Chesapeake states, while landlords sought to keep them at home. "Boundless settlements," a letter in the Maryland *Gazette* warned in 1785, will open "a door for our citizens to run off and leave us, depreciating all our landed property and disabling us from paying taxes."

A rapidly growing population pressed on landed resources in New England as well. In the typical town of Kent, Connecticut, one hundred fathers and 109 adult sons lived on the town's 103 farmsteads. Previous generations of Kent parents had subdivided their lands to provide for their many offspring; now their small farms would support only a single heir. Yeomen families faced declining prospects and even the loss of their land. "The *mortgage of our farms,* we cannot think of," the farmers of Conway, Massachusetts protested,

> to be *tenants* to *landlords,* we know not who, and pay rent for lands *purchased with our money,* and converted from howling *Wilderness,* into fruitful fields, by the *sweat of our brow,* seems . . . truly shocking.

To provide for their families in these hard times, many rural residents turned to household manufactures. In the small village of Hallowell, Maine, the daughters of Martha Ballard learned to weave, as did most of the town's young women. The resulting surge in household cloth production dramatically reduced American dependence on British manufacturers. During the Revolution, artisans in the town of Lynn, Massachusetts, had likewise raised their output of shoes. By 1789, the town turned out 175,000 pairs of shoes each year, and by 1800, no fewer than 400,000 pairs. The efforts of these women and men laid the foundation for American self-sufficiency and prosperity. As Alexander Hamilton noted proudly in 1792, the countryside was "a vast scene of household manufacturing . . . in many cases to an extent not only sufficient for the supply of the families in which they are made, but for sale, and even, in some cases, for exportation."

Merchant entrepreneurs such as Ebenezer Breed of Lynn, Massachusetts, directed many of these rural enterprises. They employed farm women and children to sew the soft uppers of shoes or to spin yarn, and rural males to weave cloth for market sale. Their entrepreneurial activities helped many Americans to maintain their standard of living during the commercial and agricultural recession of the 1780s.

This new capitalist system of production for market also increased economic conflicts. Rural workers and merchant entrepreneurs were indispensable to each other, but their interests—like those of merchants and farmers—were not always identical. Many backcountry farmers went into debt to expand household production or provide farmsteads for their children. As debts increased, so too did defaults and law suits.

The courts directed sheriffs to sell the property of bankrupt farmers and artisans to pay merchant creditors and court costs.

Commercial debt had been a feature of American life since the 1760s. "Mark any Clerk, Lawyer, or Scotch merchant," warned North Carolina farmer Herman Husband. "We must make these men subject to the laws or they will enslave the whole community." Actually, merchants usually had the law on their side so, during the 1760s, Husband and his followers intimidated judges, closed courts by force, and broke into jails to free their arrested leaders. Antimerchant sentiment during the 1770s pushed forward the independence movement in Virginia, where Scottish traders had extended credit to more than thirty-two thousand tobacco planters. And it appeared yet again in western Massachusetts in the 1780s. Between 1784 and 1786, the Hampshire County Court heard 2,977 debt cases. Angry Massachusetts farmers defended their property from seizure by closing the courts.

Farmers—like women and slaves—now used the democratic-republican heritage of the American revolution to justify their actions. They met in extra-legal conventions and spoke of the "Suppressing of tyrannical government." Led by Revolutionary War veteran Captain Daniel Shays, these farmers eventually rose in outright rebellion. As the Massachusetts aristocratic-republican Fisher Ames lamented, "The people have turned against their teachers the doctrines which were inculcated in the late revolution."

The republican ideology of liberty and equality had raised the expectations of a majority of "the People" while leaving them in an inferior social position. In 1787, American women were still legally subordinate to males, and most blacks were still legally enslaved. Legally-mandated taxes and court proceedings threatened the livelihoods of thousands of yeomen farmers and artisans. Yet "the People" also included lawyers like Ames and James Winthrop, established merchants like Bostonian James Warren, slaveowning planters like Thomas Jefferson, and shoe-industry entrepreneur Ebenezer Breed. As James Madison astutely argued in *Federalist* No. 10,

> A landed interest, a manufacturing interest, a mercantile interest, a moneyed interest, with many lesser interests, grow up of necessity in civilized nations, and divide them into different classes, actuated by different sentiments.

Madison's goal at the Philadelphia Convention had been to create a public arena in which this "variety of parties and interests" could pursue their own goals without invading "the rights of other citizens."

Participants and Spectators

Like James Winthrop, many Americans doubted that the Philadelphia Constitution represented the correct constitutional formula. The Constitution was ratified only by narrow majorities in the major states of Virginia (89 to 79), Massachusetts (187 to 168), and New York (30 to 27). Yet by July 4, 1788, the Constitution had become the supreme law of the land, and thousands of Philadelphians turned out for a celebratory parade. A band played "The Federal March," and a float carried an oversized framed reproduction of the Constitution itself.

The parade also demonstrated social and political divisions

outlined in Madison's *Federalist* No. 10. Most of the five thousand participants marched not as individual republicans, but as members of distinct occupational or social groups. Farmers cast seed before them. Weavers operated a loom on their horse-drawn float, while printers ran a press. Behind the floats marched groups of artisans and professionals—barbers, hatters, lawyers, clergymen, and political leaders. Most blacks, women, and white laborers watched from the sidewalks.

All of these Americans joined together to cheer their republican revolution and their new national constitution. But many remained as spectators, both of the parade and of the political process. And those citizens who participated did so with a heightened sense of their respective social identities and economic interests. The United States began its history with a society legally divided by gender and race, and with a polity divided by class position and economic interest.

Two hundred years later, Americans remain sharply divided by race and by economic and social inequalities, although united by their Constitution and their republican ideology. Now, as then, the meaning of liberty and equality remains the subject of intense debate and of political struggle.

James A. Henretta is Priscilla Alden Burke Professor of History at the University of Maryland, College Park. He is the coauthor of a new survey textbook, *America's History* and the author of *The Evolution of American Society, 1700-1815* (1973). The working title of his present research is "Law and the Creation of the Liberal State in America, 1770-1860."

The Philadelphia Convention and the Development of American Government: From the Virginia Plan to the Constitution

Pauline Maier

The Virginians arrived early. Gradually other delegates drifted into Philadelphia, drawn from the far reaches of the United States to take up what they knew would be a work of historic importance. The plan of government proposed by the constitutional convention would, said James Madison, "decide for ever the fate of Republican Government." Should the convention fail to repair the "defective systems" then in effect, the people would in time renounce the blessing of self-government "and be ready for any change that may be proposed to them." If the American republic failed, Roger Sherman added, mankind might well "despair of establishing Governments by Human wisdom and leave it to chance, war and conquest." Upon the convention's work depended, in short, the future of the American people and "the cause of Liberty throughout the world."

James Madison

The significance of the event helped draw a remarkable group of people to Philadelphia in the spring and summer of 1787. Of the fifty-five delegates who attended the convention, eight had participated in the constitutional conventions of their states, seven had been governors, and thirty-nine—more than 70 percent of the total—had served in the Continental Congress. One of every three had been in the Continental Army, which also increased their commitment to the United States as a nation.

The average delegate was forty-two years old, but the most brilliant of them were even younger. Alexander Hamilton of New York was thirty, James Madison of Virginia—"the father of the Constitution"—thirty-six. James Wilson of Pennsylvania, whose contributions to the convention rivaled Madison's, was eight years older than Madison. He had, however,

33

Benjamin Franklin

arrived from his native Scotland only in 1765. As a result, like the younger delegates, he learned the art of American politics under the popular institutions of the Revolution, not the old colonial system. That was important. Such men were not only practicing political scientists, fascinated with the challenge of constructing institutions so the American republic could survive longer than any republic in times past; they were experienced politicians who knew how to get things done in a democratic system.

The list of delegates also included several older Americans

who brought considerable prestige to the convention, particularly Benjamin Franklin and George Washington, the ex-commander of the Continental Army and the most respected person in the United States. Some notable Americans were absent: John Adams and Thomas Jefferson, for example, were serving their country as diplomats in Europe. Even so, when Jefferson reviewed the convention's membership he characterized it as "an assembly of demigods."

Certainly the distinction of the delegates was out of keeping with the work of a convention "for the sole and express purpose of revising the articles of confederation," as the Continental Congress said in February 1787. From the beginning, some people doubted that so distinguished a set of delegates would gather for so limited a task. "I smelt a rat," Patrick Henry explained when asked why he had refused to attend the convention. Later he and other Anti-Federalists would charge that the convention conspired to undermine the American Revolution by destroying the states and replacing them with a great "consolidated government" like that that the British had tried to establish in the years before 1776.

Henry had cause for suspicion. Many delegates expected to do more than amend the Articles of Confederation; after all, in September 1786 the Annapolis Convention had called for a convention in Philadelphia to "take into consideration the situation of the United States" and "devise such further provisions as shall appear to them necessary to render the constitution of the federal government adequate to the exigencies of the Union." Most delegates agreed that the central government had to be given substantially more power—more, perhaps, than could be accomplished by revising the Articles of the Confederation. What the Philadelphia convention proposed was, however, not a reincarnation of the British Empire, but what Madison later described as "a new Creation—a real nondescript," namely, the American federal system.

No delegate had such a system clearly in mind when the convention first assembled in May 1787. It emerged during the convention, which adopted a plan proposed by Virginia as the foundation for its deliberations, then thoroughly revised and expanded that plan in creating the federal constitution. Only after the convention dissolved did the "founding fathers" understand what they had accomplished.

Adopting the Virginia Plan

Between May 25 and 29 the convention elected its president, Washington, and secretary, Major William Jackson, and defined its basic rules of proceeding. Each state's delegation would vote as a unit, and seven states would constitute a quorum. (At the time that rule was adopted only nine states were represented, though in the end all the original thirteen states except Rhode Island would participate in the convention.) Moreover, the convention's proceedings were to be secret: the "yeas" and "nays" on specific proposals would not be recorded so delegates could more freely change their opinions, and nothing said in the convention was to be communicated to the outside world "without leave." Finally the convention turned to its main business.

Gov. Edmund Randolph of Virginia took the floor. He spoke of the crisis that led to the calling of the convention and "the necessity of preventing the fulfilment of the prophecies of the American downfall"; he summarized what was essential in any revised governmental system, and why the Articles of Confederation, though the best that could be achieved eleven years earlier, "in the then infancy of the science, of constitutions, & of confederacies," were no longer adequate. Finally, Randolph proposed to replace the Confederation with a new plan of government—the Virginia plan. It consisted of fifteen resolves outlining a new national government that would include a bicameral legislature with power to "legislate in all cases to which the separate States are incompetent, or in which the harmony of the United States may be interrupted" by separate state laws. The new legislature would, moreover, be able to "negative," or veto, state laws that in its opinion violated the articles of Union, and to use force against states that failed to fulfill their duties under those articles. The Virginia plan also provided for a separate "National Executive" and a "National Judiciary." The new scheme of government was to be ratified by special conventions, elected by the people of the various states for that purpose.

Edmund Randolph

Both Randolph's remarks and his proposal showed the influence of James Madison, who was perhaps the most knowledgeable student of government among the delegates at Philadelphia. Madison had prepared carefully for the convention by studying the history of all previous confederations in history, their strengths and defects, and by examining with equal care the "vices" of American government in the 1780s. From those studies Madison sought ground rules for the revision of American institutions. His conclusions shaped the

Virginia plan.

The convention immediately resolved itself into a committee of the whole "to consider of the state of the American Union," and in that role it discussed rigorously the Virginia plan from May 30 through June 13, revising and expanding the original Randolph proposals. Meanwhile, more delegates arrived, many of whom were uncomfortable with the direction of change in which the convention had apparently committed itself. Finally, on June 15, William Paterson of New Jersey presented to the convention an alternative plan, one that better represented the views of several "small state" delegates. It became known as the New Jersey plan.

The Virginia and New Jersey plans differed in their provisions for representation. According to the Virginia plan, representation in both houses of the national legislature would be proportional to population or contributions to the national treasury. Under the New Jersey plan, each state would continue to be represented equally, as was true in the Confederation's Congress. To delegates from states like Virginia that had relatively large populations, or that expected their populations to grow substantially in the future, the principle of proportional representation had been "improperly violated" in the Confederation. "As all authority was derived from the people," James Wilson argued, "equal numbers of people ought to have an equal n[umber] of representatives, and different numbers of people different numbers of representatives ... Are not the Citizens of Pen[nsylvania] equal to those of N[ew] Jersey? does it require 150 of the former to balance 50 of the latter?" The delegates from Delaware, however, said they were bound by their instructions to consent to no change in the system of equal state representation, and "in case such a change should be fixed on, it might be their duty to retire from the Convention." New Jersey was equally insistent: under a system of proportional representation, Paterson argued, the small states would be "swallowed up" by large states. If the small states would not confederate on a plan of proportional representation, Wilson replied, Pennsylvania "& he presumed some other States" would confederate on no other. Disagreement over the system of representation was, in short, profound, and explains in part why the "small state" delegates developed the New Jersey plan.

The supporters of the New Jersey plan were, however, no less determined than those of the Virginia plan to enhance significantly the powers of the central government, and so to

George Washington

give it, as David Brearly of New Jersey said, "energy and stability." Like the Virginia plan, the New Jersey plan granted the central government power to raise its own revenue and to regulate commerce, powers that had been denied the Confederation Congress. Although it would have continued the unicameral legislature of the Confederation, the New Jersey plan authorized the establishment of a separate Executive branch and of a "federal Judiciary" whose members would hold office "during good behavior," such that, in the end, the institutions it proposed would have resembled those of the Virginia plan. Moreover, all acts of Congress made under the powers vested in it and all treaties ratified under the authority of the United States would be "the supreme law of the respective States," and the federal Executive would have power "to call forth [the] power of the Confederate States . . . to enforce and compel an obedience to such Acts, or an observance of such Treaties" on the part of states or bodies of men within any state who interfered with the execution of such laws and treaties.

According to the supporters of the New Jersey plan, the proposals of the Virginia plan had little chance of being ratified. "Our object," Paterson said, "is not such a Government as may be best in itself, but such a one as our Constituents have authorized us to prepare, and as they will approve." As a result, the New Jersey plan was drafted in a way that made it seem more in keeping with the announced purposes of the convention: it proposed to "revise" as well as to correct and enlarge the Articles of Confederation "to render the federal Constitution adequate to the exigencies of Government, & the preservation of the Union." The government proposed under the New Jersey plan would therefore have remained "federal" in the language of the day. That is, it would have remained a Confederation of sovereign states (though the New Jersey plan violated the "federal" nature of the Confederation by providing that the central government could enforce its authority on individuals directly). In proposing the Virginia plan, Randolph had argued that a union "merely federal" in that sense was insufficient to provide for the "common defence, security of liberty, & gen[era]l welfare." A "*national* Government" was necessary, he said, one that would be "supreme."

On the same assumption, Alexander Hamilton proposed, during discussions of the New Jersey plan, the establishment of a still more clearly "consolidated" national government. "Two Sovereignties can not co-exist within the same limits," he said, repeating the established wisdom of his time. So he would have placed "compleat sovereignty in the general Governm[en]t," and reduced the states to administrative units of that new-formed sovereign nation. For him, the New Jersey plan would not work: "no amendment of the Confederation, leaving the States in possession of their Sovereignty," could possibly satisfy the country's needs. Nor did Randolph's proposals go far enough: "What even is the Virginia Plan, but pork still, with a little change of the sauce?"

Hamilton's plan, however, went too far: it was never seriously considered by the convention, no doubt because, as he admitted, it had no chance of being accepted at that time by a people whose attachments to the states remained strong. But did the New Jersey plan have any better prospect? All previous attempts to increase the Confederation's power by amendments to the Articles of Confederation had failed to get the necessary unanimous state support, and therefore Paterson's plan, George Mason argued, "never could be expected to succeed."

The convention's decision on June 19, by a vote of 7 to 3, to proceed on the basis of the Virginia plan was a critical one. It meant that the delegates had agreed to cut loose from the Confederation and follow Washington's advice to adopt "no temporizing expedients," but probe the defects of the current system "to the bottom, and provide a radical cure." They were, however, no more ready than the proponents of the New Jersey plan to go so far that their proposal would have no chance of ratification. In revising and developing the Virginia plan, they had to find ways to answer accusations that they "meant to abolish the State Governm[en]ts altogether," to devise a system of government, as Madison later put it, that would "avoid the inefficacy of a mere confederacy without passing into the opposite extreme of a consolidated gov[ernmen]t." In doing that, they provided the foundations for a new definition of the word "federal," one that allowed a genuine sharing of power between two levels of government.

Revising the Virginia Plan

The Virginia plan was in no way a complete plan of government. As originally presented, it included blanks for the convention to fill: Randolph's proposals, for example, specified only that members of the first branch of the national legislature "be elected by the people of the several States every _____ for the term of _____; to be of the age of _____ years at least...." Moreover, many specific provisions in the plan were clearly there mainly to focus debate. They may have represented the best thoughts of the Virginia delegation before the convention met, but even members of that delegation sometimes changed their minds in the course of the convention's debates. Madison, for example, decided soon after the Virginia plan was presented that the use of force against states would be a mistake because it "would look more like a declaration of war, than an infliction of punishment." In any case, the Virginia plan was far briefer than a constitution: clearly it would have to be expanded and organized and written in an appropriate form before the convention's work was done.

After its vote of June 19, the convention focused its attention again on the Virginia plan, which it had already expanded from the original fifteen to nineteen resolutions. By July 26 the convention had agreed upon twenty-three resolu-

William Jackson

tions, many of them longer than any of those originally proposed by Randolph. The convention then adjourned until August 6. Meanwhile, a Committee of Detail expanded Congress's resolutions into a draft constitution, which the convention again debated and changed. Finally, on September 8, another committee was appointed "to revise the style of and arrange the articles which had been agreed to by the House." Even after that Committee of Style completed its work, and on through September 17, when the convention finally dissolved, the delegates made further important revisions. The result was a constitution that, though built on the Virginia plan, was strikingly different from its parent document. Above all, the convention more carefully divided and balanced power among the three branches of the central government, and between the states and the nation.

The most pressing issues before the convention concerned the legislature, the subject of Article I of the constitution. Dangerous divisions over representation were finally healed on July 16 with the convention's "Great Compromise," which allowed the states equal representation in the Senate. Representation in the House of Representatives would, however, be proportional to the number of free persons, including those bound to service for a term of years but excluding "Indians not taxed," and three-fifths "of all other Persons." Direct taxes were to be apportioned in the same way. Moreover, all money bills were to originate in the lower house, and a census would be taken every ten years so representation and taxation could be allocated appropriately.

The "other persons" mentioned were, of course, slaves. The "three-fifths" ratio was taken from a proposed amendment of 1783 to the Articles of Confederation; it was not the result of a separate compromise at the convention. The effect of counting three-fifths of a state's slave population in determining its representation in the House of Representatives was, however, to increase the power of those Southern states that had argued so strongly for proportional representation in both parts of the legislature. They had done so because they expected the population of the South to grow more rapidly than that of the North. Ironically, that expectation proved wrong: in the early nineteenth century the Northern population—and so Northern representation in the House of Representatives—rapidly outran that of the South. As a result, the Senate, with the equal representation of states that the Southern delegates so opposed, proved the most important branch of the legislature for the cause of "Southern rights."

How would the legislators be chosen? According to the Virginia plan, the people would elect the lower house, which would then elect the upper house from candidates nominated by the state legislatures. The convention agreed that the House of Representatives should be popularly elected: that, Madison argued, would help establish a "necessary sympathy" between the people and their government. Representatives' terms were set at two years, but senators were given six-year terms in the hope that they would bring "due stability and wisdom" to the legislature. The convention gave state legislatures the right to elect senators, which made the Senate more independent of the House of Representatives than it would have been under the Virginia plan and so a more effective check upon that body, but tied the Senate more closely to the states. Later, however, the convention decided that senators would vote individually, not as state units.

Defining the powers of Congress was a task of enormous importance, but one that provoked little controversy. After some deliberation, the convention abandoned the Virginia plan's vague statement that Congress could act where the states were "incompetent" or where separate state legislation would interrupt "the harmony of the United States" for a very specific summary of Congress's rights. Much of that summary was simply taken from the Articles of Confederation. Congress was also given critical new powers, starting with the all-important "power to lay and collect taxes" and "to regulate commerce," and the major residual authority "to make all Laws which shall be necessary and proper" for carrying out "all . . . Powers vested by this Constitution in the Government of the United States, or any Department or Officer thereof." It was denied certain powers—to pass bills of attainder or ex post facto laws, for example. But the prohibitions on the states were even more important. The states were denied the right to "coin Money; emit Bills of Credit; make anything but gold and silver Coin" legal tender, or pass laws "impairing the Obligation of Contracts," all of which they had done in the 1780s, undermining the rights of property and provoking fear for the future of the republic. In the end, the powers of the states were so severely curtailed and those of Congress so enhanced that, Madison noted, the central government would hold "powers far beyond those exercised by the British Parliament, when the States were part of the British Empire."

The convention quickly decided to invest the executive

power—Article II of the constitution—in a single person, despite the objections of Edmund Randolph. Had it thereby created an "elective Monarchy" or, as Wilson argued, a responsible public servant who would be a "safeguard against tyranny"? Unlike a king, the president would be impeachable, and so removable from office for violations of his trust. The convention also set the president's term of office at seven years, after which he could not be reelected. Gradually, however, the president was given far more than the "general authority to execute the National laws" and the other "Executive rights vested in Congress by the Confederation" that the Virginia plan mentioned. The president could veto acts of the legislature (though that veto could be overridden by a two-thirds vote in Congress), and he could do so by himself, without the "Council of Revision" specified in the Virginia plan. He would be "Commander in Chief of the Army and Navy of the United States, and of the Militia of the several States." With the advice and consent of the Senate, he could make treaties and appoint ambassadors, judges, and other federal officers. A seven-year term seemed too long for so powerful an executive. In part for that reason, the convention cut it to four years and eliminated the ban on reelection.

The Virginia plan's provision for letting the legislature elect the president also seemed increasingly unsatisfactory given the convention's inclination to make the president so powerful. Election by Congress would lead to "cabal and corruption." Moreover, as Madison noted, experience in the states "had proved a tendency in our governments to throw all power into the Legislative vortex." State executives were "in general little more than Cyphers; the legislatures omnipotent." Clearly "the preservation of Republican Gov[ernmen]t ... required" that the executive provide an "effectual check ... for restraining the instability & encroachments of the legislature." It seemed unlikely that the executive could be adequately independent of the legislature to provide such a check if it were elected by Congress.

But how else could the president be elected? By the people, James Wilson argued; but others said the candidates would be unknown to the people at large. That problem was, Wilson said, "the most difficult of all on which we have had to decide." It was resolved, finally, though not entirely satisfactorily, by entrusting election of the president to a body of electors equal to the number of senators and representatives states were entitled to send to Congress who would be chosen according to a method defined by their state legislatures. The electors would meet in their states and vote for two persons; the ballots would be collected and counted by Congress. Later, with the development of political parties, presidential electors would be elected by popular vote rather than by the state legislatures and all of a state's electoral votes would go to that candidate who won a majority of popular votes within the state. The states then became a much more prominent part of presidential elections than the delegates at Philadelphia had expected.

Under the Virginia plan, the judicial power—Article III of the constitution—would have consisted of "one or more supreme tribunals" and "inferior tribunals ... chosen by the National Legislature." Instead the convention called for a single supreme court and "such inferior Courts as the Congress may from time to time ordain and establish." Judges would, moreover, be chosen by the president with the Senate's consent, not by the legislature. In the constitution, as in the Virginia plan, the independence of judges would be secured by giving them tenure in office during good behavior, and forbidding the reduction of their salaries while they remained on the bench.

The convention also adopted a critical passage, slightly revised, from the New Jersey plan, declaring that the constitution as well as laws and treaties made under its authority were "the supreme Law of the Land" and binding state judges to uphold them, "any Thing in the Constitution or Laws of any State to the Contrary notwithstanding." That, in effect, provided an effective substitute for the Virginia plan's congressional negative on state laws, which critics had condemned as impractical. There would, they argued, be too many laws for Congress to review, and the proposal "would disgust all the States." "A law that ought to be negatived will be set aside in the Judiciary departm[en]t," Gouverneur Morris said, "and if that security should fail, may be repealed by a Nation[a]l law." Madison remained unconvinced; a congressional veto of state laws still seemed to him "essential to the efficacy & security of the Gen[era]l Gov[ernmen]t." Virginia, Massachusetts, and North Carolina were in the minority when the convention agreed to deny Congress that power.

Finally, the Virginia plan proposed that the convention's recommendations "be submitted to an assembly or assemblies ... expressly chosen by the people to consider & decide thereon." The convention agreed, and provided further that when nine state conventions had ratified the constitution it would go into effect over the people of those states (Article

VII). The fate of the constitution would not therefore be decided by the state legislatures, which, as Rufus King noted, lost power under its provisions and so would "be most likely to raise objections." Nor would a single state, or even four states, have power to block the constitution's establishment. When, moreover, nine states had ratified, the pressure on the others (which were expected to include New York and Virginia) would be intense: they would have to decide not whether they preferred the Articles of Confederation or the constitution, but whether they would join the new-formed nation or remain apart from it.

Most important, the ratification provisions assured that the new government would be firmly founded upon "the supreme authority of the people themselves." A system of government ratified by the legislatures, Madison argued, could be at best a league or treaty, like the Articles of Confederation; the authority of "a *Constitution*" had to be "founded on the people." Thus the opening words of the new constitution: "We the people of the United States . . . do ordain and establish this Constitution for the United States of America."

A New Form of Government

The convention had accomplished much of what it set out to do. It had divided power between the states and the nation, taking from the states those powers they had abused in the past, and creating a central government with power sufficient to serve the needs of the Union. In designing the new central government, the convention also created independent executive and judicial branches to check the power of the legislature. At each step in its proceedings the convention drew on the lessons of history, including that of the Confederation and the American state constitutions. "Experience must be our only guide," John Dickinson had said; "Reason may mislead us."

But what kind of government had the convention adopted? Not a "federal" government in the sense of a Confederacy, or a "consolidated" national government. Most delegates agreed on the need for strengthening the central government and believed they could do that safely. The history of all previous confederacies had proven, Madison claimed, that such governments were endangered more by "anarchy" than "tyranny," by the "disobedience of . . . members" rather than "usurpations of the federal head." The convention was nonetheless forced repeatedly to negotiate compromises between those who thought the states "should be considered as having no existence" with respect to the general government, and those who sought repeated affirmations of the states' continued importance. Even when the delegates agreed to eliminate the word "national" from the constitution, they did so for differing reasons. The result was a system of government that conformed to no previous model and which satisfied no one completely. To Madison and Wilson, for example, the constitution's provision for equal state representation in the Senate constituted a new "vice" of the American system, an error of design that would lead to "disease, convulsions, and finally death itself." The constitution included no reference to a "perpetual Union," as had the Articles of Confederation, perhaps because its future seemed so troubled.

Elbridge Gerry

On the final day of the convention, Benjamin Franklin, the convention's only octogenarian, offered his colleagues counsel. "I confess," he said in a speech read for him by James Wilson, "that there are several parts of this constitution that I do not at present approve, but ... the older I grow, the more apt I am to doubt my own judgment, and to pay more respect to the judgment of others." A general government, he thought, was necessary for the United States, and he questioned, "whether any other Convention we can obtain, may be able to make a better Constitution.... Thus I consent ... to this Constitution because I expect no better, and because I am not sure that it is not the best. The opinions I have had of its errors, I sacrifice to the public good." He urged the other delegates to do the same, to "doubt a little" of their "own infallibility," and work "heartily and unanimously" for the constitution's ratification.

Three of the delegates who remained in Philadelphia rejected Franklin's advice—Elbridge Gerry of Massachusetts and two Virginians, Edmund Randolph and George Mason, whose discontent witnessed how far the convention had moved from the original Virginia plan. However, thirty-nine signed the constitution and campaigned for its ratification (as, in the end, did Randolph).

In the state ratification debates, moreover, the Federalists, under the leadership of James Wilson, developed a coherent justification of the new American governmental system. Provisions hammered out as compromises emerged as positive virtues. Neither the states nor the central government was "supreme," as the Virginia plan had put it, because in the American republic the people alone were sovereign. And a sovereign people could parcel out responsibility for state and national government, creating separate, concurrent jurisdictions over distinct spheres that could "no more clash than two parallel lines can meet," each with complete authority for the tasks delegated to it. This conception of the state and central governments as independent agencies of the people, separate but equal, provided the intellectual foundation for modern American federalism, a system of government that, as Madison understood, had no historical precedent and so was a "new Creation."

After two hundred years, it is tempting to celebrate the Federalists' intellectual and political accomplishments as if they were the end of the story. With justice, it should also be remembered that the conclusions Madison and his colleagues drew from past history in the 1780s were brought into question by the experience of the 1790s: eleven years after the convention "the father of the Constitution" had come to fear tyranny from the central government far more than anarchy, and he proposed, in the Virginia Resolutions of 1798, a role for the states in judging the constitutionality of Congress's laws. In the end, the future of the republic was decided not at Philadelphia so much as at Appomattox, by a war fought for much the same reason as that for which the constitutional convention met—to assure that "government of the people, by the people, for the people, shall not perish from the earth."

Pauline Maier is professor of history at the Massachusetts Institute of Technology. She is the author of *The Old Revolutionaries: Political Lives in the Age of Samuel Adams* (1980).

"Outcast" Rhode Island—
The Absent State

John P. Kaminiski

"Twelve states sent delegates; Rhode Island did not attend." This statement has been and will be repeated over and over again as we celebrate the Bicentennial of the United States Constitution. By now it has become a well-known fact that only Rhode Island refused to appoint delegates to the Constitutional Convention that met in Philadelphia during the summer of 1787. But few know why Rhode Island remained aloof.

The fundamental cause of Rhode Island's behavior lay in economics. As in other states, Rhode Island's economy had been thrown into turmoil by the Revolutionary War. Postwar depression in Rhode Island had caused the state to polarize politically and in April 1786, the Mercantile party, which favored strengthening Congress's powers, was thoroughly repudiated at the polls. The Country party, which promised a program of debtor relief, won overwhelming victories in both the legislative and gubernatorial elections.

In May 1786 the Country party began implementing its antidepression program, which centered around the issuance of £100,000 in paper money to be loaned by the state primarily on real estate collateral. The enormous amount of money issued, suspicion of paper money brought about by bad wartime experience with continental currency, and the requirement that creditors accept the paper in payment combined to guarantee that the currency would decline in value. In fact, depreciation was exactly what Country party leaders wanted. With a depreciated currency, debtors—both public and private—could more easily pay their obligations, contracted originally in more valuable currency like gold or silver. One dollar in gold in 1786 would buy several times more than one dollar in paper, but as legal tender the paper would be equal to gold in paying off old debts. The state thus would be able easily to pay its huge public

49

debt, which had gravitated into the hands of a relatively few merchant-speculators. These few had been reaping large profits from interest paid by the state at the expense of farmers impoverished by the taxes levied to meet these obligations. Farm bankruptcies and foreclosures became common. The short-term goal of the Country party was "To Relieve The Distressed." A long-term goal was to redeem the entire state debt with almost worthless paper money. This redemption began in December 1786 and was completed less than three years later.

By early 1787, the Country party's program was well established and a large majority of Rhode Islanders expressed approval at the spring elections. A vociferous minority, however, denounced the paper-money program. Nationally, Rhode Island's policies gained notoriety and a wave of verbal abuse assaulted the state. Newspapers in particular were filled with denunciations of "Rogue's Island." Some even demanded the abolition of the state as a political entity, proposing to divide its territory between Connecticut and Massachusetts. The more Rhode Island was censured, the more Rhode Islanders as a whole supported the Country party and derided the interfering Congress.

The desire to give Congress power to control the radical economic policies of some of the states served as a central reason for calling the Constitutional Convention. Rhode Island's radicalism stood out above all others. Congress itself had denounced Rhode Island's paper money in 1786 when it refused to accept the currency in payment of the congressional requisition. Many Americans agreed with George Washington's description of Rhode Island as "outcasts from the Society." Thus, Rhode Islanders knew that the Constitutional Convention was aimed, in part, at them. On the other hand, as long as the Articles of Confederation remained in operation, Country party leaders knew that their economic program would be immune from congressional interference. The unanimity required of the states to amend the Articles or to grant additional powers to Congress meant that Rhode Island could exercise a veto over any proposed change.

On 14 March 1787, the Rhode Island Assembly met and read the congressional resolution of 21 February calling the Constitutional Convention. A motion to appoint delegates to the Convention was rejected by a substantial majority of those present. During the first week of May 1787 another legislative session convened and assemblymen from Providence and Newport urged a reconsideration of an appointment to the Convention. The Assembly approved the appointment by a majority of two, but the Upper House voted it down by a two-to-one majority.

In response to this second rejection, twelve merchants and tradesmen from Providence who opposed the state's economic program took matters into their own hands. With General James M. Varnum, a Rhode Island delegate to Congress, as emissary, they sent a letter to the Constitutional Convention that expressed their distress at Rhode Island's decision: "Deeply affected with the evils of the present unhappy times," the merchants wrote, they thought it proper to tell the Convention of the hope "of the well inform'd throughout this State" that Congress might be given additional powers over commerce and taxation. The group asked that the Convention allow Varnum "to take a seat with them; when the Commercial Affairs of the Nation are discuss'd." On 28 May the Constitutional Convention read the letter but refused the request.

In mid-June, the Rhode Island Assembly again turned down a proposal to send delegates to Philadelphia. In this instance, the Upper House voted "yea" and the Assembly "nay." But the apparent reversal was owing to some political chicanery. The Country party, in control of both houses of the legislature by sizable majorities, decided that it was politically opportune for its members in both houses to be able to say to some of their constituents that they had supported sending delegates to the Convention, but to be able to say to other constituents that they had opposed the appointment of delegates. The apparent flip-flop by the houses was in reality a well-orchestrated move that allowed Country party legislators to be on both sides of this issue.

Two days after the last rejection, General Varnum wrote to George Washington, president of the Constitutional Convention, fuming. Varnum wanted Washington to know "that the measures of our present Legislature do not exhibit the real character of the State. They are equally reprobated & abhor'd by Gentlemen of the learned professions, by the whole mercantile body, & by most of the respectable farmers and mechanicks. The majority of the administration is composed of a licentious number of men, destitute of education, and many of them void of principle. From anarchy and confusion they derive their temporary consequences, and this they endeavor to prolong by debauching the minds of the common people, whose attention is wholly directed to the Abolition of debts both public & private."

All over the country, people decried Rhode Island's action. On 2 September Francis Dana, a Massachusetts delegate to the Constitutional Convention who was unable to attend because of illness, wrote his fellow Convention delegate Elbridge Gerry that Rhode Island's "neglect will give grounds to strike it out of the Union & divide [its] Territory between [its] Neighbours.... Therefore a bold politician wou'd seize upon the occasion [of its] abominations and anti-federal conduct presents for annihilating [it] as a separate Member of the Union. I think they are now fully ripe for the measure, and that the other Members of the Union, nay all Mankind, must justify it as righteous & necessary."

In response to the widespread disapproval, Governor John Collins called the legislature into special session in mid-September 1787. A joint legislative committee was appointed to draft a letter to Congress explaining why the legislature had refused to appoint delegates to the Convention. The letter, adopted on 15 September, acknowledged the "many severe and unjust sarcasmes propagated against us" for failing to appoint Convention delegates, but it asserted that the legislature could not appoint such a delegation because a state law provided that only the people could elect delegates to Congress. A legislative appointment to the Convention that intended to propose amendments to the Articles of Confederation was felt to be a violation of the spirit of this law. (The Committee did not explain the discrepancy between this position and the fact that each house of the legislature on different occasions had believed that it was proper to appoint delegates to the Constitutional Convention.) Nevertheless, the legislature, it said, looked forward to joining "with our Sister States in being instrumental in what ever may be advantageous to the Union, and to add strength and permanance thereto, upon Constitutional principles." The Assembly deputies from Newport and Providence entered an official protest to this letter stating that "the Legislature have at various times agreed to Conventions with the Sister States," and the appointment of delegates to these conventions had never been considered "inconsistent with or any Innovation upon the Rights and Liberties of the Citizens of this State." On 17 September Governor Collins forwarded both the letter and the protest to Congress where they were read a week later.

Why then did Rhode Island oppose the Constitutional Convention? First and foremost, Rhode Islanders believed that the Convention would take some decided action against the radical economic policies of the state legislatures. Country party leaders, unused to federal involvement, did not want to participate in such an inhospitable assembly. Their primary goal was to redeem the state debt with depreciated state currency; little else mattered. Their aloofness, they hoped, might even lessen the authority of the Convention by denying it an unanimous representation of the states. Country party leaders worried little about the actual implementation of anti-Rhode Island measures. They saw no need to fight these anticipated discriminatory measures in the hostile arena of the Convention when Rhode Island knew that it could veto any change in the Articles of Confederation proposed by the Convention.

But the strategy backfired. Rhode Island's failure to appoint delegates to the Constitutional Convention proved advantageous to advocates of a new constitution. The obstinacy of Rhode Island demonstrated clearly that the newly proposed Constitution could not be ratified by all of the states as required by the Articles of Confederation. Rhode Island's absence thus helped persuade the Constitutional Convention to provide that ratification by nine states would be sufficient to establish the Constitution among the ratifying states.

Rhode Island's obstreperousness continued. Its legislature refused on seven occasions to call a state convention to consider the Constitution. Not until January 1790, after all of the state debt had been redeemed, was a ratifying convention called. The Convention met during the first week of March 1790 and proposed a bill of rights and amendments to the Constitution that were submitted to the people for their consideration in town meetings. The Convention then recessed until late May.

The continued failure of Rhode Island to ratify the Constitution exasperated Congress. On 13 May 1790 the United States Senate passed a bill to boycott the wayward state. No American ship could enter Rhode Island, and no Rhode Island ship could enter the United States. The bill also prohibited land transportation and provided that the recalcitrant state pay Congress $25,000 by December 1790 in payment of Rhode Island's share of the expenses of the old Confederation government.

Now under siege from Congress, Rhode Islanders began to press for ratification. On 24 May 1790, the day that the state Convention reconvened, a Providence town meeting instructed its Convention delegates on their course of action should the Constitution be rejected again. The delegates were ordered to confer with delegates from Newport and other towns in applying to Congress for protection if and when the towns seceded from the state. Rhode Island had had enough— it could no longer stay out of the Union. On the 29th of May 1790 the Convention voted 34 to 32 to ratify the Constitution. The fourteen-month separation was over—Rhode Island was again one of the United States.

John P. Kaminiski is the editor of *The Documentary History of the Ratification of the Constitution and the Bill of Rights 1787-1791,* at the University of Wisconsin, Madison.

Who Was Who in the Constitutional Convention: A Pictorial Essay of Its Leading Figures

Margaret Horsnell

It all began on May 25, 1787, a rainy Friday morning, as the delegates assembled at the State House in Philadelphia where eleven years earlier the Declaration of Independence had been voted and signed. Now these delegates were about to participate in another event of major significance: the Constitutional Convention.

Of the seventy-four delegates who were selected to attend the Convention, only fifty-five eventually participated and, of those, only thirty-nine signed the completed document. The following are paintings and engravings, made around the time of the Convention, of eleven of the men who played key roles in shaping and presenting plans of government, and in hammering out compromises that were crucial to the successful completion of that extraordinary document.

George Washington

As the first order of business, George Washington was unanimously elected as the presiding officer. He was fifty-five years old, a striking figure—over six feet tall—elegant, energetic, and graceful. Among the delegates as well as among most Americans, Washington had won an unparalleled reputation by his service as the commander of the Continental Armies. Washington spoke only once during the convention and then on a very minor issue. His most important function at the Convention was to serve as a symbol of probity and legitimacy. William Pierce, a fellow delegate who wrote brief biographical sketches of all the members of the Convention, observed of Washington, "Having conducted these states to independence and peace, he now appears to assist in framing a Government to make the People happy."

Edmund Randolph

The first serious debate of the Convention was initiated when Edmund Randolph introduced the Virginia plan. Randolph, a member of one of the first families of Virginia, only in his early thirties, had already been elected governor of Virginia. The introduction of the Virginia plan changed the course of the Convention because, rather than revising the Articles of Confederation as the delegates had been instructed, the delegates now began to debate the merits of a new scheme of government.

Although Randolph played an active role in the Convention's deliberations, he refused to sign the completed document alleging that he was concerned about the "indefinite and dangerous powers given to Congress." These reservations were apparently overcome after the Constitution was ratified because Randolph accepted the position of attorney general in Washington's first cabinet.

John Rutledge

Planter, lawyer, businessman, head of the aristocratic South Carolina delegation, John Rutledge served with particular skill as the chairman of the Committee of Detail. That committee pieced together, from various motions that had come before the Convention, the first draft of what was to

become the Constitution. In the process, the committee converted the general law-making power of Congress into eighteen specific powers beginning with the power to tax and ending with the "Necessary and Proper" clause.

The committee also placed a number of restrictions on the power the states might exercise. By granting some power to the national government and withholding some power from the state governments, the committee had come up with a partial solution of how to divide sovereignty between the states and the national government, thereby laying the foundations for the federal system.

Roger Sherman

Roger Sherman, delegate from Connecticut, was one of the pivotal figures in the Constitutional Convention. Sherman introduced a compromise that reconciled the Virginia and the New Jersey plans. A typical product of Yankee New England, Sherman was hard working and honest, an astute self-educated lawyer. Although he came from modest circumstances, he had worked his way up the social ladder. In general he thought the government under the Articles of Confederation satisfactory; yet he also realized that it needed adjustments to remedy specific defects. William Pierce described Sherman as "awkward . . . and unaccountably strange in his manner. But in his train of thinking there is something regular, deep, and comprehensive."

To Sherman, politics was the art of compromise. Therefore, not surprisingly, he introduced the Great Compromise that would break the deadlock the Convention had been struggling with for more than six weeks. The controversy centered on the question of whether representation was to be based on population or whether each state was to be equally represented. Sherman's solution was one he had brought up eleven years earlier during the debate on the Articles of Confederation, namely that representation should be based on two different principles. The lower house should be apportioned according to population and in the upper house the states would be equally represented. This compromise was accepted by the delegates on July 16.

James Wilson

James Wilson was one of the most influential members of the Pennsylvania delegation. Along with James Madison, Wilson was probably the most sophisticated political thinker at the Convention. Pierce said of him "Mr. Wilson ranks among the foremost in legal and political knowledge."

As the debate on representation in the legislative body developed, the question of how slaves were to fit into the new scheme of government came up. At this point Wilson proposed that apportionment in the lower legislative body should also include three-fifths of all other persons—namely slaves. The question of whether slaves should be counted as people for the purposes of representation was not new. The three-fifths formula had been recommended by the Congress under the Articles of Confederation in 1783 and had become known as the "federal ratio." Apparently Wilson believed that the three-fifths compromise on slavery was the price that had to be paid for the support of the Deep South for popular representation in the legislative bodies. At any rate, the three-fifths compromise on slavery set the stage for the Great Compromise.

Gouverneur Morris

Gouverneur Morris spoke more than any other delegate at the Convention. He was witty, sophisticated, an aristocrat to the core. Morris had little faith in the common man and therefore favored property qualifications on suffrage. Pierce says of him that he was "one of those Genius's in whom every species of talents combine to render him conspicuous and flourishing in public debate, [yet] with all those powers he is fickle and inconstant, never pursuing one train of thinking."

As a member of the Committee of Style, it was Morris who put the finishing touches on the Constitution. Perhaps his most important contribution in this area appears in the Preamble. The original Preamble, written by the Committee of Detail, after the phrase, "We the People," listed each of the states; Morris changed the language by deleting the states' names and substituting "United States." The Preamble would thus begin: "We the People of the United States." Given Morris's conservative predilections, it is unlikely that this change in phrasing was motivated by a desire to increase popular participation in the new frame of government; it may however have been introduced as a means of legitimizing the activities of the Convention. The opponents of the Constitution could not claim that the new government was based upon "aristocratic" principles if the authority to originate that government rested with the people. Whether it was intentional or not, by this fortuitous shift of phrase another step was taken in transferring the sovereign power from the states to the people.

By Monday, September 17, 1787, the delegates at the Convention had completed their work, and Madison made this

closing entry in his journal: "The Constitution being signed by all the Members except Mr. Randolph, Mr. Mason, and Mr. Gerry who declined giving it the sanction of their names, the Convention dissolved itself by an Adjournment sine die ———."

George Mason

Ranked with Washington and Jefferson, George Mason was an immensely influential political figure in the state of Virginia. A wealthy planter-aristocrat and slave owner, he opposed the extension of slavery. He wrote the famous Virginia Declaration of Rights, which was an eloquent statement of human freedom and which, after the Constitution was ratified, served as a basis for the Bill of Rights. Pierce described Mason as "a Gentleman of remarkable strong powers, [who] possesses a clear and copious understanding."

During the Convention, he actively supported the provisions of the Constitution prohibiting the suspension of the right of habeas corpus by Congress, prohibiting the use of bills of attainder (legislation that punishes an individual without trial or conviction in ordinary judicial proceedings), and prohibiting the use of ex post facto laws. On September 12, Mason suggested that a general bill of rights be added to the Constitution. He observed that "it would give great quiet to the people." Elbridge Gerry, a delegate from Massachusetts, concurred. However, Roger Sherman spoke against the bill of rights on the grounds that it was unnecessary because the state governments had declarations of rights that were not repealed by the Constitution. The Convention voted down the addition of a bill of rights.

The failure of the Convention to provide any basic list of guaranteed rights and the extension of the slave trade for twenty years turned Mason against the Constitution and he refused to sign the document. Later in the Virginia Ratifying Convention, Mason became one of the principal spokesmen opposing the acceptance of the document.

William Paterson

On June 15, William Paterson introduced the New Jersey plan—which was the small states' response to the Virginia plan. Paterson, delegate from New Jersey, was educated at Princeton and trained as a lawyer. He had a profound respect for property rights. Paterson believed that freedom could flourish only in a stable economic environment. Like other moderate nationalists, Paterson realized that it was necessary to increase the power of the central government; yet he also wished to protect the rights of the states. William Pierce characterized him as "one of those kind of men whose powers break in upon you, and create wonder and astonishment."

Luther Martin

Ornery and brilliant, Luther Martin was one of the most fascinating personalities at the Convention. An unyielding advocate of the rights of the states, Martin confounded the delegates by providing the original language for the Supremacy Clause. Born in the backcountry of New Jersey, Martin was from modest circumstances. Blessed with an outstanding mind, he made his way to Princeton where he became one of the top scholars in his class. At the Convention Martin spoke frequently, and to many delegates tiresomely, on the issue of states' rights. For Martin, the states were sovereign entities. The states and not the people were the basic building blocks within the political system. Since each of the states was an equal independent unit, any plan to diminish the equality of the states was anathema to Martin.

Perhaps his most important contribution was made on July 17. At that time the delegates were discussing how

disputes between the national and the state governments were to be resolved. Martin, a fervent advocate of states' rights, made the following astonishing motion: "that the acts of Congress and treaties shall be the suspreme law of the respective states . . . and the judiciaries of the several states shall be bound thereby in their decisions. . . ."

The language of this motion was subsequently modified and eventually this provision became known as the "Supremacy" clause. Although this clause appeared to grant additional power to the national government, the question of what agency of government would overturn state laws that conflicted with national laws was left unresolved. Martin pointed out that at the time he made this motion it was not established that there would be an inferior national court system; therefore he assumed that the state courts would settle any disputes that might arise.

On September 4, Martin left the Convention in disgust. He refused to sign the document declaring that the Constitution would create a consolidated "kingly government."

William Samuel Johnson

Sophisticated, dignified, William Samuel Johnson was from one of the most socially prominent and wealthy families of Connecticut. Throughout the Convention, Johnson had been an active behind-the-scenes participant. As the Convention wound to an end, Johnson offered a proposal that squarely raised for the first time the issue of the jurisdiction of the Supreme Court.

The question of judicial review—the right of the Supreme Court to overturn laws that are not constitutional—was never really resolved during the Convention. The closest the delegates came to deciding the issue occurred during a debate on the organization of the Court. At that time, Johnson offered an amendment that stated that "the jurisdiction of the Supreme Court shall extend to all cases arising under this Constitution and the laws passed by the Congress of the United States." According to Madison, the delegates accepted this provision with the understanding that the jurisdiction of the Supreme Court extended to only those cases involving the judiciary and not to cases involving the president or the Congress.

James Madison

At the Convention, the modest but gifted James Madison played dual roles: as the reporter of the proceedings and as one of the principal authors of the document. Because the delegates took an oath of secrecy, there were no official records of the de-

bates of one of the most important events of American history. William Jackson, the official secretary, seems to have kept only a simple record of motions and votes. But James Madison became the Convention's most assiduous chronicler. Madison attended all of the meetings and positioned himself in front of Washington so that he could more easily follow the proceedings. As a result of his prodigious labors, Madison's "notes" have become the principal source of information of these extraordinary and secret meetings.

Not only did Madison record what happened but he shaped the substantive issues of the Convention. Madison enthusiastically supported a strong national government and the abandonment of the Articles of Confederation. It was his philosophy of government, embodied in the Virginia plan, that set the tone for the Convention. Pierce said of him, "Every person seems to acknowledge his greatness. He blends together the profound politician, with the scholar."

SUGGESTED ADDITIONAL READING

Bernard Bailyn, *The Ideological Origins of the American Revolution* (1967).

Catherine Drinker Bowen, *Miracle at Philadelphia* (1966).

Christopher Collier and James Collier, *Decision in Philadelphia: The Constitutional Convention of 1787* (1986).

John Hope Franklin, *From Slavery to Freedom* (1979).

Linda K. Kerber, *Women of the Republic: Intellect and Ideology in Revolutionary America* (1980).

Forrest McDonald, *Novus Ordo Seclorum: The Intellectual Origins of the Constitution* (1985).

Richard B. Morris, *Witnesses at the Creation: Hamilton, Madison, Jay, and the Constitution* (1985).

Jack N. Rakove, *The Beginnings of National Politics: An Interpretive History of the Continental Congress* (1979).

Clinton Rossiter, *1787: The Grand Convention* (1966).

David P. Szatmary, *Shays' Rebellion: The Making of an Agrarian Insurrection* (1980).

Carl Van Doren, *The Great Rehearsal: The Story of the Making and Ratifying of the Constitution of the United States* (1986).

Gordon S. Wood, *The Creation of the American Republic, 1776-1787* (1969).

Alfred E. Young, ed., *The American Revolution: Explorations in the History of American Radicalism* (1976).

Margaret Horsnell is a professor of history at American International College in Springfield, Mass.

Thomas Jefferson and the Constitution

Merrill D. Peterson

In the Declaration of Independence, Thomas Jefferson set forth in bold, round terms the political philosophy of the new nation. The principle that governments derive their just powers from "the consent of the governed" became the cornerstone of American constitutionalism. It opened an age of constitution making both in the states and in the confederation. The creation of new republican government was, Jefferson said in 1776, "the whole object of the present controversy," for although independence might be achieved, without it the revolution would fail in the higher goal of securing human freedom and self-government. For the rest of his life Jefferson was involved in the making and remaking of constitutions and, of course, in their interpretation. As a constitutionalist, he is generally associated with theories of extreme suspicion of governmental power and strict construction of written constitutions. And this characterization is true. But it is only part of a much more complex truth. Jefferson was a democrat. He trusted the people to rule themselves. He was a philosopher of the Enlightenment, who distrusted the boasted "wisdom of ancestors," welcomed progress, and was receptive to change. This double commitment to preservation and to change proved difficult for Jefferson, and it is probably impossible for us. Yet it lay at the core of Jefferson's thought and it remains, in a sense, the basic dilemma of American constitutionalism.

The forty-four year old Jefferson was United States minister to France when the federal convention met at Philadelphia in 1787. For three years he had seen the infant republic scoffed, kicked, and jeered from London to Algiers, all respect for its government annihilated by the opinion of its weakness and incompetence. He had been frustrated in his diplomacy at Versailles, a friendly court, and had gone begging to Dutch banks for loans to keep the confederation afloat. Jefferson was,

65

Thomas Jefferson

therefore, a warm advocate of a stronger government, one more national in character, and endowed with requisite powers to command influence and respect abroad as well as at home. Seeing a roster of the convention delegates, he exclaimed, "It is really an assembly of demigods," and he eagerly awaited the results of their deliberations.

When the finished work reached Paris in the fall, Jefferson was initially shocked and dismayed. "How do you like our new constitution?" he addressed his diplomatic friend and colleague, John Adams, in London. "I confess there are things in it which stagger all my dispositions." He had, of course, looked for a reinvigorated confederation rather than a bold new frame of government. Moreover, he pondered the constitution in Europe, where tyranny, not anarchy, was the problem, where the curtain had just gone up on the French Revolution, and where he had come to appreciate as never before the inestimable blessings of American liberty. He thought that the delegates had overreacted to Shays's Rebellion. Some months earlier, discussing the Massachusetts insurrection with Adams and members of his family, who were terrified by it, Jefferson declared philosophically, "I like a little rebellion now and then. It is like a storm in the atmosphere." This libertarian spirit, more congruous with the hopes of 1776 than the hopes of 1787, separated Jefferson from Adams and many of the framers of the Constitution. Nevertheless, the more Jefferson studied the Constitution the more he approved of it.

However, he voiced two major objections. First, the perpetual reeligibility of the chief magistrate opened the door to monarchy. Most of the evils of European government were traceable to their kings, he said; and a president of the United States reeligible every fourth year would soon become a king, albeit an elective one. These fears were little felt at home, however, chiefly because of the universal confidence of George Washington, whose election to the presidency was a foregone conclusion. So Jefferson suspended this objection and concentrated on the more important one, the omission of a bill of rights, in which he was supported by the mass of Anti-Federalists.

At first he unwittingly played into the game of using the demand for a bill of rights to delay or defeat ratification of the Constitution. His suggestion in a private letter that four states withhold assent until the demand was met contributed to the initial rejection of the Constitution in North Carolina. Actually, Jefferson always supported speedy adoption by the necessary nine states; and when Massachusetts opted for unconditional ratification with recommended amendments, Jefferson quickly endorsed the plan. Meanwhile, he employed his persuasive powers to convert his friend James Madison, the Federalist leader, to the cause of a bill of rights. Acknowledging the inconveniences and imperfections of parchment guarantees of liberty, conceding the theoretical objection to the denial of powers that had not been granted, Jefferson still insisted that "a bill of rights is what the people are entitled to against every government on earth, general or particular, and what no government should refuse, or rest on inference."

Jeffersonian Theory

The dominant feature of Jefferson's constitutional theory was the juxtaposition of "strict construction" of the fundamental law with readiness to accommodate change through the ongoing consent of the people. During the 1790s, as the emerging leader of the opposition Republican party, Jefferson appealed to the letter of the Constitution to curb Federalist excesses and he rose to the presidency in 1801 on a platform of state rights and limited government. Not surprisingly, this negative part of Jefferson's constitutional theory occupied so large a place in public debate that the positive part was all but forgotten. Yet the negative assumed the positive: a constitution should be strictly adhered to by mere law-making authorities because the constitution-making authority of the people is always available to introduce change either by amendment or by convention.

In 1789, the first year of the French Revolution and the first year of the new government under the Constitution, Jefferson set forth the theory that each generation should make its own constitution; and while he never found a way to reduce the theory to practice he never abandoned it. He abhorred the idolatry of constitutions. "I am certainly not an advocate for frequent and untried changes in laws and constitutions. . . . But I know also," he declared in a memorable letter, "that laws and institutions must go hand in hand with the progress of the human mind. As that becomes more developed, more enlightened, as new discoveries are made, new truths disclosed, and manners and opinions change with the change of circumstances, institutions must advance also, and keep pace with the times. We might as well require a man still to wear the coat which fitted him when a boy, as civilized society to remain ever under the regimen of their barbarous ancestors." Yet, despite this progressive outlook, self-appointed Jeffersonians throughout American history have sought to impede the wheels of progress by invocations of strict construction and the sanctity of constitutions.

Jefferson had first wrestled with the problem of securing the means of change together with the benefits of a written fundamental law in connection with the Virginia constitution of 1776. In June, while he was drafting the Declaration of Independence in Philadelphia, Jefferson also drew up a plan of government for Virginia and sent it to the revolutionary convention in Williamsburg. The relationship of one state paper to the other was that of theory to practice, principle to application. Jefferson therefore included a number of liberal reforms in the draft constitution. None of these appeared in the constitution adopted for Virginia, however. Jefferson at once became the constitution's severest critic, not alone because of its conservative character but because it failed to meet the test of republican legitimacy. The "convention," so-called, that adopted it was the revolutionary successor of the House of Burgesses, elected in April to perform the regular business of government. How, then, could it frame a supreme law binding on government itself?

Making this objection, Jefferson was not being frivolous. He was groping toward the conception of constituent sovereignty in which the government actually rises upon "the consent of the governed." In his draft constitution he proposed a form of popular ratification—a radical idea of 1776. He also included a provision for future amendment by the consent of the people in two-thirds of the counties all voting on the same day. This was unprecedented. Only two of the first state constitutions contained an amendment power, both by the legislature solely. Jefferson made the omission of any provision for constitutional change a leading count in his indictment of

Draft copy of the Declaration of Independence

the Virginia frame of government.

In 1783 when Jefferson drafted a more elaborate constitution for a reform convention that, alas, never materialized, he adopted a process of periodic revision and reform by way of popularly elected conventions. The plan of government was published in his book *Notes on the State of Virginia.* It was the proposal to "new model" (i.e., revise) constitutions more or less regularly that Madison singled out for criticism in the 49th *Federalist* paper. Madison pointed to the twin dangers of "disturbing the public tranquillity" by too frequent recurrence to the people and depriving the government of the veneration essential for its stability. Such considerations might be disregarded in a "nation of philosophers." "But," Madison sighed, "a nation of philosophers is as little to be expected as the philosophical race of kings wished for by Plato." This undoubtedly expressed the prevailing political wisdom. Jefferson, while he did not stand alone, showed greater receptivity to institutionalized constitutional change and more openness to popular will and opinion than any of his eminent contemporaries.

Yet in the political battles of the 1790s involving the United States Constitution, Jefferson associated himself with principles of strict construction, and this negative half of the equation entered deeply into emerging Republican ideology almost to the exclusion of the positive emphasis on change. The issue was drawn in the conflict between the two giants of the Washington administration, Jefferson, secretary of state, and Alexander Hamilton, secretary of Treasury.

As part of his financial plan for the new nation, Hamilton had proposed to Congress the incorporation of a great national bank. The bill was passed in 1791, but only after serious questions of constitutionality were raised. The president, in some doubt, asked his secretaries for opinions. Jefferson returned a brisk twenty-two hundred word brief against the bill. The Constitution established a government of delegated powers; no power to incorporate a bank had been delegated, nor could it be fairly inferred from any other power. The bank bill therefore breached the limits of the Constitution. "To take a single step beyond the boundaries thus specially drawn around the power of Congress," Jefferson warned, "is to take possession of a boundless field of power, no longer susceptible to any definition." In response to this opinion Hamilton enunciated the doctrine of "implied powers," under which Congress was authorized to employ all requisite means in the exercise of its limited powers. Persuaded by Hamilton's long and powerful argument, Washington signed the bill into law.

And so the Constitution, three years young, ceased to be immutable. It was not until 1819, however, in the opinion of the Supreme Court upholding the constitutionality of the Second Bank of the United States, that Hamilton's doctrine became the cornerstone, indeed the triumphal arch, of American law. The idea of "a living constitution," one that is continually accommodated to changing national circumstances, needs, and demands through legislative, executive, and, above all, judicial interpretation, was born when Chief Justice John Marshall declared in *McCulloch v. Maryland* that the Constitution is "intended to endure for ages to come, and consequently, [is] to be adapted to the various crises of human affairs." Increasingly, Article III, which described the judicial power, eclipsed Article V, the amendment power, as the agency of constitutional change. The Supreme Court, as Woodrow Wilson later remarked, became "a constituent convention in continuous session."

Jefferson, of course, could never accept this development. He rejected the cornerstone upon which the whole astounding edifice of American constitutional law would be built. He opposed not the end of change, but rather the means of achieving it through loose construction or interpretation of the Constitution. He restated his position many times, as in the Kentucky Resolutions of 1798 denouncing the Alien and Sedition laws enacted by the Federalist majority during the undeclared war with France (1798-1800). These famous resolutions invoked the authority of a state to declare acts of Congress unconstitutional, thereby embodying the doctrine of strict construction in the doctrine of state rights.

Jefferson as President

Jefferson entered the presidency in 1801 pledged to restore the government to the original principles of the Constitution. The difficulties he encountered may be illustrated first by his efforts to curb the federal judiciary, and second by the Louisiana Purchase. He had always favored an independent judiciary as the guardian of individual liberties against legislative and executive tyranny. But in the "crisis of '98" the courts became abettors of tyranny, upholding the Alien and Sedition Acts—the destroyers rather than the guardians of liberty, the usurpers rather than the enforcers of the Bill of Rights.

The power of the partisan judiciary had been increased by the Judiciary Act passed in 1801, in the waning hours of the Adams administration. The act created many new judgeships and expanded the jurisdiction of the federal courts. The Federalists, Jefferson believed, had retired to the judiciary as a stronghold from which to assail his administration, and he promptly called for repeal of the Judiciary Act, which he accomplished in 1802. The case of *Marbury v. Madison* in 1803, which arose on a technical point from the Judiciary Act, pitted Chief Justice John Marshall, a staunch Federalist, against the Republican president. Jefferson objected to the decision not because the court asserted the ultimate power to interpret the Constitution, for in fact it did not go that far, but because Marshall traveled out of the case, pretending to a jurisdiction he then disclaimed, in order to administer a slap to the chief magistrate for violating constitutional rights.

With regard to judicial review, Jefferson consistently held to the theory of "tripartite balance," under which each of the coordinate branches of government has an equal right to decide questions of constitutionality for itself. Such a theory was as necessary to maintaining the separation of powers, in his opinion, as the doctrine of state rights was to preserving the division of authority in the federal system. Jefferson's repugnance to judicial supremacy in constitutional matters was also grounded in democratic principles. Federal judges had no accountability to the people and ought not, therefore, be the ultimate interpreters of the sovereign will. He sought to secure greater accountability through impeachment and an amendment making judges removable, but nothing came of the amendment and impeachment proved an embarrassing failure from which he withdrew. In the end, though he held the judiciary at bay, Jefferson was unwilling to push his principles to conclusion and he left the foundations of judicial power undisturbed for Marshall to build upon when the time was ripe.

The great foreign affairs triumph of his administration, the Louisiana Purchase, was spoiled for Jefferson by his conviction that it was "an act beyond the Constitution." Nothing in the Constitution authorized the acquisition of foreign territory, much less the incorporation of that territory and its inhabitants into the Union, as provided by the treaty with France. Jefferson drafted a constitutional amendment—"an act of indemnity"—to sanction the treaty retroactively. "I had rather ask an enlargement of power from the nation...," he wrote to a Virginia senator, "than to assume it by construction which would make our powers boundless. Our peculiar security is in the possession of a written Constitution. Let us not make it a blank paper by construction." Congress was less

Monticello

scrupulous, however, and when it declined to follow him, the president acquiesced. A revolution in the Union perforce became a revolution in the Constitution as well.

Jefferson later defended the unconstitutional actions of Brig. Gen. James Wilkinson in the suppression of the Burr Conspiracy in the southwest in 1807. Wilkinson accused Aaron Burr of plotting the secession of the Louisiana Territory. To meet the threat, the general turned New Orleans into an armed camp, subverted the civil authority, and placed several of Burr's associates under military arrest. Yet Jefferson justified these actions under his own version of "executive prerogative." Strick observance of written law was not always the highest duty. "To lose our country by scrupulous adherence to written law," he wrote, "would be to lose the law itself, with life, liberty, property, and all those who are enjoying them with us, thus absurdly sacrificing the ends to the means." So it is incumbent on high officials, like Wilkinson in 1807, to risk themselves on great occasions when the safety of the nation or other paramount interests are at stake. In Jefferson's thinking, actions of this kind, which were exceptional and uncodified, were preferable to false and tortuous constructions of the Constitution, which permanently corrupted it.

In retirement at Monticello from 1809 until his death seventeen years later Jefferson repeatedly contronted the problem of constitutional preservation and change. He knew there could be no preservation without change, no constructive change without preservation. He again declared his belief, formed in 1789 in the shadow of the fallen Bastille, that each generation, representing a new constituent majority, should make its own constitution. The American republic was an experiment in liberty and self-government, and it would survive only as long as the people kept it responsive to change. "Nothing is unchangeable but the inherent and inalienable rights of man," he intoned. Changes should be made by constitutional convention or by specific amendment as prescribed in Article V. As president, Jefferson had advocated the Twelfth Amendment approved in 1804 separating the balloting for president from that for vice president, and several others that were stillborn. Now, from Monticello, he advocated amendments authorizing federal internal improvements, the direct election of the president, and the two-term limitation on presidential eligibility. None made progress. Finally, not long before his death, he "despair[ed] of ever seeing another amendment to the Constitution," and declared, "Another general convention can alone relieve us."

Jefferson continued to the end to reject constitutional change by construction or interpretation. In the wake of the Panic of 1819, which threw his private affairs into hopeless disorder, he reacted sharply against the course of consolidation in the general government, above all the bold nationalism of the Supreme Court as exhibited in such decisions as *McCulloch v. Maryland,* in which the court took a broad view of the powers of the national government and authorized the creation of the Second Bank of the United States. "The judiciary of the United States is the subtle corps of sappers and miners constantly working under ground to undermine the foundations of our confederated fabric," Jefferson wrote in 1820. "They are construing our Constitution from a co-ordination of a general and special government to a general and supreme one. This will lay all things at their feet. . . ." Only by combining the theory of constituent sovereignty with the rule of strict construction would it be possible, Jefferson believed, to maintain constitutional government on the republican foundation of "the consent of the governed."

In our time, of course, Americans have accepted, wittingly or unwittingly, the idea of a "living constitution," and passive or "implied consent" has replaced the active and real consent of the original theory of government founded on civil contract. This outcome is owing to many things—the responsiveness of modern government to public opinion, the technical complexities of present-day government, and the anachronistic character of the political language of natural rights, contract, and popular sovereignty. How Jefferson's philosophy might have come to terms with these changes, it is impossible to say. We should remember, nevertheless, that his philosophy, for all its jealousy of power, for all its opposition to judicial construction, was not rigid and conservative but enlightened, progressive, and democratic in outlook.

Merrill D. Peterson is Thomas Jefferson Foundation Professor, Corcoran Department of History, University of Virginia. He is the author of many works on Jefferson, including *Thomas Jefferson and the New Nation: A Biography* (1970).

II. Public Reception of the Constitution

The Federalist

Jean Yarbrough

On September 17, 1787, after four months of deliberation and compromise, the Federal Convention concluded its business in Philadelphia and forwarded a copy of the proposed Constitution to Congress for further action. According to the new plan of government, nine states would have to ratify the Constitution before it could go into effect. Immediately after adjournment, Alexander Hamilton, New York delegate to the Convention and one of the Constitution's chief supporters, launched an ambitious newspaper campaign to secure ratification in his home state.

Both supporters and opponents of the Constitution recognized the pivotal importance of New York. Not only did New York provide the crucial link between the New England states and the rest of the country, but it was the seat of government under the Articles of Confederation. A negative vote in New York would surely affect the outcome in other states. Yet, important as New York was, it would not be an easy state to carry. Both Robert Lansing and Robert Yates, New York's other two delegates at Philadelphia, had walked out of the Convention in protest, while Gov. George Clinton organized the opposition at home. Unanimously elected president of the New York Ratifying Convention, Clinton would use his considerable influence inside the Convention and "out of doors" in an effort to defeat the proposed Constitution.

Because time was short, Hamilton enlisted the aid of fellow New Yorker John Jay in preparing the essays. Jay, though not a delegate to the Federal Convention, was a prominent New York statesman who had served as secretary for foreign affairs under the Articles of Confederation. After several other possibilities had fallen through, Hamilton invited James Madison to join them. Madison, a leading force at the Convention, was now in New York as Virginia's representative to the Confederation Congress. Between October 1787 and May 1788, the three produced eighty-five essays under the title, *The Federalist.* It is now generally agreed that Hamilton wrote fifty-one papers, Madison twenty-six, and Jay (owing to illness) five. The remaining three papers, tracing the history of past confederacies, are the joint collaboration of Madison and Hamilton.

Following a common eighteenth-century practice, the authors did not reveal their identities but signed the papers under the pseudonyms, "Publius." Americans of that day recognized that the reference was to Publius Valerius Publicola, who, according to the account in Plutarch's *Lives,* had saved the Roman Republic. The choice of "Publius" suggested that, like their ancient namesake, the authors of *The Federalist* papers would save republicanism in America by reconstituting it on sounder principles.

Although *The Federalist* is the most important writing in American political thought, it is, more precisely, an exercise in political rhetoric than political philosophy. Unlike the great treatises of political philosophy by, say, Aristotle or Hobbes, Publius is not engaged in a disinterested pursuit of the truth. The authors of *The Federalist* do not explore such questions as "What are the proper ends of political life?" or "What form of government best promotes these ends?" Rather, they take as their starting point the principles set forth in the Declaration of Independence (which are themselves derived from Locke, the Scottish moral philosphers, and others), that the purpose of government is to protect the natural rights of man. Moreover, their work is circumscribed by the knowledge that a republican government, organized on federal principles, is the only form of government Americans will accept. The purpose of *The Federalist,* then, is to persuade the people, by reason when possible and by appeals to passion and prejudice when necessary, that the Constitution establishes a republic, and that this republic is "sufficiently federal" to secure their rights.

John Locke

But if *The Federalist* has a practical political agenda, it is by no means simply a tract for the times. Indeed, it is doubtful that *The Federalist* had much of an impact upon the ratification drive in New York. As the political scientist Clinton Rossiter has written: "Promises, threats, bargains and face to face debates, not eloquent words in even the most widely circulated newspapers, won hard-earned victories for the Constitution in the crucial states of Massachusetts, Virginia and New York." Ultimately *The Federalist's* claim to greatness lies in its authoritative explosition of the new Constitution and of the principles underlying it.

The first seal of the United States, 1782

At the bottom of *The Federalist*'s defense of the proposed Constitution is a view of human nature that may best be described as realistic. The authors of *The Federalist* rejected the popular Enlightenment view that man was basically good, and corrupted only from without by faulty institutions such as monarchy or mercantilism. Overthrow these institutions, it was widely believed, and men can live together in harmony with little or no government. Although Publius agreed that these institutions were flawed, the authors of *The Federalist*[1] held that the causes of human quarrelling could not be blamed simply on external conditions. The roots of discord and faction are "sown in the nature of man" (No. 10). Thus, in answer to the question, "Why has government been instituted at all?" Publius replied: "Because the passions of man will not conform to the dictates of reason and justice without restraint" (No.

**The Federalist's View
of Human Nature:
"If Men Were Angels. . ."**

---

[1] *The Federalist* essays will be referred to by their numbers in parentheses after quotations.

15). Since no arrangement of the social order could ever make men good, government, with its ultimate threat of coercion, would always be necessary.

Americans, blessed by Providence with the most favorable external conditions (No. 2), must learn that man is no better in the New World than in the Old. Publius is one of the first to deny "the myth of American exceptionalism." Americans, he warns, have no claim to "an exemption from the imperfections, weaknesses, and evils incident to society in every shape" (No. 6). To believe otherwise is to indulge in "the deceitful dream of a golden age."

> But if men are not good, neither does Publius regard them as simply evil. In one of the longest statements on human nature in *The Federalist,* Publius suggests that human nature partakes of both the admirable and the base and that republican government would be indefensible if men were simply degenerate.
>
> As there is a degree of depravity in mankind which requires a certain degree of circumspection and distrust: So there are *other qualities* in human nature, which justify a portion of esteem and confidence. Republican government presupposes the existence of these qualities in a higher degree than any other form. Were the pictures which have been drawn by the political jealousy of some among us, faithful likenesses of the human character, the inference would be that there is not sufficient virtue among men for self-government, and that nothing less than the chains of despotism can restrain them from destroying and devouring one another (No. 55).

Yet although republican government "presupposes" a certain capacity for virtue, elsewhere in *The Federalist* Publius makes it clear that republican government cannot *rely* on morality for its preservation. All too often, these "better motives" fail just when they become most necessary. Moreover, the promotion of virtue by the national government would require a degree of political interference in private matters inconsistent with republican liberty.

Instead, *The Federalist* seeks to ground republican government on the most reliable aspect of human nature: self-interest. By self-interest, Publius means that most men, if left alone, will naturally seek to satisfy their own interests and desires, rather than look to the well being of the whole. In a society such as the one Publius hopes to shape, this means that most men will seek a comfortable material existence. Although some men will continue to pursue the more aristocratic desires for glory and power, Publius understands that the desire for material well-being is the modern democratic passion *par excellence*. Publius does not condemn any of these selfish impulses, or even try to moderate them. For *The Federalist* is confident that improvements and discoveries in "the new science of politics" (No. 9) will enable them to channel these desires toward the public good.

Chief among these discoveries is "the enlargement of the orbit" of republican government. Opponents of the Constitution, citing the authority of the French political philosopher Montesquieu, had insisted that republican government could not be expanded beyond the size of the states. Smallness was

The Classical Republican Tradition and "the Extended Republic"

Alexander Hamilton

essential because it preserved a sense of community and made it possible for citizens to discern the common good. In an extended republic, the people would be too remote from the centers of power to participate in public affairs, and government would fall into the hands of private interests.

Publius responds in *Federalist* No. 9 by arguing that the states are far too large to meet the requirements of classical republicanism. Strict adherence to this principle would require that the states, too, be broken up into city-sized republics. Having demonstrated the inapplicability of the small republic argument to the Anti-Federalist cause, Publius then proceeds in *Federalist* No. 51 to turn the small republic argument on its head. In that paper, he argues that "the *larger* the society, provided it lie within a practicable sphere, the more duly capable it will be of self-government." For *The Federalist* the chief danger to republican government comes not from the decline in civic virtue but, on the contrary, from the all too active involvement of the majority in schemes of oppression against the minority. According to Publius, the great advantage of the extended republic is that it permits majority rule while discouraging majority faction, or the tyranny of the many over the few. The minority Publius had in mind was principally the propertied few, but it applies with equal force to religious, racial, and ethnic minorities.

The Extended Republic and "The Multiplicity of Sects and Interests"

This proposition, that a large republic is better able to protect liberty and hence to govern itself, rests on two premises. First, by extending the size of the country, the number of religious sects, political parties, and economic interests would be so multiplied that no one group could force an unjust majority to oppress others. As Publius explains, in a large, pluralistic society, a coalition of the majority "could seldom take place on any other principles but justice and the general good" (No. 51). Here again, we note the crucial distinction between majority faction and majority rule.

But for social pluralism to work to maximum advantage, it is not enough simply to extend the sphere of republican government; the Constitution must encourage a large *commercial* republic. By commerce, Publius does not mean unrestricted laissez faire, for he regards "the regulation of these various and interfering [economic] interests" as "the principal tool of modern legislation" (No. 10). What *The Federalist* has in mind, very loosely, is a system of free enterprise, in which government policy and social mores encourage the people to acquire, possess, and most important, *increase* their property and wealth.

In its defense of a commercial republic, *The Federalist* challenges still another tenet of the republican creed. For the classical tradition eschewed commerce and insisted that its citizens remain poor so that nothing could distract them from their singleminded devotion to the common good.

Having substituted self-interest for virtue as the ground or "spring" of republican government, Publius is more sanguine about the prospect of a commercial republic. As he explains in *Federalist* No. 10, the cure for the evils of majority faction lies in the division of society into different *kinds* as well as amounts of property. Rich and poor must view each other not simply as opposing classes, but as members of different economic interests and occupations: creditors, debtors, farmers, merchants, manufacturers, etc. Since only commerce can give this "variety and complexity to the affairs of a nation" (No. 56), Publius seeks to encourage a commercial republic.

"Inventions of Prudence": Representation and the Separation of Powers

The second reason that a large republic is more capable of self government is that it attracts more qualified representatives. In small republics, such as the states, representatives were drawn from smaller, more homogeneous constituencies and frequently did nothing more than mirror the "local and particular" views of the majority. By contrast, in the extended republic, electoral districts would necessarily be larger, increasing the likelihood that only the most "fit characters" would be elected. And once in office, these representatives would "refine and enlarge" rather than merely "reflect" their constituents' views. On the political level then, the advantage of the large republic consists in "the substitution of representatives whose enlightened views and virtuous sentiments render them superior to local prejudices and schemes of injustice" (No. 10). Nevertheless, Publius does not believe the large republic *guarantees* the election of "enlightened statesmen." He recognizes full well that such leaders "will not always be at the helm." Thus an additional advantage of the large electoral district is that even if less qualified men are chosen, the sheer diversity of interests and opinions that they represent, as well as the necessity to compromise in order to obtain a legislative majority, will compel them to enlarge their views. So, by virtue of the "refined" representation that the large republic encourages, self government becomes good government. It is for this reason that Publius makes representation the *sine qua non* of republican government. Republican government is nothing more—and nothing less—than a government in which "a scheme of representation takes place" (No. 10).

If the extended republic makes possible a certain kind of representation, representation in turn makes possible the principle of separation of powers. In a pure democracy, where the people exercise all political power directly, no such division of legislative, executive, and judicial powers is possible. Publius, citing Thomas Jefferson, regards the concentration of political power in the same hands as the very "definition of despotic

James Madison

government" (No. 48).

Publius does not claim to have discovered the separation of powers, but the Constitution does modify the principle significantly. Prior to 1787, the separation of powers was part of the theory of the mixed regime. According to this older view, which was given its fullest practical embodiment in the Roman Republic and later the British Constitution, political power was parcelled out to different hereditary classes in society. For example, in England, the monarch exercised executive power while the aristocracy and democracy shared legislative powers. By distributing political powers among these hereditary classes, the theorists of the mixed regime hoped to secure the benefits of monarchy, aristocracy, and democracy while avoiding their defects.

What makes the American Constitution unique is that it severs the separation of powers from the separation of classes or orders. Instead the Constitution establishes a democratic republic in which every branch of government—and not just the lower house of the legislature—represents the people. Within this wholly democratic framework, Publius hopes to secure the advantages of a mixed regime. As he explains in No. 37, by creating a single executive, independent of the legislature, the Constitution encourages energy and dispatch in that branch. Similarly, by reducing the size of the Senate and extending its terms of office, the Constitution promotes certain other aristocratic qualities—stability, wisdom, dignity—so often lacking in popular governments. In this way, the separation of powers by itself approximates the virtues of a mixed regime while remaining true to its republican form.

Still, the main purpose of the separation of powers is to prevent one branch from encroaching upon the powers of the others. According to Publius, the greatest danger to liberty in a "representative republic" comes not from the executive, but from the legislature. Because its constitutional powers are broader, and because it controls the raising and spending of money, the legislature stands in need of the greatest checks. "The provision for defense must . . . be made commensurate to the danger of attack" (No. 51). Accordingly, the Constitution divides legislative power between the two houses of Congress, each elected independently of the other and responsible to different (though democratic) constituencies. As a further precaution, the Constitution equips the executive with one-sixth of the legislative power through the veto. Finally, the Constitution encourages an independent judiciary to ensure the

John Jay

impartial administration of the laws. By giving to each branch "the necessary constitutional means, and personal motives to resist the encroachments of the others" (No. 51), the Constitution puts teeth into the principle of separation of powers. Here again, Publius reiterates his view that the Constitution cannot rely primarily upon the "better motives" of moral and patriotic leaders to maintain the proper separation of powers, but must appeal instead to each individual's self interest. In perhaps the most famous passage of *The Federalist*, Publius connects the separation of powers with his realistic view of man:

> Ambition must be made to counteract ambition. The interest of the man must be connected with the constitutional rights of the place. It may be a reflection on human nature that

such devices should be necessary to control the abuses of government. But what is government itself but the greatest of all reflections on human nature? If men were angels, no government would be necessary. If angels were to govern men, neither external nor internal controls on government would be necessary (No. 51).

The Constitution not only divides power horizontally among the three different branches of government, it also divides power vertically between the federal government and the states. This vertical distribution—or federalism—in which power is constitutionally distributed between two levels of government, each of which is supreme in its own sphere, is the most novel of the framers' inventions. Prior to 1787, federalism was synonymous with confederalism. Federalism in this more traditional sense referred to a league of small republics, united for limited security purposes. The states retained full sovereignty over their internal affairs and were represented equally in the federal alliance. Confederalism was a vital component of the small republic tradition, according to which only the state governments could preserve republican liberty.

But in 1787, a new generation of Americans, having witnessed first hand the defects of state sovereignty under the Articles of Confederation became convinced a modification of the traditional federal principle was necessary if liberty was to be secure. Accordingly, the new federal principle invested at the Constitutional Convention forms a mean between confederation based on state sovereignty and a consolidated central government based on national sovereignty. The Constitution, Publius concedes, is "partly federal, partly national" (No. 39).

But is it "sufficiently federal" to preserve the republican liberty? In *Federalist* No. 39, Publius examines the new government from five different perspectives—its foundation, sources of power, operation and extent of powers, and the amendment process—to convince his critics that it is "sufficiently federal." His discussion makes it clear the extent to which federalism—in its contemporary meaning—suffuses the political order.

Starting with the amendment process, Publius argues that the foundation of government is a federal act since the Constitution rests on the unanimous consent of the people in the states. No state can be compelled to join the Union without its consent.

The Compound Republic: "Partly Federal, Partly National"

Considering next the sources from which the ordinary branches of government are derived, Publius concludes that they are mixed. The House of Representatives is national because it represents the people and not the states. On the other hand, the Senate, especially as originally conceived, is the most "federal" branch, since it represents each state equally regardless of its size or population. Because the president is chosen by the electoral college, rather than by direct popular vote, Publius regards the source of executive powers as essentially federal. Indeed, it is worth noting that, even today, there is no federal office that is elected by a simple majority of the people as a whole.

Turning next to the operation of the new government, Publius concedes it is unambiguously national. The federal government will have the power to legislate directly over individuals. Publius regards this provision as essential, for the government would not *be* a government if it lacked the power to legislate and enforce its decisions.

The amending power Publius considers partly federal and partly national. Although the states have the power to alter the Constitution, the amendment process does not, as traditional federal theory would have it, require the unanimous consent of the states. By contrast with the ratification process, the sovereignty of the dissenting states is here breached.

Finally, "perhaps most importantly, federalism provides some check" upon the extent of national powers. Since the federal government is "an incomplete" national government, the states are necessary to perform those tasks that are inconvenient or undesirable for the federal government to perform. The federal principle holds that the absorption of these powers by the federal government would dangerously concentrate political power.

It is true that the Constitution does not explicitly enumerate which powers are reserved to the states. For this reason, the division between state and federal jurisdiction has been more a political than a constitutional issue. Nevertheless, modern federalism preserves, however loosely, the division of power necessary for republican liberty. In this way, it accords with the central theme of *The Federalist*, that liberty is best preserved not by limiting political power, but by properly distributing it.

Conclusion   Although the immediate aim of *The Federalist* was to secure the ratification of the Constitution in New York, it remains unclear how successful the papers were in achieving

In the PRESS,
and speedily will be published,
THE

FEDERALIST,

A Collection of Essays written in favor of the New Constitution.

By a Citizen of New-York.

Corrected by the Author, with Additions and Alterations.

This work will be printed on a fine Paper and good Type, in one handsome Volume duodecimo, and delivered to subscribers at the moderate price of one dollar. A few copies will be printed on superfine royal writing paper, price ten shillings.

No money required till delivery.

To render this work more complete, will be added, without any additional expence,

PHILO-PUBLIUS,

AND THE

Articles of the Convention,

As agreed upon at Philadelphia, September 17th, 1787.

☞ *As very few more copies will be published than subscribed for, those who are desirous of possessing the Federalist through all its numbers, will be as expeditious as possible in transmitting their names to John M'Lean, printer, Norfolk, and to A. Davis, printer, Richmond, the work being already far in progress, and may be expected out in a very short time.*

Norfolk, January 16, 1788.

this goal. On June 21, 1788, while the New York Ratifying Convention was just beginning its deliberations, New Hampshire became the ninth state to ratify the Constitution. Shortly thereafter, Virginia voted to join the Union, and on July 26, 1788, with the new Constitution already a certainty, New York followed suit.

But the enduring claim of *The Federalist* does not rest primarily on its role in securing ratification. Though written in haste, under the pressure of editorial deadlines, *The Federalist* was from the outset regarded as the most authoritative explication of the principles underlying the Constitution. And two hundred years later, there is no reason to revise this view.

SUGGESTED ADDITIONAL READING

David F. Epstein, *The Political Theory of "The Federalist"* (1986).
Clinton Rossiter, ed., *Federalist Papers* (1986).

Jean Yarbrough is associate professor of political science at Loyola University of Chicago and director of the honors program. She is now at work on a manuscript entitled "Moral Foundations of the American Republic."

The Constitutional Thought
of the Anti-Federalists

Murray Dry

Although they claimed to be the true federalists and the true republicans, the men who opposed the Constitution's unconditional ratification in 1787-1788 were called Anti-Federalists. The leading opponents from the major states included Patrick Henry, George Mason, and Richard Henry Lee from Virginia, George Clinton, Robert Yates, and Melanchton Smith from New York, John Winthrop and Elbridge Gerry from Massachusetts, and Robert Whitehill, William Findley, and John Smilie from Pennsylvania. They all agreed that the document produced by the Convention in Philadelphia was unacceptable without some amendments. Since most state constitutions contained bills of rights, the need for a similar feature for the national constitution formed the Anti-Federalists' most effective argument against unconditional ratification. The national Bill of Rights is the result of that dialogue.

Nevertheless, the Anti-Federalists' major contribution to the American founding lay more in their critical examination of the new form of federalism and the new form of republican government than in their successful campaign for a bill of rights. The Anti-Federalists sought substantial restrictions on federal power, which the amendments subsequently adopted did not provide. Suspicious of a strong national government, these opponents nevertheless failed to agree on an alternative constitutional arrangement. Still, the legacy of the Anti-Federalists persists in our constitutional debates over federalism and republican government.

Anti-Federal constitutionalism finds its most thoughtful and comprehensive expression in the *Letters of the Federal Farmer* and the *Essays of Brutus,* attributed to Richard Henry Lee and Robert Yates, respectively. Although authorship remains uncertain, these writers covered all major constitu-

93

tional questions in a manner that required, and received, the attention of "Publius," the pen name adopted by Alexander Hamilton, James Madison, and John Jay, authors of the famous *Federalist* papers.

This essay will discuss Anti-Federal constitutionalism in three parts: federalism; the separation of powers; and the bill of rights.

Republican Government and Federalism

The Anti-Federalists claimed to be the true federalists because they were the true republicans. Consequently, we begin with their account of republican government and its relation to federalism.

The Anti-Federalists believed that to maintain the spirit of republican government, which was the best defense against tyranny, individuals needed to know one another, be familiar with their governments, and have some direct experience in government. Only then would the citizenry possess a genuine love of country, which is the essence of republican, or civic, virtue.

The Anti-Federalists espoused the then traditional view of republican government, reflected in the first state constitutions, which emphasized the legislative branch of government. With the first federal constitution, the Articles of Confederation, the states, through their legislatures, retained effective control of federal men and federal measures. The delegates to Congress were chosen by the state legislatures and were subject to being recalled. The federal power to raise taxes and armies not only required a vote of nine states, but, even after such a vote, it depended on state requisitions, which meant that the federal government depended on the good will of the states to execute the law.

In stark contrast, the Constitution proposed by the Federal Convention in 1787 provided the basis for a strong national government. Elections to the House of Representatives were by the people directly, not the states, and the federal powers over taxes and the raising of armies were completely independent of the state governments. This new form of federalism necessarily produced a new form of republicanism, the "large republic." Furthermore, Publius did not shrink from providing a positive argument in support of it. *Federalist* 10 justified the new form of republicanism, not only as the price of union but as the republican remedy to the disease of majority faction, or majority tyranny.

Because the Federalists saw a major danger not from the

Cartoon ridiculing the Anti-Federalists, 1793

aggrandizing of the ruling few, but from the tyranny of the majority, they sought to restrain the influence of that majority in order to secure individual rights and the permanent and aggregate interests of the community. Such restraint was to be achieved through a large extended sphere; that is, the constituencies of the federal government. These would be larger and more diverse than the constituencies of the states, and so would make majority tyranny more difficult, since more negotiation and compromise would be needed for any single faction to become part of a majority. In addition, the increased competition for office would produce better representatives and a more effective administration throughout the government.

Perhaps because he took republican government for granted, as a given in America, Publius understood it to require only that offices of government be filled directly or indirectly by popular vote. Furthermore, the representation of the people was satisfied by the fact of election, regardless of the contrast between the wealth and influence of the elected and the electorate.

To the Anti-Federalists, the people would not be free for long if all they could do was vote for a representative whom they would not know and who would be very different from them.

Because the Anti-Federalists emphasized participation in government, they argued that a small territory and a basically homogeneous population were necessary for a notion of the "public good" to be agreed upon. The Anti-Federalists did not insist that every citizen exercise legislative power. But they did emphasize representation of the people in the legislatures and on juries. By "representation" they meant that the number of people in a legislative district must be small enough and the number of districts large enough so that the citizens will know the people they are voting for and be able to elect one of their own—one of the "middling class." This latter phrase referred to the large number of farmers of modest means. A substantial representation of this agricultural middle class was possible even in the large states and necessary for the character of the governors to reflect the governed. Under the proposed constitution, argued the Anti-Federalists, this kind of representation would be impossible at the federal level, where the districts would contain at least thirty thousand people.

Likewise, by participating in local jury trials, in civil as well as criminal cases, the people in their states acquired a knowledge of the laws and the operation of government, and thereby, argued the Anti-Federalists, they become more responsible citizens. It was feared that this responsibility would be lost when cases were appealed to the proposed national supreme court, which had jurisdiction on appeal over all questions of law and fact.

Since the Anti-Federalists believed that republican government was possible in the states but not in one single government for the entire country, only a confederacy, that is, a federal republic, could safeguard the nation's freedom. They understood such a form of government to have a limited purpose, primarily common defense. Hence, those who became Anti-Federalists originally favored limited amendments to the Articles of Confederation, rather than an entirely new constitution. When a new constitution became inevitable, they hoped to limit the transfer of political power from the states to the national government. They claimed to be the true republicans and the true federalists because they understood republican government to require a closely knit people attached to their government. They sought to grant only so much power to the federal government as was absolutely necessary to provide for defense. In this way, the distribution of governmental power, as between the nation and the states, would correspond to the distribution of representation. And while the Anti-Federalists did argue for an increase in the federal representation, that by itself would not have satisfied the requirement of republican government, as they saw it, since the people would always be more substantially represented in their state governments. According to the Anti-Federalists, the Federalists were not federalists but consolidationists; and the ultimate effect of the Constitution would be to reduce the states to mere administrative units, thereby eliminating republican liberty.

Already fearful of the Constitution's threat to republican liberty, the Anti-Federalists vehemently objected to the large number of specific powers granted to Congress, especially the taxing power and the power to raise armies. They found the undefined grants of power in the "necessary and proper" and the "supremacy" clauses (I,8,18 and VI,2) alarming as well. The government, Brutus claimed, "so far as it extends, is a complete one, and not a confederation," and "all that is reserved to the states must very soon be annihilated, except so far as they are barely necessary to the organization of the general government." With the power to tax virtually unchecked, Brutus lamented that "the idea of confederation is totally lost, and that of one entire republic is embraced." The Anti-Federalists attempted to draw a line between federal and state powers, conceding to the federal government only those powers that were necessary for security and defense. Their most common tax proposal would have limited the federal government to a tax on foreign imports, leaving internal taxes, both on individuals and on commodities, to the states. This limitation would guarantee the states a source of revenue out of reach of the national government. If this federal tax source proved insufficient, the Anti-Federalists proposed turning to the states for requisitions, as was the case under the Articles of Confederation.

Brutus warned, as well, that the power "to raise and support armies at pleasure . . . tend[s] not only to a consolidation of the government, but the destruction of liberty." The Anti-Federalists generally took the position that there should be no standing armies in time of peace. Brutus proposed a

Federalism and the Constitution: The Legislative Powers

Patrick Henry

limited power to raise armies to defend frontier posts and guard arsenals to respond to threats of attack or invasion. Otherwise, he maintained, standing armies should only be raised on the vote of two-thirds of both houses.

Publius's rejection of this position was complete and uncompromising. The "radical vice" of the Confederation had been precisely the dependence of the federal power on the states. The universal axiom that the means must be proportional to the end required that the national government's powers be adequate to the preservation of the union. (*Federalist* Nos. 15, 23)

The Separation of Powers and Republican Government

The separation of powers refers primarily to the division of power among the legislative, executive, and judicial branches of government, but it also includes bicameralism, or the division of the legislature into a house of representatives and a senate. In this part, we begin with the Anti-Federalists' general approach to the separation of powers, which will be followed by accounts of their views on the senate, the presidency, and the judiciary.

The Anti-Federalists attacked the Constitution's separation of powers from two different perspectives. Some, such as Centinel (a Pennsylvania Anti-Federalist), alleged that there was too much mixing and not enough separation; others, like Patrick Henry and the Maryland Farmer, asserted that there were no genuine "checks" at all. The first position opposed the special powers given to the senate and the executive. The second argued that a true separation of powers depended upon social divisions not available in the United States, such as a hereditary nobility as distinct from the common people. The English Constitution drew on such divisions; social class checked social class in a bicameral legislature, and each was checked, in turn, by a hereditary monarch. While the Federalists celebrated the filling of all offices by election directly or indirectly, some Anti-Federalists, including Patrick Henry, argued that such elections would result in the domination of the natural, or elected, aristocracy in all branches of government, not a true "checks and balances" system.

The Senate

The Anti-Federalists feared that an aristocracy would emerge from the senate, taking more than its share of power. A small number of individuals, elected by the state legislatures for six years, and eligible for reelection, shared in the appointment and treaty-making powers with the executive, as well as in the law-making process with the house of representatives. In order to prevent senators from becoming an entrenched aristocracy, the Anti-Federalists favored an amendment requiring rotation in office and permitting recall votes by the state legislatures. They also favored a separately elected executive council, which would have relieved the senate of its share in the appointment power. None of these proposals was adopted.

The Executive

Anti-Federal opposition to the office of president was surprisingly limited. While Patrick Henry asserted that the constitution "squints toward monarchy," most of the Anti-Federalists accepted the unitary office and the "electoral college" mode of election.

The eligibility of the president to run repeatedly for office, however, did provoke substantial opposition, as did the absence of a special executive council, which would have shared the appointment power. Whereas Publius had argued that reeligibility provides a constructive use for ambition, Federal Farmer replied that once elected a man will spend all his time and exercise all his influence to stay in office. The executive council would have weakened the power of the Senate, which concerned the Anti-Federalists even more than the president's power.

No Anti-Federalist expressed concern about the general phrase "the executive power," perhaps because it was unclear whether this was a grant of power or merely the name of the office. Some questioned the "commander in chief" clause, the pardoning power, and the authority to call either of both houses into special session. But in light of the difficulties of governing without an independent executive, which the country experienced under the Articles of Confederation, and the common expectation that George Washington would become the first president, the Anti-Federalists let their objections go.

The Judiciary   While many Anti-Federalists failed to discuss it, Brutus's account of the judicial power anticipated the full development of judicial review as well as the importance of the judicial branch as a vehicle for the development of the federal government's powers, both of which he opposed. By extending the judicial power "to all cases, in law and equity, arising under this Constitution," Article III permitted the courts "to give the constitution a legal construction." Moreover, extending the judicial power to equity as well as law (a division made originally in English law) gave the courts power "to explain the constitution according to the reasoning spirit of it, without being confined to the words or letter." Hence, Brutus concluded that "the real effect of this system will therefore be brought home to the feelings of the people through the medium of the judicial power."

Under the judicial power, the courts would be able to expand powers of the legislature and interpret laws in a way Congress did not intend. Brutus interpreted the grant of judicial power to all cases arising under the Constitution as a grant of "judicial review." He opposed this grant, because he thought the judges, who were appointed for life, should leave it to Congress to interpret the constitutional reach of its powers.

Richard Henry Lee

That way, if Congress misinterpreted the Constitution by overextending its powers, the people could repair the damages at the next election. Brutus approved of the framers' decision, following the English Constitution, to make the judges independent by providing them with a lifetime appointment, subject to impeachment, and fixed salaries. But he pointed out that the English judges were nonetheless subject to revision by the House of Lords, on appeal, and to revision, in their interpretation of the constitution, by Parliament. Extending the judicial power to the American Constitution meant that there would be no appeal beyond the independent nonelected judiciary. Brutus did not think that impeachment for high crimes and misdemeanors would become an effective check, and while he did not mention it, he doubtless would have regarded the amendment process also as unsatisfactory.

Anti-Federalists including Brutus objected as well to the extensive appellate jurisdiction of the supreme court. Article III section 2 may have guaranteed a jury trial in criminal cases, but on appeal, the fate of the defendant would be up to the judges. The Anti-Federalists wanted to have the right of jury trials extended to civil cases and to have the results protected against appellate reconsideration.

Finally, Brutus objected to the "Madisonian compromise," which authorized, but did not require, Congress to "ordain and establish" lower courts. Except for the limited grant of original jurisdiction in the supreme court, judicial power, the Anti-Federalists argued, should have been left to originate in the state courts.

The Bill of Rights

The Anti-Federalists are best known for the Bill of Rights, since the Constitution would not have been ratified without the promise to add it. But the Bill of Rights was as much a Federalist as an Anti-Federalist achievement. The Anti-Federalists wanted a bill of rights to curb the power of the national government to intrude upon state power; the Bill of Rights, as adopted, did not address this question. Instead, it limited the right of government to interfere with individuals, and, as such, included provisions similar to those in the bills of rights in many of the state constitutions.

When the Federalists denied the necessity of a federal bill of rights, on the grounds that whatever power was not enumerated could not be claimed, the Anti-Federalists pointed to the Constitution's supremacy and to the extensiveness of the enumerated powers to argue that there were no effective limitations on federal authority with respect to the states. None of the actual amendments, which were written up and guided through the House by Madison, followed the Anti-Federal proposals to restrict federal powers, especially the tax and war powers. As for what became the Tenth Amendment, Madison himself said that it simply clarified the existing enumeration of powers but changed nothing. Furthermore, when an Anti-Federalist tried to get the adverb "expressly" inserted before "delegated" in the amendment—"The powers not delegated to the United States by the Constitution, nor prohibited by it to the States, are reserved to the States respectively, or to the people"—his motion failed by a substantial margin.

The Anti-Federalists' demand for a bill of rights derived from their understanding of republican government. Such a form of government was mild in its operation and a public proclamation of their rights kept the people aware of them. Consequently, the Bill of Rights, even in its Federalist form, reflects Anti-Federal constitutionalism. But the amendments did not restrict the major federal powers, over taxes, commerce, and war, or in any way limit implied powers. Furthermore, as Jefferson noted, in a letter he wrote to Madison in 1789, by emphasizing individual rights, the Bill of Rights put a legal check in the hands of the judiciary. In other words, before he opposed the power of judicial review, Jefferson seemed to take its existence for granted. He argued that writing a bill of rights into the Constitution would provide judicial protection of those rights. Neither Jefferson nor the Anti-Federalists seemed to realize how a federal bill of rights, by strengthening the federal courts, would thus serve to strengthen Federalist constitutionalism.

Conclusion

The Anti-Federalists lost the ratification debate because they failed to present a clear and convincing account of a constitutional plan that stood between the Articles of Confederation, which they acknowledged were unable to provide for the requirements of union, and the Constitution proposed by the Federal Convention, which they feared would produce a consolidation of power. And yet the periodic and contemporary constitutional debates over federalism, over the extent of legislative and executive power, and over individual rights and judicial review reflect the different conceptions of republican government that were developed in the founding dialogue over the Constitution.

Any strict construction of federal power has much in

common with Anti-Federalist constitutionalism. During the founding debate, opponents of a strong national government wanted to amend the Constitution; after ratification, Anti-Federalists had no choice but to interpret the Constitution to require limited federal government. The contemporary controversies over abortion, pornography, and sexual practices among consenting adults, and the issues surrounding the religion clauses of the First Amendment reveal disagreements over the scope of individual rights, on the one hand, and the legitimacy of government maintenance of community manners and morals on the other. These controversies resemble the founding debate over republicanism, where the Federalists focused on the security of individual rights and the Anti-Federalists expressed a greater concern for the character of republican citizenship, maintained in part through religion. Through such debates, Anti-Federal constitutionalism, as applied to governmental structure and to moral qualities necessary for free government, thus remains an important part of our constitutional polity.

SUGGESTED ADDITIONAL READING

Herbert J. Storing, *What the Anti-Federalists Were For* (1981).

Herbert J. Storing, with Murray Dry, *The Anti-Federalist* (1985).

Murray Dry, "The Case against Ratification: Anti-Federalist Constitutional Thought," in Dennis Mahoney, ed., *Essays on the Ratification of the Constitution* (1987).

Gordon Wood, *The Creation of the American Republic, 1776-1787* (1969).

Murray Dry is professor of political science at Middlebury College. He is now working on a study of the constitutional evolution of American federalism.

The Constitution as Myth and Symbol

Milton M. Klein

The United States Constitution is and always has been a political symbol as well as a political document. Like the American flag and the national anthem, the Constitution expresses ideas of patriotism, nationalism, and freedom. Unlike the flag and the anthem, the Constitution also connotes the rule of law and the superiority of higher law over legislative and executive actions. It thus confers a stamp of legitimacy upon public and private behavior that has few counterparts in other countries.

As a symbol, the Constitution's appeal has been broad and multifaceted. Historians like John Fiske celebrated the document as "this wonderful work,—this Iliad, or Parthenon, or Fifth Symphony, of statesmanship." European statesmen like William Gladstone celebrated it as "the most wonderful work ever struck off at a given time by the brain and purpose of man"; and American statesmen like Andrew Johnson paid their homage to the document in his wish: "When I die, I desire no better winding sheet than the Stars and Stripes, and no softer pillow than the Constitution of my country."

There is no necessary correlation between the symbolic and the substantive meaning that the American public attaches to its objects of civil worship. Thus, while the nation paid near-universal tribute on July 4, 1986, to the Statue of Liberty as the symbolic representation of the "Golden Door" and of America as a land of freedom and opportunity for newcomers to our shore, a CBS-*New York Times* poll, at the same time, disclosed that a plurality of those questioned believed we should be more restrictive in our immigration policies.

Symbols do, however, play an important role in American political culture, perhaps more so than in others. All political systems require a sense of personal identification between the individual citizen and the political system and a sense of

105

identification among individuals within the system. In the United States, the creation of such a sense of national identity was inhibited by the absence of a long history of nationhood or the existence of bonds like a monarchy, an aristocracy, an established religion, or a common intellectual culture. While there is evidence of an emergent sense of American nationhood even before the Revolution, the prevailing sentiment of Americans was probably more like that of the New Englander who during the Revolution declared that his affections flowed in what he called their "natural order": "toward Salem,—Massachusetts,—New England,—the Union at large."

While the Constitution did not in itself create an American nationalism, it provided an extraordinarily influential symbol of national identity; and symbols are powerful ingredients in the creation of a political culture. Symbols supply an overarching sense of unity in societies that might otherwise be riddled with conflict. They evoke, as illusion or reality, the implicit principles by which a society lives; they are visible signs of an often invisible belief; they simplify and emotionalize loyalties; and they require no formal proof. What they stand for may be only partly true, or not true at all, but for those who accept them, symbols are as real and objectively verifiable as the Rock of Gibraltar. In politics, symbols serve to link the individual to the larger political order, to synchronize the diverse motivations of different individuals, and to make possible collective action. They become the "currency" of political communication. One political scientist goes so far as to insist that for most of us, "politics is . . . a passing parade of abstract symbols," and Max Lerner suggests that unless a government is naive enough to rely solely on rational appeals or brutal enough to resort to coercion, it will employ symbols to enlist group loyalty.

Symbols are vehicles for myth making, and the myth of the Constitution early augmented that document's symbolic importance. Anthropologists define myths as tales and traditions that people develop to create and reinforce social order. Like symbols, myths provide societies with coherence and direction, putting new experiences into familiar contexts. Myths strengthen tradition and endow it with greater value and prestige by tracing it back to a higher and better source. With symbols, they give a political order a sense of purpose. Political myths and political symbols are mutually supporting and reinforcing.

"Cult of the Constitution"

The events surrounding the birth of the American republic were not particularly conducive to the creation of national symbols, but the new nation shortly created three icons: George Washington, the Stars and Stripes, and the Declaration of Independence. None of these provided underpinnings for a particular political order, since the government of the United States for the first decade of its existence rested on the tenuous foundation, first, of an informal agreement by which the Continental Congress served as a limited national government and, then, of the short-lived Articles of Confederation. The Constitution provided a more solid foundation, and its framers early began to surround it with the mythology it required as the symbol of the new political order.

The creation of a "cult of the Constitution" began with the Federalists who wrote the document and fought for its ratification. The philosophical basis for the myth was both religious and secular. Jefferson described the Framers as "demi-gods" and the document itself as the "ark of our safety." The words "ark" and "covenant" were invoked frequently by those who, in speech and writing, worked to enlist emotional support for the country's new fundamental charter. The Olympian gathering of virtuous men performing a "miracle" at Philadelphia could only be likened to a supernatural event. The Constitution itself was compared to Scripture, and the Supreme Court, in time, became the temple that incarnates the sacred document.

There is also a secular foundation for the cult of the Constitution. The colonists, in their contest with Britain, steadily insisted that Parliamentary actions violated a "constitution" that governed relations between colonies and mother country and that implicitly reserved a sphere of internal autonomy for them within the broader imperial context. Resorting to their own provincial manifestations of this imperial constitution, individual colonies insisted that the fundamental law governing their relations with the mother country was fixed and immutable, invulnerable to Parliamentary legislation and the acts of British sovereigns or their viceroys in the colonies. There were basic legal rights, several New York lawyers argued as early as 1754, that were "interwoven with and part of the Political Frame and Constitution of the Province" and that could not be arbitrarily abridged or abrogated. They repeated the claim ten years later, when they charged the province's lieutenant governor with responsibility for tampering with the traditional right to trial by jury:

Is a constitution matured by ages, founded as it were on a rock, repeatedly defended against lawless encroachments by oceans of blood, meliorated by the experiences of centuries, alike salutary to princes and people, and guarded by the most awful sanctions: is such a constitution ... now to be altered or abolished, by—the dash of a pen?

By the eve of the Revolution, the idea was widespread in the colonies that constitutions were not merely descriptions of how governments operated but rather fundamental charters, anterior to statutory law and the source from which both legislatures and executives drew their authority. Further, constitutions were held to possess a special role in the preservation of liberty, since they guaranteed from governmental interference those rights that individuals possessed in nature. Conservative patriots, in the end, could justify an act of revolution precisely because, they insisted, they were the true conservators of both the British and the colonial constitutions; the British were the innovators and the real revolutionaries!

For those Americans who accepted the Lockean theory of the origin of government there was still another ground for their respect for constitutions. A constitution represented the civil contract by which societies had been formed. The idea of the inviolability of compacts was one of the most persistent arguments employed by colonials in their legal confrontation with Parliament before the Revolution. Their relationship with Britain, they contended, was founded on an original compact between the first settlers and the Crown. The compact prescribed mutual obligations and responsibilities: the settlers agreed to establish colonies in a wild continent for England's political and economic benefit; the Crown, in turn, undertook to nurture and protect the colonies and to guarantee the settlers the same personal liberties they had possessed while in England. Independence was, then, justified, as a recognition that the Crown had broken the compact, leaving the colonists legally free to pursue their own destiny as sovereign states.

Constitutions and compacts were the high ground on which the colonists sought to justify their rebellion "out of a decent respect to the opinions" of an incredulous eighteenth-century world, and the success of that rebellion gave constitutions a hallowed place in the pantheon of American political icons. The Constitution of 1787 thus began its existence with a veneration already engendered by a long colonial and Revolutionary history.

Illustration in celebration of New York's ratification on July 26, 1788. New York Packet, July 29, 1788

Ratification   None of this is to imply that the Constitution did not require careful cultivation by its earliest supporters in order for it to assume the symbolic power it came to possess. It could hardly have been an automatic symbol of unity given the limited number of persons who were involved in its making and ratification and the violent debate over its acceptance. Anti-Federalists, of course, denounced it as an instrument of centralization, authoritarianism, aristocracy, and even godlessness, and epigrammatized it as a "thirteen-horned monster," a "spurious brat," and a "heterogeneous phantom." Federalists, on the other hand, employed the rhetoric of national unity almost from the start to counter the divisiveness aroused by the Constitution's critics. In *The Federalist* papers, its authors expressed the hope that the Constitution would draw upon itself "that veneration which time bestows on everything, and without which perhaps the wisest and freest of governments" would lack stability; but supporters of the new charter of government were not content to allow time to do its work unaided. A rhetoric and a ritual of national unity were created to supply what ordinary circumstances might not.

While Anti-Federalists in 1788 insisted that the nation wanted no new constitution, the popular mood was better reflected in the sentiments of James Sullivan, a Massachusetts Anti-Federalist turned Federalist: he surmised that people expected so much from the Philadelphia convention that they would be ready to accept almost anything it offered. The outpouring of popular celebrations of the inception of the new government, even before ratification was formally secured in some states, seemed to bear out Sullivan's prediction. New York City's festivities were held three days before the Poughkeepsie Convention approved the new Constitution on behalf of the state of New York. Federalists in New York City orchestrated a huge "Federal Procession." It began in the morning and did not end until 5:30 p.m. Almost one quarter of the city's population was in the mile-and-a-half parade. Every trade and profession was represented among the marchers, and each carried distinctive banners or mounted special displays: a federal loaf by the bakers, a three hundred-gallon ale cask by the brewers; and a federal ship by the pilots and mariners. The theme was unity and prosperity, and banners carried the worlds in undistinguished but unmistakeable verse. From the pewterers:

> *The Federalist plan most solid and secure*
> *Americans their freedom will endure*
> *All arts will flourish in Columbia's land*
> *And all her sons join as one social band.*

From the butchers:

> *Skin me well, dress me neat,*
> *And send me aboard the federal fleet.*

From the chairmakers:

> *The fed'ral states in union bound,*
> *O'er all the world our chairs are found.*

And from the joiners:

> *The federal ship will our commerce revive,*
> *And merchants and shipwrights and joiners shall thrive.*

As if to mark Heaven's own dispensation on the new Constitution, Federalists reported that the weather was fair, there was neither disorder nor injury, the procession was "well conducted," and the crowd retired after the day's events "without any instance of rudeness or intemperance."

There were other processions in Boston, Charleston, Baltimore, Annapolis, Hartford, New Haven, Newport, Trenton, Albany, and Portsmouth and Salem, N.H. The theme of union prevailed everywhere. An ode especially composed for the occasion in Albany typified the sentiment:

YORKERS rejoice! Your state is SAV'D FROM BLOOD!
UNION protects her with a guardian's care;
DISCORD, that threaten'd like a raging flood,
Has spent the fruitless breath in empty air.

Bostonians held their parade on February 8, 1788, as soon as their own state had ratified the Constitution and before the requisite number of nine states had acted, but the Bay Staters were confident the new charter would go into effect. The centerpiece of their procession was a ship, the *Federal Constitution,* drawn by thirteen horses, symbolizing the embarkation of the new government on the sea of liberty. (The federal ship became the focus of most celebratory parades thereafter.) Again, observers remarked on how "Everything was conducted with the greatest order," and how "Candor, Love, Harmony, Friendship, and Benevolence" prevailed. In the rhetoric of the Federalists, the word "federal" connoted everything that was good, honest, dignified, and American.

Philadelphia's grand procession topped them all. It was held on July 4, 1788, after the ninth state had ratified, and it linked Washington, independence, and the new Constitution in a near-mystical trinity. Charles Willson Peale, the artist, and Francis Hopkinson, the writer, were the principal organizers. Peale designed a "Grand Federal Edifice" for the march. It had thirteen Corinthian columns, and around the pedestal were the words "In union the fabric stands firm." The procession also displayed a Federal ship, the *Union.* Pennsylvania's chief justice, Thomas McKean, rode on another float, carrying a copy of the Constitution and standing inside the figure of a giant bald eagle that stood thirteen feet high and sported thirteen stars and stripes. Seventeen thousand people—half the population of Philadelphia—assembled to meet the procession at its close and to dine on four thousand pounds of beef, twenty-five hundred pounds of lamb, and thirty-five hundred gallons of beer. The ode that Hopkinson wrote for the occasion reiterated the now universal theme:

And let the PEOPLE'S Motto ever be,
UNITED THUS, and THUS UNITED-FREE.

Nature cooperated once more. The sky was overcast during the procession, shielding the participants from the hot sun. A cool breeze blew all day, and "in the evening the sky was illuminated by a beautiful aurora borealis." Benjamin Rush, observing the parade, remarked with pleasure that hundreds were heard to comment that "Heaven was on the

Emblematic eagle appearing with two odes to the Constitution. New York Packet, July 25, 1788

federal side of the question."

At the close of the day's events, Rush proudly exclaimed: " 'Tis done! We have become a nation." But the Federalists could not rest on these slim laurels. The Constitution was not quite universally accepted. Albany's Anti-Federalists observed the Fourth of July by publicly burning a copy of the new frame of government; at Carlisle, Pa., they prevented a public celebration; and in Providence, R.I., armed Anti-Federalists broke up an incipient Federalist barbecue. If, as Carl van Doren has declared, the grand federal processions were "symbolic act[s] of faith in the future of the United States," the symbols would have to be reinforced over and over again during the next half-century to give them permanency.

Politicians, editors, historians, clergymen, lawyers, and educators joined in the effort to make the Constitution an emblem of national unity and virtue. Religion was invoked to demonstrate that the Constitution was as much a part of the di-

Reinforcement

vine plan as the Revolution, already sanctified in the public imagination. A Connecticut newspaper early sounded the spiritual note in proclaiming that "pious men of all denominations will thank God for having provided in our Federal Constitution an ark, for the preservation of the justice and liberties of the world." Benjamin Franklin in a geriatric burst of uncharacteristic religious zeal, expressed his certainty that so momentous an event as the creation of a new government under the Constitution could not have occurred "without being in some degree influenced, guided and governed" by divine Providence. New England preachers assured their congregations that the inauguration of the new government in 1789 was "declarative of the superintendence of God," and a Connecticut magazine challenged any true Christian to deny that Heaven itself had inspired the new government, "calculated to promote the glory of God."

The judiciary joined in the beatification of the Constitution. Judge Alexander Addison of the Pennsylvania Court of Common Pleas, dubbed by Jeffersonians "the transmontane Goliath of federalism," demonstrated the depth of his convictions in one of his jury charges in 1791:

> The laws and Constitution of our government ought to be regarded with reverence. Man must have an idol. And our political idol ought to be our Constitution and laws. They, like the ark of the covenant among the Jews, ought to be sacred from all profane touch.

The death of Washington in 1799 permitted the mythmakers to link his already widespread fame with the Constitution's efficacy. Thus, George Minot, historian and secretary of the Massachusetts ratifying convention, rhapsodized in this eulogy to the fallen hero:

> The people he has saved from external tyranny suffer from the agitations of their own unsettled powers. The tree of liberty, which he has planted and so carefully guarded ... flourishes beyond its strength.... But he comes! In convention he presides over councils, as in war he had led to battle. The Constitution, like the rainbow after the flood, appears to us now just emerging from an overwhelming commotion; and we know the truth of the pledge from the sanction of his name. The production was worthy of its authors ... you cherish it, ... and resolve to transmit it, with the name of Washington, to the latest generation, who shall prove their just claim to such an illustrious descent.

Historians and textbook writers lent their hand in the movement to canonize the Constitution. With the exception of the Anti-Federalist Mercy Otis Warren, virtually all of the early historians were ardent promoters of the new framework of government. David Ramsay conceded that the Articles served a purpose in demonstrating the need for reform. The Constitution itself, he wrote, was a "triumph of virtue and good sense, over the vices and follies of human nature." It combined "law with liberty, energy with safety, the freedom of a small state with the strength of a great empire." Ratification was the last act in the great national drama initiated by the Revolution. John Marshall, in his *Life of Washington,* did not devote much attention to the Constitution because he treated it as foreordained, but he took time to note the "imbecility" of those who wrote the Articles, which he called "absolutely unfit for use" and praised the framers as "men of enlarged and liberal minds." The Constitution he regarded as the only hope of national government; on its success depended "the union of the states, and the happiness of America."

By 1837, when the Constitution's jubilee was observed, the elements in the canonization of that document were all in place, and the Constitution had begun to weave its "word-magic" spell over the American people. The document signed in Philadelphia fifty years earlier was portrayed as the sheet anchor of national stability. It had rescued the nation from post-Revolutionary disaster. It fulfilled the wishes of the signers of the Declaration. It was the capstone of the War for Independence. It not only defined the past but shaped the present and ordained the future. And it was the work of heroes viewed in the hazy light of semidivinity. They were to be honored for their prudence, integrity, and virtue. They were to be revered as true Fathers of the Country. Indeed, their only flaw was that, in doing their work so perfectly, they had left so little for future generations to do. At best, later Americans could remain faithful to the "precious memory of the sages" who had taught them republican virtue. And the Constitution itself was the symbol of their handiwork under Providence's guidance.

Perhaps the greatest tribute to the new symbolism and mythology was the relative speed and ease with which former critics of the Constitution accepted it and joined in paying their homage to it. As Charles Pettit, a Pennsylvania Federalist put it in 1800, with some amazement, despite the intensity of political factionalism and partisan strife, "both parties profess an attachment and reverence for, the Constitution as their guide." When they differed, he noted, each charged the other "with designs to warp, subvert, and destroy the Constitution itself."

It was left only to describe the nation's half-century old charter in terms of perfection: "the most perfect social compact the wisdom of man has hitherto devised," exulted one Fourth of July orator; the "consummation" of America's history, John Quincy Adams announced in his inaugural address; the "palladium of American liberty," Story boasted in his *Commentaries on the Constitution;* the "nearest approach to supreme wisdom," Daniel Webster declaimed in the halls of Congress; and "the most wonderful instrument ever drawn by the hand of man," unparalleled in its "comprehension and precision," Justice William Johnson announced from his seat on the Supreme Court bench. In his farewell address to the nation in 1837, Andrew Jackson assured citizens that the Constitution was "no longer a doubtful experiment" and that under its superintendency, the country had preserved liberty and property and promoted prosperity. And John Quincy Adams gave a celebratory address in New York City linking the Declaration of Independence with the Constitution "as parts of one consistent whole."

An Unstable Instrument

But there was disturbing evidence that the constitutional cult would have to continue to be nurtured in the years ahead. The date the Constitution was signed, September 17, had never been celebrated as a national holiday, and it was not so observed at its jubilee. (It was not to be designated officially as a commemorative day until 1952!) The day was a Sunday in 1837, and Congress was not in session, but neither house marked the event by even so much as a word the day before or the day after. Both houses were absorbed in debates over the new banking system and the annexation of Texas. The date was ignored in the public prints, as well. Newspapers carried accounts for September 17 of a balloon ascent by a female astronaut, a twenty-four-hour horse race, nonstop, employing twelve horses over a 788-mile course, and the discovery of the remains of a mastodon in Rochester, N.Y., but not a line about Constitution Day. A new magazine launched in October 1837 to promote democratic political principles contained no reference to the anniversary of the signing of the Constitution, although it did carry a poem dedicated to the warship *Constitution.*

Daniel Webster replying to Robert Hayne in their 1830 debate on the Constitution

Why was the national symbol, so sedulously cultivated by friends of the Constitution for a half-century now ignored? For one, July 4th had already become the centerpiece of patriotic observances, utilized by temperance and peace advocates, abolitionists and war veterans, to identify American ideals with their causes. Independence and Union, the Declaration and the Constitution, Washington and the founding fathers were all merged imperceptibly in these observances, leaving little room for distinctive recognition of Constitution Day. And even the

Glorious Fourth had lost some of its old emotional appeal as it became formalized or deteriorated from a holy day to a holiday. There were editorial complaints that the celebrations had degenerated into drinking orgies, "eating, firing of guns, dancing, and quarreling." Only Americans, one writer complained, would blemish the anniversary of their birth as a nation by getting wildly inebriated.

More important in the blurring of the Constitution in the public imagination was the growing focus on the document as a yet unstable instrument of government. It could scarcely evoke unanimity as a symbol when the meaning of the Constitution was debated bitterly on the stump and in Congress. While Webster and Hayne both avowed their allegiance to the Constitution in their historic debate in 1830, the event was, in Max Lerner's words, "the climax of the attempt to solve national problems through constitutional symbols; and the attempt was a failure." Cynics like Senator William Crawford of Georgia declared himself sick of eulogies of the Constitution by advocates of national power or states' rights. "The gentlemen . . . still view it as a model of perfection. They are certainly at liberty to entertain that opinion. Every man has a right to erect his idol in this land of liberty, and to worship it according to the dictates of his conscience."

An innocuous joint resolution introduced in Congress in 1837 to appropriate $30,000 for the acquisition of certain manuscripts of James Madison dealing with the Constitutional Convention provoked a furious debate between Webster and Calhoun over whether Congress had the power to spend money, under the "general welfare" clause, for this purpose. John Niles of Connecticut noted wearily: "Who is to decide what is the true theory and exposition of the Constitution? This has been a subject of controversy from the formation of the Constitution." Americans might still agree that the Constitution was a palladium of liberty but they could not decide whether its beneficence stemmed from its character as the supreme law of a nation or as a compact among sovereign states. Benjamin Rush, who had hailed the adoption of the Constitution in 1788 as testimony to the creation of a nation, was not at all so sure twenty years later. In the midst of the international difficulties with Britain and France, Rush asked bitterly: "What shall we fight for? For our Constitution? I cannot meet with a man who loves it. It is considered as too weak by one half of our citizens and too strong by the other." And an equally despairing Daniel Webster complained in 1842 that "The Constitution was intended as an instrument of great political good; but we sometimes so dispute its meaning, that we cannot use it at all."

Resolution of the issue was not to come until the Civil War, but from that bloody conflict was to emerge a symbolism even more powerful than the one first created by the Federalists. The new cult of the Constitution made that document the hallmark of laissez-faire conservatism and a bulwark against radical socialism; but it also came to signify, in time, the promise of opportunity, equality, and expanding democracy for others. The meanings changed, but the symbol remained as the vehicle of the nation's life, an idealization of its best hopes and aspirations. Walter Bagehot once said that every government must contain something of the "dignified" or "majestic" principle to give cohesive force to its existence. For a nation that had eschewed the monarchies, aristocracies, and established churches that were emblematic of European societies, perhaps the Constitution, signifying the rule of law, was not such an inappropriate symbol.

Milton M. Klein is professor of history emeritus at the University of Tennessee, Knoxville. He is the author of *The Politics of Diversity: Essays in the History of Colonial New York* (1974) and general editor of the thirteen-volume *History of the American Colonies* (1973-1986).

III. *Ratification and the Inauguration of the Government*

"Our Successors Will Have an Easier Task": The First Congress under the Constitution, 1789-1791

Joel H. Silbey

The First Congress under the Constitution got off to a late start. Scheduled to meet on March 4, 1789, in New York City, the temporary national capital, on that date no quorum was present in either house. As a result, no business could be transacted; moreover, the eight senators (of twenty-two) and thirteen representatives (of fifty-nine) who were there at the scheduled time had a long wait. The House did not achieve a quorum until April 1; five days later, on the sixth, the twelfth senator, Richard Henry Lee of Virginia, finally arrived to form the necessary majority of that chamber.

The month-long delay was hardly an auspicious beginning, even allowing for the difficulties of travel, late elections in some states, and unresolved contests for some seats in others. It strongly recalled the dilatoriness, inattention, and what Rep. Fisher Ames referred to as "the languour of the old confederation," which the new government was to replace. Nevertheless, once it settled down to work, this first Congress found its feet and accomplished an enormous amount. In its three sessions, from April 1789 to March 1791, it established the foundations of the new government, addressed some of the ambiguities in the Constitution, and set the whole republican experiment on its permanent course. The Constitution had left a great deal unsaid or unclear about the nature of the new government. The First Congress provided the initial opportunity to put flesh on bare bones. The men sitting in New York took up the heavy task successfully. They were guided by the notion, in the words of one of their number, "that it is proper for the legislature to speak their sense upon those points on which the Constitution is silent."

Fisher Ames

123

Organizing

Most of the members of the First Congress were not strangers to the rigors of legislative life in their raw, new country. As was to be expected, they were members of the ruling social and political elites of their day. Either they had inherited high social status and wealth, or they had made their way significantly up the social ladder on their own. Lawyers, planters, land speculators, and merchants, many were graduates of the most prestigious colonial colleges and British universities. Schooled in the English parliamentary tradition, several had served in their state legislatures and in the Continental Congress. Twenty had participated in the Federal Convention, several in the state ratifying conventions; half of them had been politically active in the revolutionary period. Among them were two future presidents as well as many who would shape the political world during the next decade and more. Fisher Ames, Elbridge Gerry, and Rufus King sat with James Madison in the House, while Robert Morris and James Monroe joined past and future in the Senate. As Fisher Ames summed them up, there were "few shining geniuses ... many who have experience, the virtues of the heart, and the habits of business." It would be "quite a republican assembly. It looks like one. Many who expected a Roman Senate ... will be disappointed."

Robert Morris

Ideologically, the members of Congress were almost of one mind. Most had been supporters of the Constitution and had helped in the ratification struggles in their states over the past two years. The Constitution's opponents, the Anti-Federalists, were few in number. This did not prevent great controversy since definitions of the nature of the republic and the powers of the government varied among the pro-Constitution forces as events in this first Congress amply demonstrated. But, at the outset at least, there was general good will and a hope that all would contribute effectively to the success of the new government.

Despite the cold and damp of a New York City spring, once settled in Congress got down to business without fuss. "There is the most punctual attendance of the members at the hour of meeting," Massachusetts's Fisher Ames wrote, "Three or four have had leave of absence, but every other member actually attends daily, till the hour of adjourning. There is less party spirit, less of the acrimony of pride when disappointed of success, less personality, less intrigue, cabal, management or cunning than I ever saw in a public assembly." The business-like, conscientious behavior remained. The rest did not. Congress moved very slowly at first owing to the newness of its situation, and "the novelty and complexity of the subjects of Legislation." Its members were, Madison pointed out to Thomas Jefferson, "in a wilderness without a single footstep to guide us. Our successors will have an easier task."

A chronology of Congress's activities from 1789 to 1791 suggests the variety and range of the matters covered. In the first session, it was inevitable that members of Congress would be preoccupied by definition and institution building. Each House's first action was to read and file its own credentials and inform the other that it was organized. This operation was followed by a joint meeting in the Senate chamber to open and count the electoral votes for president and vice president.

Rufus King

Shortly after the winners were notified, John Adams arrived to preside over the Senate as vice president on April 21. On April 1, the House had elected Frederick Muhlenberg, of a prominent Pennsylvania family, as its first Speaker. George Washington arrived two days after Adams, took the oath of office on April 30, and delivered his inaugural address in the gallery in front of the Senate chamber.

As Congress began to sort itself out in these spring months, each house elaborated sets of internal rules of procedure to guide it through its daily business. The two houses drew upon the precedents of either Britain's House of Commons or the colonial assemblies or the state legislatures in which members had earlier served. The major locus of activity became each chamber's Committee of the Whole House on the State of the Union. It was there that the principles, directions and boundaries of the legislative agenda were established. After a member requested permission to introduce a bill, and such was given, the subject was debated in the Committee of the Whole. Bills were then sent to special committees for final drafting into refined language reflecting the previous debates. There were only two standing subject committees in the First Congress: the Committee on Elections, and a Committee on Enrolled Bills; the rest were ad hoc.

Before and after the daily sessions, these committees, then as now the life-blood of legislative activity, met to advance the legislative business before them. Early on, certain people were viewed as experts in particular subject areas and they usually were appointed to the relevant committees. Oliver Ellsworth of Connecticut, one of the acknowledged legislative activists, for example, served on twenty-two committees in the first session, and thirty-six in the second, compared with an average of eleven for all senators. Robert Morris and Richard Henry Lee were other active committee members in these years. Committees did not stay out long. The select committee on the Bill of Rights, chaired by James Madison, was appointed on July 21, 1789, and reported exactly a week later, on the 28th. Finally, there were conference committees that had to be appointed when the two houses disagreed on the wording of a bill as frequently happened in the First Congress.

Defining Relationships

What Congress had to do was clear enough. After organizing itself and settling its procedures, a vast array of business confronted the members. The matters to be dealt with ranged from the symbolic to the substantive. In the first instance, such concerns involved defining relationships. What titles shall there be in the new republic? What shall be the meaning of the appointing powers of president and Congress? What shall be the relationship between executive departments and Congress? Is one house superior to the other; does each have a distinctive role? From the vantage point of two hundred years, much of this seems remote to important matters; other aspects anticipate themes still present in the 1980s.

The long debate over titles clearly had substantive implications. The Senate wanted the president to be called, "His Highness the President of the United States, and Protector of the Rights of the Same." The House demurred and the first congressional conference committee ever appointed had to deal with this issue. The Senate's aggressive presiding officer, John Adams, made his position clear: without such titles there would be an important lack of dignity and respect for their new republican institutions. To the House of Representatives the question was one of violating the essentials of republican simplicity. The whole thing was not worked out until the Senate agreed to go along with the House's referral of the chief executive as just "Mr. President."

In a similar vein, the members engaged in long debates over how to treat each other, the procedures for receiving messages from each other, and how the president was to be received when he came to give his annual report on the State of the Union. Finally, there was debate over whether the president would be mentioned in the enacting clause of the bills passed. These matters clearly echoed practices of the English Parliament, with its Address from the throne and the formal response to it, and the English constitutional position that their governing authority was the "King in Parliament" so that both warranted mention in legislation.

Congress omitted mention of the president in its bills, but that one decision could not clarify the still ambiguous relationship between the chief executive and the national legislature. Madison had few qualms about the relationship at the outset. "In our government," he said, it was "less necessary to guard against the abuse in the Executive Department . . . because it is not the stronger branch of the system, but the weaker."

Nevertheless, Washington's attempt to negotiate directly with the Senate over an Indian treaty provoked great tensions and fears. The treaty negotiations and drafting were primarily the president's responsibilities. He determined to include the Senate in them as well, taking a broad view of that body's

Frederick Muhlenberg

constitutional duty to advise and consent to treaties. But, as Washington viewed it, the Senate's response was not helpful. He appeared in the Senate chamber on a warm August day in 1789 to be met with much silence and some hostility. A number of senators felt that he was out of place. Their historical memories of the long years of conflict between the English king and Parliament, particularly the former's efforts to bend the legislature to his will, and of the battles between the colonial governors and their legislative assemblies, remained strong. The president wished in this instance, one senator claimed, "to bear down our deliberations with his personal authority and presence. Form only will be left to us." Such men were determined to protect legislative independence from the executive, especially against any indications of pressure on their considerations.

This attempt at face to face discussion in the Senate chamber was awkward. Washington did not repeat it. Rather, written communications between the executive and legislative branches became the established procedure. But the president was not passive in using the Senate as a consultive body in foreign and military affairs when and as he saw fit to do so. He wrote frequently to ask advice before treaties were finalized. The Senate responded more freely than it had when he came in person but always remained somewhat distant and cautious toward his requests.

President Washington also consulted members of Congress directly about appointments to executive office, willingly receiving from them suggestions of both acceptable and unacceptable appointees. That procedure worked well. One matter that became contentious involved the constitutional provision that the Senate advise and consent to individual executive appointments. Did such responsibility carry with it the implication that senators also had to agree when the president wished to remove someone they had previously aproved? Some senators claimed that they had this right. Washington strongly demurred, arguing that such a process would effectively prevent him from carrying on the government with people of his own choosing. For a time, a vigorous debate developed, presaging a later controversy in the Reconstruction era when Congress impeached President Andrew Johnson over the same dispute—whether or not he could remove an official from office without the Senate's consent. This particular debate in the first Congress petered out as only a few senators chose to try to make an issue of their right to advise on removals. But the argument, together with several similar ones, reveals a great deal about the uncertain powers of the different branches of the government caused by often ambiguous constitutional provisions, as well as the tendency of some members to be defensive about their own powers and suspicious of the president's intentions.

Legislation

In addition to these definitional and status problems, Congress began to consider and pass an enormous amount of substantive legislation. Here, perhaps, lies much of the importance of this First Congress (although its members would have argued that their wrestling with definitions, procedures, and limits on power were just as critical for the future). On May 19, 1789, for example, Rep. James Madison moved the creation of a Department of Foreign Affairs, one of Treasury, and one of War. Later, several other bills, including those to create the offices of attorney general, postmaster general, superintendent of the Land Office, the governor of the Northwest Territory, were also introduced. There was an attempt to add to the list a Home Department, concerned with a range of administrative duties, patent and copyright registration, the census, etc. Most of these subsequently wound up in the Department of Foreign Affairs, renamed with the broader title of Department of State. Congress also passed the Judiciary Act of 1789, establishing a federal court system, detailing federal judicial procedures, and recognizing the power of judicial review over legislation enacted by Congress.

All of these bills passed by the summer and early fall of 1789. They elaborated the structure of the federal government rapidly and effectively, creating the foundations on which the execution of national authority rested thereafter. It was a notable achievement especially for the House of Representatives, which held the initiative in these early days and did most of the work. During its three sessions the First House of Representatives considered 142 different bills (other than private ones, introduced by individual members for some limited or special purpose), the Senate only 24. In the first session, the Senate originated only the Judiciary Act. As a result, the irascible Sen. William Maclay of New Hampshire complained in his journal of his chamber's comparative idleness.

At the center of this activity was the acknowledged floor leader and administration spokesman in the House of Representatives, the "Father of the Constitution," James Madison of Virginia. Fisher Ames said of Madison that he "speaks low, his person is little and ordinary." But his physical stature did not limit his imagination or effectiveness, first as the leader of the constitutional forces, then as the close confidant of Washington, and, later, as the emerging leader of the anti-administration group in Congress. Among the first representatives to arrive for the first session, he quickly began that round of activities that led him at one point to be engaged not only in shaping legislation and caucusing to work out compromises, but also in writing messages to himself as he drafted both the House's response to the president's address and the president's reply to that response—not to mention parts of the original Address itself. He was a busy man.

Madison was also one of the central participants in the two other major areas of legislative activity in this Congress beyond the establishment of the government itself. He worked vigorously to undercut opposition to the new government by moving early to incorporate changes and clarifications in the Constitution. He took a campaign promise he had made seriously and pressured the House to take up the amendments to the Constitution he had fashioned out of the several hundred suggestions made by state ratifying conventions and local political meetings. Amost all of these suggestions sought limits on the power of the central government, many in favor of individual rights. Madison reduced the number of suggestions, seventeen of which he shepherded through the House of Representatives. The Senate reduced these further to twelve (largely by combining several), which were submitted to the states where ten were finally ratified as the Bill of Rights. (The two that were not ratified limited members' ability to raise their own salaries and set stringent restrictions on the apportionment of seats in the House.)

This major achievement of the First Congress passed with some angry debate but relatively little opposition. Most members of Congress accepted the need to reassure those still suspicious of any expansion of central government power. Madison and others believed that the rights enumerated in these amendments already clearly existed and did not need to be spelled out as constitutional provisions. But they accepted the amendments' need in political terms, as part of the legitimating reassurances necessary to bolster support for the federal government and its activities. This massive affirmation of personal liberties against government power, in short, passed largely due to political calculations and requirements—things that do not lessen the amendments' importance but places their passage into perspective as a specific part of the national building agenda dominating this Congress.

Economic Policy

The most contentious area of legislative activity in these years involved economic policy, especially the wide-ranging program aggressively pushed by Secretary of the Treasury Alexander Hamilton. The Hamiltonian program was designed to give the federal government authority to raise revenue, regulate commerce, and establish national authority in the economic sphere more clearly than had been the case earlier. James Madison was deeply involved from the first, originally throwing his support behind notions of building up national economic strength. Before long, however, he moved into opposition to the ambitious goals of Hamilton, creating an era of conflict in Congress different from its early, harmonious, days.

Discussion began quietly enough. In the first session, in the spring of 1789, Madison brought onto the floor a tariff bill and a bill to regulate foreign trade, and he then began to formulate plans for an excise tax bill, all designed either to raise revenue for the new government or to establish its role in external trade relations. Some of these programs provoked opposition by economic groups negatively affected by particular tariff rates or unhappy with other specific provisions they considered detrimental to their economic well being. Madison worked assiduously and successfully to meet objections by amendment and compromise, to build coalitions, and to shepherd the whole package through. By the end of the first session, in late September 1789, Congress had given the federal government a number of important revenue resources to help it operate.

Hamilton was more concerned, however, with domestic economic matters. He detailed his program in January 1790 in his *Report on Public Credit,* drafted at Congress's direction. Hamilton's recommendations included the funding of the national debt, the federal government's assumption of the outstanding state debts (to permit the accumulation of development capital), and the establishment of a national bank to carry on directly the federal government's financial activities and to regulate indirectly the general economy. Eventually, Congress adopted most of Hamilton's program. Some of it Madison supported, some of it went through in the form of legislative compromises fashioned between Madison and the administration. The most famous of these bargains was the agreement by the Virginian and his colleagues to support the assumption of state debts in return for the establishment of the national capital on the Potomac—a choice Washington and other Southerners very much wanted but which New York and Pennsylvania members of Congress strongly opposed. Hamilton benefited from the powerful impulse at work to make the new government successful, to find means to bring people together, to compromise different points of view, all hallmarks of this Congress in its early months. As Sen. William Smith of South Carolina put it, "Much harmony, politeness and good humor" characterized this assembly. Madison and other nationalists had a great stake in making the new system work.

But, as bill followed bill to carry out Hamilton's program, another legacy of this Congress emerged: stable political alignments. Opposition to Hamilton grew stronger and more bitter, finally including Madison and Secretary of State Thomas Jefferson as well. Both broke with the Washington administration over the reach of this national economic agenda. As their resistance developed, the congressional arena became

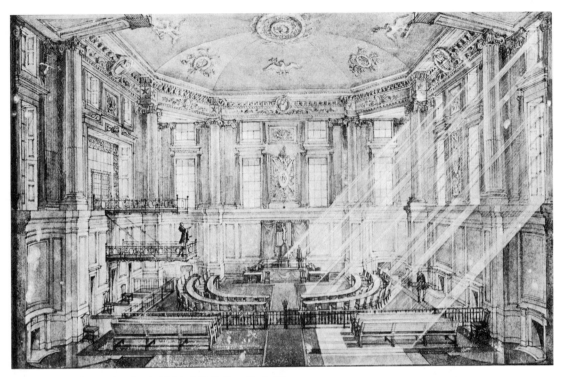

Interior of the House chamber in Federal Hall, New York City

more divided than it had ever been and more angry. Fisher Ames referred to the second session from January to August 1790, when much of this controversy began to develop, as "a dreadful one" with its "discord of opinions," and "labyrinth" of intrigues, cross pressures, anger, and division.

In fact, real policy differences existed and so political matters provoked conflict. The United States was a pluralist society of many groups with different, and often antagonistic, economic interests. These different economic groups and regional interests now faced each other over the shape and impact of national economic policy. The internal economic rivalries within the nation were appearing on the floor of the First Congress as they had appeared during the time of the Articles of Confederation. Further, and critically, there were strong indications that this contentiousness was more than temporary since it reflected not only the local, sectional, and regional economic differences endemic in the American republic but also basic ideological differences over the role, purpose, and extent of the powers of the national government.

The battles over the Hamiltonian program proved deep and searing. It had become apparent, to everyone's great relief, that the dangerous sectional divisions of the earlier years had not intensified. As Madison noted to Jefferson, "members from the same State, or the same part of the Union are as often separated on questions from each other, as they are united in opposition to other States or other quarters of the Continent." At first, too, voting blocs were very volatile, swiftly changing from issue to issue. But as time passed and the controversy over the Hamiltonian program sharpened and deepened, several distinct lines of cleavage became noticeable in Congress.

There were two kinds of polarities, a division over strong government versus weak government, and then sectional/regional differences on economic and development issues. Three voting blocs emerged in the first session representing the Eastern, Southern, and Middle states. Different ones appeared later, particularly, and ominously for national stability, the much feared North-South one. By the end of the First Congress, whatever had gone before, a hardening of positions was occurring. The House then had thirty-nine pro-administration members and twenty-seven who were anti-administration. Full consolidation into political parties, a situation that was to characterize the next decade, had not yet occurred but was becoming visible. This was yet another heritage this Congress left to its successors and to history: an important structure of disagreement and conflict.

Conclusion   "Tomorrow," James Madison wrote to his brother on March 2, 1791, "will put an end to our existence." The First Congress adjourned the next day. It had come a long way. It had filled out the government framework, instituted a system of national revenue, attended to the debts of the Revolution, set up a judiciary, begun to establish a presence in foreign relations, paid attentions to our borders and relations with the Indian tribes. It created a whole range of administrative agencies, and it had passed a Bill of Rights. It founded a national bank and located a permanent capital. In terms of the long view, the First Congress had reminded every one that America was a fractious entity, that Americans readily divided along ideological, local, and sectional lines when provoked by government activity, that the extent of the reach and powers of the national government remained an area of contention; it showed too that there were vigorous proponents of the many positions present on the floor of the national legislature and that Congress would be a major focus in the defining and shaping of the battles over the future of the country. It was not a bad beginning.

Joel H. Silbey is President White Professor of history at Cornell University. He is the author of *The Partisan Imperative: The Dynamics of American Politics before the Civil War* (1985), and one of the editors of *The History of American Electoral Behavior* (1978).

The Birth of the Federal Court System

David Eisenberg, Christine R. Jordan,
Maeva Marcus, and Emily F. Van Tassel

As the first justices of the Supreme Court were preparing to undertake their duties, President Washington wrote to them expressing his feelings about the importance of the job they were about to begin. "I have always been persuaded that the stability and success of the National Government and consequently the happiness of the People of the United States, would depend in a considerable degree on the Interpretation and Execution of its Laws," Washington observed. "In my opinion, therefore, it is important that the Judiciary System should not only be independent in its operations, but as perfect as possible in its formation."

The founders of the new nation believed that the establishment of a national judiciary was one of their most important tasks. Yet Article III of the Constitution of the United States, the provision that deals with the judicial branch of government, is markedly shorter than Articles I and II, which created the legislative and executive branches. Moreover, at the Constitutional Convention the delegates spent relatively little time discussing judicial power. Instead they left the resolution of those issues on which they could not easily agree to the Congress that would come into being after the new frame of government was approved. Thus the story of the development of judicial power under the Constitution concerns much more than an understanding of the text of Article III.

The Constitution had not sprung full blown from the crucible of revolution but instead resulted from a growing recognition throughout the states that the Confederation was inadequate and that a stronger national government was needed if the United States was to survive. The lack of an independent judiciary to decide controversies of a national and

Article III

137

international nature contributed to the Confederation's weakness. Congress had set up the very limited Court of Appeals in Cases of Capture to hear disputes involving ships seized during the Revolution, but it did not meet regularly and had no power to enforce its decrees.

Thus the concept of a national judiciary was a new one in the late 1780s and its embodiment in Article III a cause of much concern. The structure of the judiciary was a rock upon which the Constitution could founder when it went before the states for ratification; hence Federalist efforts had focused on creating a constitutional framework that would give wide latitude to Congress to flesh out the particulars of a court system. By creating a structure that left all the details of form and content to congressional discretion, Federalists hoped to allay—or at least postpone until after the Constitution was safely ratified—Anti-Federalist fears that the national judiciary would swallow up the state courts.

Article III of the Constitution created a federal "judicial Power" but defined it in only the broadest of terms. Section 1 provided that power "shall be vested in one supreme Court, and in such inferior Courts as the Congress may from time to time ordain and establish." Section 2 specified the types of cases to which the federal judicial power extended, giving the Supreme Court original jurisdiction to hear "all Cases affecting Ambassadors, other public Ministers and Consuls, and those in which a State shall be a Party." In all other categories enumerated in the section, cases would originate in lower courts but could be brought to the Supreme Court on appeal, subject to "such exceptions, and under such Regulations as the Congress shall make." Hence the Constitution left to congressional discretion the content and extent of the appellate jurisdiction of the Supreme Court, and by implication the entire jurisdiction of any lower federal courts that might be established.

The text of Article III set down certain basic principles, but the debates during the ratification process indicated that in many states there was dissatisfaction with the broad language of the judicial article and a strong demand for some additional constitutional safeguards. In his *Federalist* No. 78, Alexander Hamilton downplayed the importance of the federal judiciary by denominating it the "least dangerous" of the three branches; in No. 80 he reminded his readers that any inconvenience suggested by the generality of the plan should not condemn it, as

Oliver Ellsworth

the national legislature will have ample authority to make such *exceptions,* and to prescribe such regulations as will be calculated to obviate or remove these inconveniences. The possibility of particular mischiefs can never be viewed, by a well-informed mind, as a solid objection to a general principle, which is calculated to avoid general mischiefs and to obtain general advantages.

Ideas as to what those inconveniences might be, and how best to deal with them began to circulate well before any lawmaker had so much as dipped his quill into the inkwell. Soon after the Constitutional Convention adjourned in September 1787, people were expressing fears that an extensive federal court system would prove too expensive, drag hapless defendants hundreds of miles from home, and undermine state sovereignty and individual liberties.

Anti-Federalist forces led by two Virginians—George Mason, who had refused to sign the Constitution, and Richard Henry Lee, who had refused to attend the Constitutional Convention—began an immediate campaign in the press and in the state ratifying conventions to have the federal judicial power amended before ratification of the Constitution. Recalling the harsh treatment meted out by colonial governors and British Vice-Admiralty judges in the years prior to the Revolution, Anti-Federalists were particularly concerned with protecting the rights of the criminally accused. They called for a bill of rights to include protection of the right to a grant jury indictment, to a speedy and public trial by an impartial jury drawn from the vicinage (i.e., vicinity in which the crime was committed), to know the cause and nature of accusations, to confront witnesses and compel them to appear in court, to assistance of counsel, to due process of law, and to protection against self-incrimination, double jeopardy, excessive bail, fines, and cruel and unusual punishment. In noncriminal cases, Anti-Federalists also wanted as much jury protection for the individual as possible: jury trials in all civil cases, protection for jury verdicts by limiting appellate courts' power to review juries' factual determinations, and the right to due process under the law.

In addition to a written guarantee of individual rights, Anti-Federalists favored a number of explicit proposals to limit the power of the federal courts. At least half the state ratifying conventions recommended limiting or abolishing diversity jurisdiction—a jurisdiction based solely on the fact that the parties are citizens of different states. A proposal to restrict appeals to the Supreme Court to cases involving only large sums of money also gained considerable support during the ratification process of 1787-1788. Another Anti-Federalist proposal, which came to have support among some cost-conscious Federalists as well, was the use of state courts as lower federal courts. Roger Sherman of Connecticut, a member of the Constitutional Convention and soon to be a member of the First Congress, endorsed just such an idea in his essay "A Citizen of New Haven," published on January 1, 1787. Even such a leading Federalist as James Madison, on the eve of his election to the House of Representatives in January 1789, acknowledged the need for some sort of bill of rights to protect individual liberties and some sort of restriction on appeals in the federal courts. As early as March 15, 1789, the staunch Massachusetts Federalist Fisher Ames reported from New York to a friend in New England that a judicial plan was being discussed by three or four persons that would limit diversity suits and suits involving foreigners to cases where the sum in controversy was over five hundred dollars. He further commented that the great objectives of low cost and allaying state-federal jealousies might best be accomplished by narrowing rather than expanding federal jurisdiction.

The Judiciary Act of 1789

It fell to the First Congress to interpret the various sections of Article III and to take into consideration the amendments demanded by several states as the price of ratification. By drawing up the Bill of Rights and enacting the Judiciary Act of 1789, the First Congress met the concerns of many. It was able to establish a working judicial system that pleased no one completely, but which could be changed as experience showed it to be necessary or desirable.

While the House of Representatives began its work on the first important piece of financial legislation, a revenue system, the Senate, acknowledging the pivotal role that the federal court system must play in the new government, began its legislative work by appointing a committee to prepare a judiciary bill. The committee as formed on April 7, 1789, consisted of one senator from each state: Oliver Ellsworth of Connecticut, William Paterson of New Jersey, Caleb Strong of Massachusetts, Richard Henry Lee of Virginia, Richard Bassett of Delaware, William Maclay of Pennsylvania, William Few of Georgia, and Paine Wingate of New Hampshire. Charles Carroll of Maryland and Ralph Izard of South Carolina, arriving late for the opening of Congress, were added

Richard Henry Lee

to the roster six days later.

Only Ellsworth, Paterson, and Strong, of the ten committee members on whom the judiciary's fate depended, could claim any sizable technical legal expertise; but most had a strong political and legislative background. Six had been members of the Continental Congress (Ellsworth, Few, Carroll, Izard, Wingate, and Lee). Five had been members of the Constitutional Convention (Ellsworth, Strong, Paterson, Bassett, and Few). Five had been members of their state ratifying conventions (Ellsworth, Strong, Few, Bassett, and Izard). Nearly all had held a variety of state offices. Politically all were Federalists with the exception of Richard Henry Lee, a leading Anti-Federalist and a harsh critic of an expansive federal judiciary, and William Maclay, who was elected by Pennsylvania to represent the state's agricultural interests.

The combination of extensive legal experience and firsthand knowledge of the Constitution seems to have been a key factor in determining who would write the bill; for it was the three men with both characteristics—Ellsworth, Paterson, and Strong—in whose handwriting the first draft appeared. Ellsworth, in particular, dominated the proceedings, from the first page of handwritten text, through the debates, to the final conference with the House. "This vile bill is a child of his," fumed the irascible diarist, William Maclay, "and he defends it with the care of a parent, even in wrath and anger." Maclay's disgruntlement aside, Ellsworth was eminently qualified for the job of creating a bill that, after all the politics were exhausted, still had perforce to deal with a multitude of arcane details. Ellsworth's background included service on the Continental Congress Committee on Appeals (giving him firsthand experience with the problems of appellate jurisdiction in a federal system); he had also been a member of the Governor's Council and a state court judge in Connecticut, as well as a member of the Constitutional Convention and the Connecticut ratifying convention. Caleb Strong had served in the Constitutional Convention and the Massachusetts ratifying convention. William Paterson had been attorney general of New Jersey and had also been present at Philadelphia for the drafting of the Constitution.

Within three weeks the committee had drafted a set of guiding principles that clearly reflected the concerns raised during the ratification debate over limiting federal court jurisdiction. The resolutions indicated that the committee favored a small judiciary and had already adopted the idea of limiting noncriminal cases tried in federal courts to those involving large sums of money. The structure created by the committee included a Supreme Court and two levels of lower federal courts. The draft bill specified a six-judge Supreme Court, to convene twice yearly in the national capital. During the months when they were not sitting as the Supreme Court, the justices were made responsible for hearing trials and appeals on circuit in the several states, sitting in pairs in conjunction with a district court judge. The district court judges would come from the courts established in each state as federal trial courts, responsible primarily for hearing admiralty cases. The circuit court's jurisdiction in noncriminal cases was restricted in most instances to cases of at least three hundred dollars or more. Appeals to the Supreme Court could only be made in cases involving amounts above two thousand dollars. Finally, the committee gave the Supreme Court explicit powers of judicial review over state supreme court decisions involving federal law. There seemed to have been a consensus that only cases involving substantial amounts of money should be subject to federal appellate review unless an interpretation of the federal Constitution, a statute, or a treaty were in question.

The drafting efforts of Paterson, Ellsworth, and Strong culminated in a first reading before the full Senate on June 12. When printed for distribution and Senate debate, the bill ran sixteen pages. District court jurisdiction, which was to give rise to the greatest debate in both houses, had been fleshed out in more detail. In addition to exclusive original jurisdiction over all civil admiralty and maritime cases, district courts were also given jurisdiction over some other lesser federal matters. The committee made trial by jury protections explicit in several situations, among them criminal cases and suits brought by the United States for amounts over one hundred dollars. Similarly, jury trials were required in civil and criminal cases in the circuit courts and in original Supreme Court cases involving individuals who were United States citizens. It is clear that Richard Henry Lee wanted his jury trial protections incorporated at every possible point.

William Few

After agreeing to report the committee bill, Richard Henry Lee then leveled an Anti-Federalist attack at the jurisdiction of the district courts. On the opening day of debate, June 22, Lee moved to limit the district courts to admiralty jurisdiction. Simply stated, Lee's proposed amendment called for the judiciaries of the several states to serve as lower federal courts in most instances. While many people believed that state courts could handle the business that might be assigned to lower federal courts, opponents of this view argued that state control over the application of federal law would result in diminished popular confidence that national laws were being executed impartially. State judges who held office only for specified terms could not be relied upon to be independent, and appeals to the Supreme Court would have to be allowed in large numbers of cases to ensure the enforcement of national interests. Moreover, some argued that as soon as state judges exercised federal powers they would become federal judges, with life tenure and secure salaries as mandated by the second clause of Article III section 1. Why Lee chose to introduce his amendment after apparently having gone along with the committee in setting up a lower court system is not known. Perhaps Lee felt obligated to bring this proposal to the attention of the full Senate because he had been so directed by the Virginia legislature. The oddity is increased by the fact that

Virginia had just enacted a restriction on its courts forbidding them to try causes arising under the laws of the United States.

Even Maclay, who had been on the committee with Lee and who would join Lee in voting against the bill in its final form, did not support Lee on this point. Maclay joined with the Federalists in believing that the Constitution's scheme would be thwarted unless the federal courts could adjudicate other issues besides admiralty—such as taxation, duties and imports, naturalization, coinage, counterfeiting, and treason. He also made the longstanding Federalist point that the state judges would not enforce federal laws. William Paterson may have advanced some of the additional reasons against using state courts as federal tribunals: his personal notes reflect that he though the elective office of most state judges was not compatible with the constitutional requirements of tenure during good behavior and fixed salaries. Paterson agreed that state judges should not be relied upon to enforce federal criminal laws or the collection of federal revenue. The Federalist majority, many of whom had already rejected the notion of state courts as lower federal courts in their correspondence with constituents, followed this view.

The Bill of Rights   At the same time that the Senate was considering the judiciary bill, the House had taken up the subject of a bill of rights. As originally proposed by James Madison on June 6 it included several amendments pertaining to the judicial system. Deemed most important were those protecting the rights of the criminally accused: the right to grand jury indictment, to a speedy and public trial by an impartial jury of the vicinage, to know the cause and nature of accusations, to confront witnesses and have compulsory process to produce them, to assistance of counsel, to due process, and to protection against self incrimination, double jeopardy, excessive bail, fines, and cruel and unusual punishment. With the exception of the jury of the vicinage, which was struck by the Senate, all of these became parts of the Fifth, Sixth, and Eighth Amendments. Madison's list also included the three judicial system amendments considered most important by the Anti-Federalists: a guarantee of jury trial in common law cases (that is, suits governed by earlier judicial decisions rather than by statutes) above twenty dollars; a prohibition on the reexamination of the facts found in a case by the trial court except by the restrictive rules of the common law (which meant that jury decisions would not be easily overturned); and a monetary restriction on all appeals to the Supreme Court. The Senate removed this last provision, but the first two became the Seventh Amendment. The Senate also voted down a requirement for unanimous jury verdicts and the grant of a right to make jury challenges. Moreover, that body refused to agree to what Madison considered the most important of all: a prohibition against state violations of fundamental rights, including trial by jury.

Although Madison had received House approval of his amendments as the only ones to be discussed, members continued to attempt additions. The most extreme judicial amendments offered were those of Thomas Tudor Tucker of South Carolina to limit lower federal courts to admirality jurisdiction and to prohibit any federal jurisdiction over diversity cases, suits involving foreigners, and suits involving land grants from two different states. Unsuccessful in that effort, Tucker, on the last day of debate again tried, but failed, to limit the lower courts to hearing only admirality cases.

Having postponed consideration of the judiciary bill until after passage of a bill of rights, the House began debate on the former on August 27. Despite heavy speculation that Madison would lead the attack he failed to do so and few substantive changes were made. Tucker renewed his attempts, made without success during the bill of rights debates, to eliminate the district courts. He was joined in this by Samuel Livermore of New Hampshire; their proposal engendered more debate than any other issue, but ultimately went down to defeat. In his closing speech on the bill, delivered on September 17, Madison summed up the views of most of his colleagues that the bill, however imperfect, was the best they could get at this late date in the session, and that it could always be changed as experience proved necessary.

The only direct evidence of interaction between the two houses as they considered the judiciary bill and the bill of rights is a letter of September 24 from Madison to Edmund Pendleton, discussing the bill of rights. "It will be impossible I find to prevail on the Senate to concur in limitation on the value of appeals to the Supreme Court," complained Madison,

> which they say is unncessary, and might be embarrassing in questions of national or Constitutional importance in their principle, tho' of small pecuniary amount. They are equally inflexible in opposing a definition of the locality of Juries. The vicinage they contend is either too vague or too strict, too vague if depending on limits to be fixed by the pleasure of the law, too strict if limited to the County.... The

Charles Carroll

Senate suppose also that the provision for vicinage in the Judiciary bill, will sufficiently quiet the fears which call for an amendment on this point.

On September 19 the Senate had proposed a compromise to the judiciary bill that allowed the trial jury in capital cases to be drawn from the county in which the crime was committed. It was adopted by the House on September 21, the same day that a joint conference committee of Reps. Madison, Sherman, and Vining, and Sens. Ellsworth, Paterson, and Carroll was appointed to resolve the differences over the bill of rights. Three days later on September 24, as the conference committee was agreeing to limit constitutional protection to a jury of the district, President Washington signed the Judiciary Act into law. Although little hard evidence exists to suggest that the Judiciary Act and the Bill of Rights were deliberately fashioned to complement each other, the fact is that together they took care of most Anti-Federalist concerns about the judiciary under the Constitution.

Probably none of the Judiciary Act's provisions captured the spirit of balancing state and federal interests that informed the creation of the Act better than Section 34. The section stipulated, simply enough,

> [t]hat the laws of the several States except where the Constitution, treaties or statutes of the United States shall otherwise require or provide, shall be regarded as rules of decision in trials at common law in the Courts of the United States in cases where they apply.

While the First Congress may well have intended "laws of the several states" merely as a shorthand for all the laws then in effect, including the unwritten common law, it is equally possible that the framers meant "laws" to refer only to statutes, leaving the federal courts free to fashion common law remedies of their own. Even if the drafters did intend that "laws" include the common law of the several states, they may have wished merely to permit, not to compel, the federal trial courts to apply state common law. Still another possibility is that the bill's framers deliberately worded the provision vaguely so as to leave its meaning open to future judicial interpretation. Its literal meaning notwithstanding, the thirty-fourth section was written, like the other sections, in the spirit of reconciling national interests with those of the various states. The enactment of the Judiciary Act of 1789 marked the culmination of an effort to implement federal law adequately and yet in a manner least detrimental to state policies and practices.

Conclusion

The passage of the Judiciary Act of 1789 was crucial to the growth of the federal judiciary. The remarks of Associate Justice Samuel Chase, in a 1799 opinion, sum up its importance. "The notion has frequently been entertained," noted Chase,

> that the federal courts derive their judicial power immediately from the Constitution; but the political truth is that the disposal of the judicial power (except in a few specified instances) belongs to Congress. If Congress has given the power to this court, we possess it, not otherwise; and if

Congress has not given the power to us or to any other court, it still remains at the legislative disposal.

The generality of Article III of the Constitution raised questions that Congress had to address in the Judiciary Act of 1789. These questions had no easy answers, and the solutions to them were achieved politically. The First Congress decided that it could regulate the jurisdiction of all federal courts, and in the Judiciary Act of 1789 Congress established with great particularity a limited jurisdiction for the district and circuit courts, gave the Supreme Court the original jurisdiction provided for in the Constitution, and granted the Court appellate jurisdiction in cases from the federal circuit courts and from state courts where those courts' rulings had rejected federal claims. The decision to grant federal courts a jurisdiction more restrictive than that allowed by the Constitution represented a recognition by the Congress that the people of the United States would not find a full-blown federal court system palatable at that time.

For nearly all of the next century the judicial system remained essentially as established by the Judiciary Act of 1789. Only after the country had expanded across a continent and had been torn apart by civil war were major changes made. A separate tier of appellate circuit courts created in 1891 removed the burden of circuit riding from the shoulders of the Supreme Court justices but otherwise left intact the judicial structure.

With minor adjustments it is the same system we have today. Congress has continued to build on the interpretation of the drafters of the first judiciary act in exercising a discretionary power to expand or restrict federal court jurisdiction. While opinions as to what constitutes the proper balance of federal and state concerns vary no less today than they did nearly two centuries ago, the fact that today's federal court system closely resembles the one created in 1789 suggests that the First Congress performed its job admirably.

The authors have all been associated with the *Documentary History of the Supreme Court of the United States, 1789-1800.*

The "Great Departments":
The Origin of the Federal Government's
Executive Branch

Richard Allan Baker

In its first years the executive branch of the federal government consisted essentially of the president and his three principal advisers—a modest beginning. Among these advisers—the secretaries of Treasury, state, and war—Treasury Secretary Alexander Hamilton ranked first, combining superior administrative skills with a sparkling intellect. Secretary of State Thomas Jefferson, who would rather have remained minister to France, took second place in this exclusive company. And the congenial Henry Knox, preoccupied with his wife's gambling debts, served without noticeable distinction as secretary of war. Playing significant supporting roles, but apart from these chiefs of the "Great Departments," were Postmaster General Samuel Osgood and Attorney General Edmund Randolph.

At the 1787 Constitutional Convention, delegates demonstrated little interest in the specifics of executive department organization. Once they had determined the powers and responsibilities of the presidential office, they simply assumed that an administrative structure would form to continue the basic governmental functions of finance, foreign relations, and defense that existed under the Articles of Confederation. The Constitution's only explicit reference to this structure appears in Article II, section 2 with the provision that the president ". . . may require the opinion, in writing, of the principal officer in each of the executive departments, upon any subject relating to the duties of their respective offices. . . ."

For several months after George Washington took his oath of office on April 30, 1789, he served as virtually the entire executive branch. Caretakers left over from the Confederation government awaited presidential and congressional

149

The first cabinet

initiative: John Jay as secretary of foreign affairs, Henry Knox as secretary of war, and Samuel Osgood, who looked after the country's post offices. The old Treasury Board continued to manage the nation's finances.

On June 8, 1789, while waiting for Congress to pass legislation establishing the three major departments, Washington asked each of the acting secretaries for a written survey of the "real situation" within their agencies. He urged them to provide a "clear account ... as may be sufficient (without overburdening or confusing the mind which has very many objects to claim its attention at the same instant) to impress me with a full, precise, and distinct *general idea* of the affairs of the United States, so far as they are comprehended in, or connected with that department."

In his relations with the embryonic executive departments, President Washington proved to be a capable administrator. His military command and staff experience became apparent in his manner of reviewing proposals of subordinates, in outlining plans for them to expand, and in his pursuit of opinions regarding the constitutionality of legislation and policy decisions. Thomas Jefferson later described Washington's managerial style: "If a doubt of any importance arose," wrote Jefferson, the president "reserved it for conference. By this means, he was always in accurate possession of all facts and proceedings in every part of the Union, and to whatsoever department they related; he formed a central point for the different branches; preserved a unity of object and action among them; exercised that participation in the suggestion of affairs which his office made incumbent upon him; and met himself the due responsibility for whatever was done."

Initially, Washington consulted with his department heads, individually or collectively, as circumstances dictated. Within four years, however, this group began to meet regularly and became known as the president's "cabinet." He worked with the cabinet much as he had with his senior officers during the Revolutionary War, often changing his own plan in the face of adverse opinion from his advisers. In the early years, the president encouraged opposing views and he got them in abundance in bitter clashes between Secretary of State Thomas Jefferson and Treasury Secretary Alexander Hamilton. By 1793, as the burdens of the presidency increased, Washington concluded that henceforth he would avoid advisers "whose political tenets are adverse to the measures which the general government are pursuing."

The Treasury Department

Alexander Hamilton

The statute creating the Treasury Department contained greater detail than those establishing the Departments of State and War, yet all three were remarkably brief. Treasury was the largest of the three cabinet agencies and, during the early years of the new government's existence, it grew at a faster rate than the other two. Congress singled out that agency for special attention by providing a direct tie between it and the legislature. Unlike the heads of the other two departments, who were to carry out their duties "in such manner as the President of the United States shall, from time to time order or instruct," the Treasury secretary was given a specific congressional mandate. The statute provided that he "digest and prepare plans for the improvement and management of the revenue, and for the support of the public credit" and that he "make report, and give information to either branch of the legislature, in person or in writing . . . respecting all matters referred to him by the Senate or House of Representatives, or which shall appertain to his office." The act contained no explicit provision for presidential supervision of the secretary. Six days after Hamilton became Treasury secretary, the House of Representatives abolished its Committee on Ways and Means. This action suggested that the House intended the secretary to take the initiative in the formulation and implementation of general financial policy: preparing revenue measures, drafting public reports, managing financial operations, and placing public funds in banks and other financial institutions.

Even before the department was officially established, Congress assigned it operational control of the customs service, light houses, and sailing vessel registration. Beyond its initial financial duties, the department soon acquired responsibility for administering a $12 million loan for conducting land surveys. Customs collectors took on the additional tasks of paying military pensions and purchasing army supplies.

The department's large number of employees reflected its broad responsibilities. At the end of 1789, its central office included six chief officers, three principal clerks, twenty-eight clerks, and two messengers. Within a year, that number had nearly doubled. By 1801, the Treasury Department employed more than half of all federal government workers, including a field staff of sixteen hundred revenue collectors.

The combination of Alexander Hamilton's leadership and the Treasury Department's vital function in raising revenue made that agency preeminent. Hamilton had actively campaigned for the position well in advance of his September 1789 appointment. While many friends urged him to avoid the Treasury—with the nation's finances in a "deep, dark, and dreary chaos"—and run for the Senate, or seek nomination as chief justice of the U.S. Supreme Court, Hamilton believed that he was one of the few men available who possessed the training and experience to accomplish this difficult task. When Robert Morris, financier and senator, advised the president to select the thirty-two-year-old Hamilton, whom he described as "damned sharp," Washington immediately sent his name to the Senate, where confirmation quickly followed.

With a growing family to support, and a promising law practice under way, Hamilton realized that he was endangering his personal financial security by taking the modestly compensated $3,500-per-year post. After a month on the job, he commented, "I hazarded much, but I thought it was an occasion that called upon me to hazard."

A gifted administrator and a fiscal genius, Hamilton had been involved in the affairs of government since 1777 when, at the age of twenty, he was appointed Washington's military aide. Five feet, seven inches tall, he maintained a strict military bearing, heightened by a touch of arrogance. A man of vast energy and deep intellect, Hamilton understood the possibilities for planned economic development under governmental direction. Above all, he preferred action to contemplation. One biographer observed that "Hamilton's credo was audacity and yet more audacity. While others temporized, calculated the risks and paused in indecision, Hamilton acted."

His intense ambition, his passion for order and efficiency, together with his tendency to meddle in the operations of other cabinet agencies, made him the administrative architect of the new government. The combination of special congressional powers vested in the Treasury Department, the president's relative inexperience in financial affairs, and Hamilton's expertise placed him in a stronger position than the secretaries of war and state to pursue a course of his own choosing. One member of Congress commented, "Congress may go home. Mr. Hamilton is all-powerful and fails in nothing he attempts."

The State Department

Compared with Treasury, the State Department remained relatively small and restricted in the scope of its activities throughout the nation's formative years. The secretary of state conducted foreign negotiations on a highly personal basis. These relations were so delicate that no secretary considered the possibility of delegating them to subordinates. With ministers in only five capitals—Paris, London, Lisbon, The Hague, and Madrid—there was little need for an administrative staff greater than a half-dozen clerks.

Unlike the close ties Congress set between itself and the Treasury secretary, it left the secretary of state to the president's supervision and did not even require an annual report from him. The only issue that troubled legislators in devising this statute was the president's authority to remove the secretary. This question provoked the first major crisis in relations between the legislative and executive branches under the new Constitution.

For days in June 1789 a debate raged in the House of Representatives as to whether the president should seek the Senate's advice before removing officers whose initial nominations had received Senate review. The debate focused on the right of Congress to specify conditions for the operation of an executive agency, including conditions for its chief's removal, as long as those conditions did not conflict with provisions of the Constitution. It also raised the question of whether the president would be required to share administrative authority with the Senate. On a close vote, both chambers agreed that the president could remove the officers subject to Senate confirmation without Senate concurrence.

Although President Washington was content to leave management of the nation's finances to the Treasury secretary, he displayed no such detachment in the realm of foreign affairs. The president routinely consulted close associates on foreign policy matters but did not necessarily include the secretary of state in the discussions. Jefferson expressed his frustration, on one occasion, writing that as "Secretary of State to the United States, I can not receive any communication on the part of foreign ministers but for the purpose of laying it before the President, and of taking his orders upon it."

The act of July 27, 1789, which established the Department of Foreign Affairs as the first executive agency, provided only the briefest outline of its duties. They included "Correspondence, commissions, and instructions to ministers and consuls; negotiations with public ministers from foreign states or princes; memorials or other applications from foreign ministers or other foreigners"; and "such other matters respecting foreign affairs as the president assigned."

Early in its existence, the State Department acquired a significant measure of responsibility for domestic, as well as foreign, affairs. Congress had specifically rejected a proposal to

The site of the first American Foreign Office, Philadelphia, 1781

create a "Home Department" in the belief that it could achieve administrative efficiency and minimize expenses by dividing these functions among the three former Confederation agencies. The major share would go to the Foreign Affairs Department as it was less burdened with work than the Treasury and War departments. Consequently, in September 1789 the Foreign Affairs Department was renamed the Department of State and given such functions as distributing federal laws to members of Congress and the states, preparing and authenticating commissions issued by the president, conducting the decennial census, granting patents and copyrights, and safekeeping government records. The department also issued instructions to federal marshals and attorneys, and coordinated the activities of federal judges.

At its beginnings, the department included two clerks.

One was in charge of the Foreign Office and the other supervised the Home Office. Housed in two rooms, this staff grew slowly with the addition of a chief clerk who carried the title of undersecretary, a part-time interpreter, a doorkeeper, and a messenger. In 1792 Congress authorized two additional clerks. By 1800 the State Department of the United States included one secretary, one chief clerk, seven clerks, and a messenger.

When Thomas Jefferson took up his duties as secretary in March 1790, the department's entire budget, including his own $3,500 salary, amounted to $8,000. Jefferson had little to do at the outset of his term, for few foreign nations maintained active embassies at the seat of government, and the president had not yet appointed permanent ambassadors to the major European posts. At that time a round-trip voyage to Europe required three months. With the exchange of correspondence so delayed, resident diplomats exercised a great deal of independence. In March 1791 Jefferson complained to the minister at Madrid, "Your letter of May 6, 1789 is still the last that we have received, and that is now two years old."

Jefferson had served as U.S. minister to France from 1785 to 1789. There he grew to appreciate that country's role in maintaining American independence of Great Britain. As secretary of state, he soon engaged in sharp political infighting with Alexander Hamilton, their mutual antagonism flaring over relations with Great Britain and France. Jefferson advocated commercial sanctions against the British to force their evacuation from posts in the Northwest. Hamilton successfully blocked this strategy, fearing a serious loss of revenue from British imports. Hostilities between the two secretaries intensified as Hamilton continued to interfere in the conduct of foreign affairs and published an anonymous series of bitter attacks on Jefferson.

When not engaged with pressing foreign business, Jefferson turned his attention and creative genius to the domestic responsibilities of his office. Among the most notable of his achievements was a lengthy and enlightening report to the House of Representatives on the topic of weights and measures. A biographer observed that his conclusions, on which the House took no action, represented "an admirable combination of arithmetic and common sense." Jefferson spent a great deal of time in the administration of patents, after Congress created that system in 1790. Under the law, patent applications were to be examined by a three-man board, composed of the secretary of state, the secretary of war, and the attorney general. As a practical matter, the work fell to the secretary of state. After the attorney general ruled on the propriety of the application forms, Jefferson determined whether the individual inventions were either frivolous, unworkable, or mere modifications of existing items in common use. During his five years in office, Jefferson granted sixty-seven patents, rejecting a great many more. In 1791, weary of the task's complexity and demands on his time, Jefferson drafted a bill relieving himself of substantive responsibilities for the patent process. Two years later Congress passed a similar measure, eliminating the examination and placing responsibility for settling disputes with the courts.

Jefferson considered these and the related duties of his office as "hateful labors." As his earlier and subsequent accomplishments testified, Jefferson's greatness lay elsewhere. While secretary of state, he operated in the shadow of George Washington, who wished to be his own foreign minister. Overcome by the drudgery of the job and his battles with Hamilton, Jefferson retired at the end of 1793.

The War Department

On August 7, 1789, Congress established the War Department and within five weeks the Senate confirmed Henry Knox as secretary of war. The department's original staff included Knox and a clerk. A second clerk was added a few years later. By 1800, when the government moved from Philadelphia to Washington, the agency's total central and field office staff had grown to eighty. The department supervised the nation's two armories: one at Springfield, Mass., and the other at Harpers Ferry, Va. It also included a quartermaster's section, a fortifications branch, a paymaster, an inspector general, and an Indian office.

The early record of the department was an unhappy one. Mismanagement and incompetence characterized its administrative actions. A committee of the House of Representatives, investigating the late 1791 Indian defeat of Gen. Arthur St. Clair's forces, determined that it resulted from improper organization of the expedition; lack of troop training and discipline; and "delays consequent upon the gross and various mismanagements and neglects in the Quartermaster's and contractor's departments." Alexander Hamilton moved to take matters into his own hands by requesting that his allies in the Senate push legislation giving his Treasury Department supervision of army supply services. Congress enacted Hamilton's measure in May 1792.

Henry Knox

Henry Knox had served since 1785 as secretary of war under the Articles of Confederation. Born in Boston, Knox concluded his formal education at the age of twelve. When the Revolutionary War began in 1775, he became an artillery colonel. In the war's subsequent campaigns, Knox distinguished himself as a military commander and became a favorite of General Washington. Still, Knox proved to be a clumsy civilian administrator, undercut by a president who considered military affairs his own greatest strength. Plagued by the pressure of gambling debts, Knox became preoccupied with land speculation schemes designed to restore his family's financial health. These ventures led to further indebtedness and numerous law suits. Knox resigned as war secretary in 1794.

The Post Office   In 1789 the nation's mail system consisted of seventy-five post offices and 1,875 miles of post roads, running principally from Boston, Mass., to Petersburg, Va. In September of that year Congress passed legislation temporarily continuing post office operations as they had existed under the Articles of Confederation. Members demonstrated no interest in creating a separate postal department, or of merging its functions with an existing department. The statute simply provided that "the Postmaster General shall be subject to the direction of the President of the United States."

In the years before 1789, the Confederation Congress viewed the post office as a vital source of governmental revenue. In 1790, the office produced a $5,000 profit on income of $38,000. In 1792 Congress specifically placed the post office within the jurisdiction of Hamilton's Treasury Department, in recognition of its revenue producing functions. This provoked a protest from Secretary of State Jefferson, who feared that "the department of the Treasury possessed already such an influence as to swallow up the whole executive powers, and that future presidents (not supported by the weight of character which [Washington] possessed) would not be able to make head against this department."

By 1796, the department's profit-producing incentive yielded to another essential function—its capacity for communicating governmental actions to all sections of the nation. As Washington advised the House of Representatives in 1792, "The circulation of political intelligence through these vehicles is justly reckoned among the surest means of preventing the degeneracy of a free government, as well as recommending every salutary public measure to the confidence and cooperation of all virtuous citizens."

In 1790 the post office consisted of Postmaster General Samuel Osgood, who earned $1,500—less than half the annual salary rate of the department secretaries—an assistant, and a clerk. His principal duties were to designate post offices, to select and maintain contact with deputy postmasters, to award contracts for carrying mail, and to keep accounts. The actual work of moving the mail fell to the deputy postmasters and contractors, whose salaries were paid by local postal revenues. Retention of competent deputy postmasters proved to be the postmaster general's greatest headache. Those part-time positions held few attractions, except in major cities. Osgood resigned in 1791 rather than move with the rest of the government from New York to Philadelphia. The post office remained a subordinate agency until 1825 when it achieved independent status as a result of presidential wishes to control politically attractive deputy postmaster appointments.

The Attorney General

Like the postmaster general, the attorney general served as a second-level presidential appointee during the federal government's early years. President Washington viewed Attorney General Edmund Randolph, who held that post from 1790 to 1794, simply as his legal adviser. Under the provisions of the 1789 Judiciary Act, which established his position, Randolph was to prosecute all suits in the Supreme Court that involved the interest of the United States government. That statute also directed him to provide legal advice to the president and department heads when they requested it. At the outset, as there were no cases before the Supreme Court, and as the president seldom sought his advice, Randolph had virtually nothing to do. Reflecting this status, the attorney general received less than half the salary of cabinet secretaries and had no government staff. He was expected to conduct official business from his personal law office and to maintain a private legal practice when he was not advising the president or other federal officials. On matters of major legal consequence, President Washington frequently by-passed his attorney general in favor of Hamilton and Jefferson. The secretary of state retained responsibility for supervising federal district attorneys. Despite his persistent efforts, Randolph was unable to acquire

Samuel Osgood

law enforcement responsibilities. He left the position in 1794 to replace Jefferson as secretary of state.

Conclusion

Washington, Hamilton, Jefferson, and Knox, along with Osgood and Randolph, by and large built successfully on the executive structure established under the Articles of Confederation and by Congress under the Constitution. These leaders of the early executive departments achieved much for the government in a nation that less than a generation earlier had suffered the dependence of colonial rule. In these formative years, the executive agencies established a high level of legitimacy and moral integrity, as well as a degree of autonomy from close legislative direction. The president clearly exercised substantial administrative authority and responsibility for conduct of the new government's official business. He effectively delegated authority to department heads and through them to their immediate subordinates and field representatives, while retaining controls over their performance. Despite Hamilton's occasional intrusions into operations of other departments, executive agency leaders formed relatively stable relationships based on precedent, law, and presidential directives. To be sure, the achievements of these men were not untouched by failure. The Post Office was slow and unreliable. The Treasury and War departments remained unable to devise an efficient system for procuring army supplies. The patent system, after a period of rigorous executive involvement, was abandoned to the courts. Despite these shortcomings, the occasion for celebrating the Constitution's two hundredth anniversary is due in great measure to the successful establishment of the early executive departments.

SUGGESTED ADDITIONAL READING

Marcus Cunliffe, *The American Heritage History of the Presidency* (1986).
Ralph Ketcham, *President above Party: The First American Presidency, 1789-1829* (1984).
Forrest McDonald, *Alexander Hamilton: A Biography* (1979).
Dumas Malone, *Jefferson and the Rights of Man* (1951).
Leonard D. White, *Federalists: A Study in Administrative History, 1789-1801* (1948).

Richard Allan Baker has served as director of the U.S. Senate Historical Office since that office was established in 1975. He was recently president of the Society for History in the Federal Government. He is the author of *Conservation Politics: The Senate Career of Clinton P. Anderson* and *Senate of the United States: A Bicentennial History*.

IV. Bill of Rights, Constitutional Adaptation, and the Future of the Constitution

James Madison and the Bill of Rights

Jack N. Rakove

James Madison went to the Federal Convention of 1787 convinced that it faced no greater challenge than finding some means of checking "the aggressions of interested majorities on the rights of minorities and of individuals." He left it still fearful that the new Constitution would not effectually "secure individuals against encroachments on their rights." In his best known contribution to American political theory, *The Federalist,* No. 10, Madison again voiced his great concern that majorities were enacting laws "adverse to the rights of other citizens," and he went on to define the protection of the individual "faculties" of men as "the first object of government."

These and other statements suggest that Madison should have welcomed the addition of a bill of rights to the Constitution. And in fact Madison can rightly be regarded as the principal framer of the Bill of Rights that the first federal Congress submitted to the states in 1789. Many members of Congress felt that he was acting with undue haste in calling for quick action on the subject of amendments. Had Madison not pressed them to consider the amendments he had introduced early in the session, the Bill of Rights might never have been added to the Constitution.

Yet even as he was shepherding the amendments through Congress in August 1789, Madison privately described his efforts as a "nauseous project." His acceptance of the need for a bill of rights came grudgingly. When the Constitution was being written in 1787, and even after it was ratified in 1788, Madison dismissed bills of rights as so many "parchment barriers" whose "inefficacy" (he reminded his good friend, Thomas Jefferson) was repeatedly demonstrated "on those occasions when [their] control is most needed." Even after Jefferson's entreaties finally led him to admit that bills of

165

rights might have their uses, it still took a difficult election campaign against another friend, James Monroe, to get Madison to declare that, if elected to the House of Representatives, he would favor adding to the Constitution "the most satisfactory provisions for all essential rights."

To trace the evolution of James Madison's thinking about the virtues and defects of a bill of rights, then, is to confront the ambiguous mix of principled and political concerns that led to the adoption of the first ten amendments. Today, when disputes about the meaning of the Bill of Rights and its lineal descendant, the Fourteenth Amendment, have become so heated— when, indeed, we often regard the Bill of Rights as the essence of the Constitution—it is all the more important to fix the relation between the Constitution of 1787 and the amendments of 1789. To do this there is no better place to begin than with the concerns that troubled James Madison.

Enumerating Rights   Much of the contemporary debate and controversy about the rights-based decisions that the Supreme Court has made over the past three decades centers on the question of whether the judiciary should protect only those rights that enjoy explicit constitutional or statutory sanction, or whether it can act to establish new rights—as in the case of abortion—on the basis of its understanding of certain general principles of liberty. We cannot know how Madison would decide particular cases today. But one aspect of his analysis of the problem of rights seems highly pertinent to the current debate. Madison's deepest reservations about the wisdom of adopting any bill of rights reflected his awareness of the difficulty of enumerating all the rights that deserved protection against the "infinitude of legislative expedients" that could be deployed to the disadvantage of individuals and minorities.

Madison's notion of rights was thus open-ended, but his ideas about which kinds of rights were most vulnerable changed over time. In 1787 he felt that the greatest dangers to liberty concerned the rights of property. The passage of paper money laws in various states revealed the depths of "injustice" to which these populist forces were willing to descend. Worse might be yet to come. At the Federal Convention, Madison told his fellow delegates that he foresaw a day when "power will slide into the hands" of "those who labour under all the hardships of life, and secretly sigh for a more equal distribution of its blessings." And even if the Constitution succeeded in checking the danger from a dispossessed proletariat, Madison thought that almost any act of legislation or taxation would affect rights of property. "What are many of the most important acts of legislation," he asked in *The Federalist,* No. 10, "but so many judicial determinations ... concerning the rights of large bodies of citizens?"

But the development of Madison's ideas of liberty long predated the specific concerns he felt about the economic legislation of the 1780s. His first known comments on political issues of any kind expressed his abhorrence at the persecution of religious dissenters in pre-Revolutionary Virginia; and his first notable action in public life had been to secure an amendment to the Virginia Declaration of Rights, the most influential of the bills of rights that had been attached to the state constitutions written at the time of independence. In 1785 Madison led the fight against a bill to provide public aid for all teachers of the Christian religion in Virginia; the *Memorial and Remonstrance against Religious Assessments* that he published in conjunction with this campaign treated rights of conscience as a realm of behavior entirely beyond the regulation of civil authority.

Majority Misrule

We thus cannot doubt Madison's commitment to the cause of protecting private rights and civil liberties against improper intrusion by the government. But all orthodox republicans in Revolutionary America shared such beliefs. What carried Madison beyond the conventional thought of his contemporaries was, first, his analysis of the sources of the dangers to individual and minority rights, and second, the solutions and remedies he offered.

Traditional republican theory held that the great danger to liberty lay in the relentless efforts of scheming rulers to aggrandize their power at the expense of ordinary citizens. The great safeguard against such threats was believed to lie in the virtue and vigilance of the people.

The skeptical Madison sought to overturn this received wisdom. In the weeks preceding the gathering of the Federal Convention in May 1787, Madison collected his thoughts in a memorandum on the "Vices of the Political System of the United States." As he saw it, the "multiplicity," "mutability," and most important, "the injustice" of the laws of the states had called "into question the fundamental principle of republican Government, that the majority who rule in such Governments are the safest Guardians both of public Good and of private rights." The experience of the states demonstrated,

Madison concluded, that neither legislative majorities nor the popular majorities whom they represented could be expected to refrain "from unjust violations of the rights and interests of the minority, or of individuals," whenever "an apparent interest or common passion" spurred such majorities to act. Religion, honor, a sense of the public good—all the virtues a good republican might hope to see operate as restraints—seemed ineffective.

It is crucial to note that Madison directed his criticism against the character of lawmaking *within the individual states;* and the logic of his analysis further led him to conclude that the greatest dangers to liberty would continue to arise within the states, rather than from a reconstituted national government. The ill effects of majority rule far more likely would emerge within the small compass of local communities or states, where "factious majorities" could easily form, than in the extended sphere of a national republic that would "be broken into a greater variety of interests, of pursuits, of passions," whose very diversity and fluidity would check each other.

The solutions Madison offered to this problem operated at two levels. He reserved his most radical proposal—an absolute national veto over state laws "in all cases whatsoever"—for the continuing need to protect individual rights against majority misrule within the states. In effect, Madison hoped the national government would serve as a "disinterested and dispassionate umpire in disputes between different passions and interests" within the states.

But Madison was also prepared to concede that the wrong kinds of majorities might still coalesce within the new Congress that the Federal Convention would create. "Experience in all the States had evinced a powerful tendency in the Legislature to absorb all power into its vortex," he reminded the Convention on July 21. Who could say whether Congress might not prove equally "impetuous"? To protect citizens against the danger of unjust *national* legislation, Madison favored establishing a joint executive-judicial council of revision armed with a veto over acts of Congress; he was also attracted to the idea of an independent and powerful Senate, insulated from both the state legislatures and the electorate, to counteract the excesses of the House of Representatives.

Madison justified all of these proposals in terms of the protection they would extend to individual and minority rights. But he went to the Convention convinced that bills of rights could add little if anything to the defense of civil liberty. None of the existing state bills of rights provided an effective check against legislative or popular excess. The problem was that bills of rights were not self-enforcing. The actual protection of the lofty principles they espoused required the existence of well-constituted governments. But if such governments did exist—or could be created—what need would they have for bills of rights?

Most of the framers at Philadelphia agreed that there was no need for adding a bill of rights to the new Constitution, but they rejected Madison's two pet proposals for a national veto and a Council of Revision. The Convention protected individual liberty only by placing a handful of prohibitions on the legislative authority of the states (notably laws impairing the obligation of contracts) or Congress (habeas corpus, ex post

**A Proposal for
a National Veto**

facto, bills of attainder). When George Mason belatedly insisted that the new Constitution required a much longer list of enumerated rights, his arguments were ignored.

The rejection of his pet scheme for a national veto on all state laws greatly disappointed Madison. During the first weeks after the Convention's adjournment, he seems to have feared that the new Constitution was fatally flawed because the new government would still lack the authority to deal with the problem of "vicious" popular and legislative majorities in the *states.* Even though the supremacy clause of the Constitution established a basis for state and federal judges to overturn laws violating individual rights, he doubted whether the judiciary could ever muster the will or political strength to withstand majoritarian excesses or the ingenuity of ambitious legislators.

When it came to the dangers that liberty might face from the *national* government, however, he was far more optimistic. Though not entirely happy with the system of checks and balances that would shape relations among the three branches, Madison thought it would discourage the enactment of harmful legislation. Moreover, he continued to rely confidently on the theory of the advantages of multiple factions he had derived just prior to the Convention. "In the extended republic of the United States, and among the great variety of interests, parties, and sects which it embraces," he wrote in *The Federalist,* No. 51, "a coalition of a majority of the whole society could seldom take place upon any other principles than those of justice and the general good." State laws might still work wholesale injustice; national laws, he believed, would not.

Anti-Federalist Clamor

As Madison threw himself into the campaign to ratify the Constitution, however, he was forced to take seriously the growing clamor for the addition of a bill of rights—especially after Jefferson wrote him to affirm *his* conviction "that a bill of rights is what the people are entitled to against every government on earth, general or particular [i.e., national or local], and what no just government should refuse or rest on inference." Had the issue of amendments been confined to matters of rights alone, Madison might have readily agreed. But fearing that many diehard Anti-Federalists hoped to exploit the call for amendments to propose major changes in the Constitution or even to promote a second convention, Madison balked at accepting Jefferson's correction.

In October 1788—more than a year after the adjournment of the Convention, and a good four months after Virginia became the tenth state to ratify the Constitution—Madison wrote Jefferson to explain why, though now willing to see a bill of rights added to the Constitution, he found no other solid reason to support it than the fact "that it is anxiously desired by others." With other Federalists—notably James Wilson of Pennsylvania—he still thought that a bill of rights was superfluous because the federal government could exercise only those powers that were expressly delegated to it—and those powers did not extend to violating individual liberties. Moreover, Madison confessed his "fear that a positive declaration of some of the most essential rights could not be obtained in the requisite latitude." Better (in other words) not to have any bill of rights than to incorporate in the Constitution weak statements that might actually leave room for the violation of the very liberties they were meant to protect.

Again, however, Madison drew his greatest doubts about the value of a bill of rights from his analysis of the problem of majority tyranny. In a monarchical regime, Madison noted, such declarations might serve as "a signal for rousing and uniting the superior force of the community" against the government. But in a republic, where the greatest dangers to liberty arose not from government but from the people themselves, a bill of rights could hardly serve to rally the majority against itself. The most Madison would concede was that a bill of rights might help to instill in the people greater respect for "the fundamental maxims of free government," and thus "counteract the impulses of interest and passion." He was willing to entertain, too, the idea that a bill of rights would be useful in case "usurped acts of the government" threatened the liberties of the community—but in his thinking, that problem remained only a speculative possibility.

Like any intellectual, then, Madison valued consistency too highly to renounce ideas to which he was deeply and personally committed. But Madison, for all his originality as a political theorist, was also a working politician. His early disappointment with the Constitution had quickly given way to the belief, as he wrote in *The Federalist,* No. 38, that "the errors which may be contained in the Constitution . . . [were] such as will not be ascertained until an actual trial shall have pointed them out." Amendments taking the form of a bill of rights might serve a vital *political* function—even though unnecessary on their merits—if they could be framed in such a way as to reconcile the moderate opponents of the Constitution without opening an avenue to a radical assault on the essential structure of the new government.

This sensitivity to the need to assuage popular opinion was reinforced by Madison's own experience in the first congressional elections of 1788-1789, when he faced a difficult fight against James Monroe. With reports abroad that Madison "did not think that a single letter of [the Constitution] would admit of a change," he found it necessary not only to return to Virginia from his seat in the Confederation Congress at New York and to travel around the district debating with Monroe, but more important, to issue public letters affirming his willingness to propose and support amendments guaranteeing such "essential rights" as "the rights of Conscience in the fullest latitude, the freedom of the press, trials by jury, security

against general warrants &c." Even then, however, he was careful to note that he had "never seen in the Constitution . . . those serious dangers which have alarmed many respectable Citizens."

Political Exigencies

Madison carried the election by a margin of 336 votes out of 2,280 cast. Four weeks into the first session of Congress, he informed his colleagues of his intention to bring the subject of amendments forward, but another month passed before he was at last able to present a comprehensive set of proposals on June 8, 1789.

Some members of Congress thought that Madison was acting from political motives alone. Sen. Robert Morris of Pennsylvania scoffed that Madison "got frightened in Virginia 'and wrote a Book' "—a reference to his public letters on amendments. But there was nothing disingenuous about Madison's June 8 speech introducing his plan of amendments. Having reconciled himself to political exigencies, Madison sought to achieve goals consistent with his private beliefs.

In typical scholarly fashion, he had culled from over two hundred amendments proposed by the state ratification conventions a list of nineteen potential changes to the Constitution. Two of his proposals concerned congressional salaries and the population ratio of the House; two can best be described as general statements of principles of government. The remaining amendments fell under the general rubric of "rights."

The most noteworthy aspects of Madison's introductory speech of June 8 is that it faithfully recapitulates the positions he had taken not only in his election campaign against Monroe but also in his correspondence with Jefferson. He took care to deal with the objections that could come from Anti-Federalists and Federalists alike, noting his reasons for originally opposing amendments, explaining why he had changed his mind, yet also leaving his listeners and readers with a clear understanding that he was acting on a mixture of political and principled motives. The central elements of his analysis of the problem of protecting rights in a republican government were all there: the difficulty of enumerating rights, the emphasis on the greater danger from popular majorities than acts of government, the risks of trusting too much to "paper barriers."

Two of his proposals deserve special notice. The first is the forerunner of the Ninth Amendment. In its graceless original wording, it read: "The exceptions here or elsewhere in the constitution, made in favor of particular rights, shall not be so construed as to diminish the just importance of other rights retained by the people; or as to enlarge the powers delegated by the constitution; but either as actual limitations of such powers, or as inserted merely for greater caution." Here Madison sought to prevent the enumeration of specific rights from relegating other rights to an inferior status—a concern that was consistent with both his open-ended notion of rights and his fear that any textually specific statement might inadvertently or otherwise create loopholes permitting the violation of liberties. As finally adopted by Congress and ratified by the states, this amendment came to read: "The enumeration in the Constitution, of certain rights, shall not be construed to deny or disparage others retained by the people."

Among all the provisions of the Bill of Rights, this somewhat mysterious formula has had perhaps the most curious history. Long ignored and disparaged because it did not identify the additional rights it implied should be protected, it was resurrected in the critical 1965 case of *Griswold v. Connecticut.* In his concurring opinion, Justice Arthur Goldberg invoked the Ninth Amendment to support the claim that state prohibition on contraception even for married couples violated a fundamental right of privacy that did not need to be specifically identified to be deserving of constitutional protection. If interpreted in Madisonian terms, this "forgotten" provision is immediately and enormously relevant to the current controversy over the extent to which judges can recognize claims of rights not enumerated in the text of the Constitution itself.

"No State Shall Violate ..."

The second proposal of particular interest—and arguably the most important to Madison—held that "No state shall violate the equal rights of conscience, or the freedom of the press, or the trial by jury in criminal cases." All the other amendments that Madison enumerated elsewhere in his speech imposed limitations on the power of the national government alone. This amendment, by contrast, proposed adding to the prohibitions on state legislative authority already found in Article VI of the Constitution these further restraints in the three critical areas of religion, speech, and criminal law. Here, in effect, Madison belatedly hoped to salvage something of his original intention of creating a national government capable of protecting individual rights within (and against) the individual states, in a manner consistent with his belief that the greatest threats to liberty would continue to arise there, and not at the

national level of government.

On this proposal Madison again met defeat. Not until the adoption of the Fourteenth Amendment in 1868 would the Constitution contain provisions that would establish a firm foundation upon which the federal government could finally act as the James Madison of 1787-1789 had hoped it would. But after a variety of procedural delays, Congress finally endorsed Madison's remaining provisions for the protection of individual liberty. All of the first ten amendments that we collectively describe as the Bill of Rights appeared, in seminal form, in Madison's speech of June 8. Among the rights he then insisted upon recognizing, Madison included: free exercise of religion; freedom of speech, of the press, and the right of assembly; the right to bear arms; and the protection of fundamental civil liberties against the legal and coercive power of the state through such devices as restrictions on "unreasonable searches and seizures," bail, "the right to a speedy and public trial" with "the assistance of counsel," and the right to "just compensation" for property.

Rethinking   Because the states retained the major share of legislative responsibility for more than another century, the Bill of Rights had little initial impact. Arguably only during the past forty years has it emerged as a central pillar of American constitutionalism—and thus as a central source of political controversy as well, as the current debate over the legitimacy of judicial "activism" in the enforcement and even creation of rights readily attests. But the question of what the prohibitions of the Bill of Rights finally mean can be answered only in part by appealing to the evidence of history.

Madison himself was one of the first to realize how ideas of rights had to be adjusted to meet changing political circumstances. His original breakthroughs in constitutional theory had rested on the conviction that in a republic the greatest dangers to liberty would arise "not from acts of government contrary to the sense of its constituents, but from acts in which the Government is the mere instrument of the major number of the constituents." He had further predicted that the greatest dangers to liberty would continue to arise within the states. Within a decade of the writing of the Constitution, however, the efforts of the Federalist administration of President John Adams to use the Sedition Act of 1798 to quell the opposition press of Madison's Republican party, in seeming defiance of the First Amendment, forced Madison to rethink his position. Now he saw more clearly how the existence of a bill of rights could serve to rally public opinion against improper acts of government; how dangers to liberty could arise at the enlightened level of national government as well as at the more parochial level of the states; and even how the political influence of the states could be used to check the excesses of national power.

Our ideas of rights and liberty have deep historical and philosophical roots that any good faith effort at interpretation must always take into account; and Madison's agency in drafting both the Constitution and its first ten amendments suggests that his views deserve particular attention and even respect. Yet just as his own efforts to understand both what the Constitution meant and how liberty was to be protected continued well after 1789—indeed literally to his death nearly a half century later—neither can ours be confined to recovering only some one meaning frozen at a mythical moment of supreme understanding. Such a moment has never existed and never will.

Jack N. Rakove is director of the American studies program at Stanford University and the author of *The Beginnings of National Politics: An Interpretive History of the Continental Congress* (1979).

The Nationalization of the Bill of Rights: An Overview

Richard C. Cortner

In the 1980s, amid heated discussion about constitutional rights, few Americans recall that for most of our history the Bill of Rights did not apply to the exercise of power by state and local governments. Until the 1920s, only state constitutions and state law prevented local governments from encroaching upon basic liberties such as freedom of speech, press, religion and the right against compulsory self-incrimination.

In 1897, however, the Supreme Court for the first time began to extend the protections guaranteed in the Bill of Rights to exercises of power by state and local governments. That first decision and others since have been based on the Fourteenth Amendment of the Constitution, adopted in 1868 in the wake of the Civil War, specifically the clause that prohibits the states from depriving any person of life, liberty, or property without "due process of law." The process by which the Court has applied most of the rights in the Bill of Rights as restrictions upon state and local governments via the "due process" clause of the Fourteenth Amendment is usually referred to as the "nationalization" of the Bill of Rights.

The Constitution that emerged from the Philadelphia convention in 1787 did not of course include a bill of rights; during the ratification struggle in the states, that omission provoked the most heated criticism of the new frame of government. To win over their opponents, the Federalist supporters of the new Constitution promised to consider amendments guaranteeing basic freedoms. Keeping that promise, the first Congress in 1789 submitted for ratification amendments making up the Bill of Rights, drafted largely by James Madison; the Bill of Rights formally became a part of the Constitution in 1791.

179

Advocates of a bill of rights feared that the new national government created by the Constitution would encroach upon personal liberties. Thus, according to the common understanding of the period, the rights specified in the Bill of Rights checked only the powers of the national government; they did not apply to powers retained by state and local governments. The U.S. Supreme Court confirmed this understanding in *Barron v. Baltimore* in 1833, and it became thereby a basic principle of constitutional law.

The Fourteenth Amendment

In 1868, the ratification of the Fourteenth Amendment in the wake of the Civil War placed new restrictions upon state power. Many of its framers entertained the hope that the Fourteenth Amendment's provisions prohibiting the states from denying persons the privileges and immunities of U.S. citizenship (the "privileges and immunities" clause) or denying them life, liberty, or property without due process of law (the due process clause) might become the bases for guaranteeing fundamental individual rights against deprivation by state and local governments.

Although Rep. John Bingham (R-Ohio) and Sen. Jacob Howard (R-Mich.) had suggested during debates on the Fourteenth Amendment in Congress that the privileges and immunities clause might apply all of the Bill of Rights to the states, interpretation of that clause by the Supreme Court denied it such an important role as a source of civil liberties. In the *Slaughter House Cases,* decided in 1873, the Court held that the most basic rights of the individual had state law and state constitutions as their source, notwithstanding the addition of the Fourteenth Amendment to the Constitution, and that the privileges and immunities clause guaranteed only a very narrow spectrum of relatively unimportant rights against deprivation by the states.

This narrow reading of the Fourteenth Amendment carried over as well to the Court's construction of the due process clause, and for a time that clause also seemed destined to become a constitutional dead letter. In 1884, in *Hurtado v. California,* the Court rejected an argument that the due process clause required the states to indict defendants in criminal cases by grand juries, a right guaranteed in serious federal criminal cases by the Fifth Amendment of the Bill of Rights; in the process, the Court adopted reasoning that denied that any right specifically guaranteed in the Bill of Rights could apply to the states via the due process clause of the

The restored chamber of the Supreme Court (1862-1935) in the Capitol

Fourteenth Amendment. The *Hurtado* case therefore appeared to foreclose the possibility that the due process clause would serve as a vehicle for the extension of the rights in the Bill of Rights to the states, just as the *Slaughter House Cases* extinguished the same potential for the privileges and immunities clause.

"Substantive Due Process"

Pressure on the Supreme Court by business interests, however, eventually undermined the reasoning adopted by the Court in the *Hurtado* case. Until 1890, due process had been commonly interpreted by the courts as essentially a procedural limitation on governmental power—that is, in taking action depriving persons of life, liberty, or property, the government must act in a manner that was procedurally fair. Due process meant that individuals had to have notice of the government's action and a hearing before the action occurred. Apprehensive about pending state regulatory legislation, business interests, particularly the railroads, now began to argue that their economic and property rights deserved more than fair governmental procedures under the due process clause, that there were some governmental actions affecting "liberty" and "property" that were illegitimate under the due process clause regardless of how such actions were carried out.

Although initially reluctant to accept this concept of "substantive due process," in an 1890 case, *Chicago, Milwaukee & St. Paul Railroad v. Minnesota,* the Supreme Court finally expanded the meaning of the due process clause to embrace substantive rights as well as procedural protections. In doing so, the Court granted broad protection to property rights and also stymied regulation of commercial enterprises by the states. But the new interpretation of due process also had a fundamental impact upon the nationalization of the *Bill of Rights. Although most of the rights in the Bill of Rights are procedural, the rights in the First Amendment are substantive. Without the Court's acceptance of the idea that the due process clause embraced substantive as well as procedural rights, the theoretical basis for the application of the First Amendment rights to the states via the Fourteenth Amendment would not have existed.

The breakthrough regarding the nationalization of the Bill of Rights occurred in 1897, *Chicago, Burlington & Quincy Railroad Co. v. Chicago.* In this case the Court held that the due process clause required the states when taking private property for a public purpose to give the owners just compensation—a right also guaranteed by the "just compensation" clause of the Fifth Amendment of the Bill of Rights. For the first time a right in the Bill of Rights had been applied to the states via the due process clause of the Fourteenth Amendment.

By its decision in the *Chicago, Burlington & Quincy Railroad* case, the Court implicitly repudiated the reasoning in the *Hurtado* case of 1884, in which it had held that no right specifically guaranteed in the Bill of Rights could apply to the states via the due process clause.

Fundamental Rights

The Court attempted to reconcile the contradiction between the two cases when the next stage of the nationalization process opened in 1908 with the decision in *Twining v. New Jersey.* In *Twining,* the Court rejected a claim that the self-incrimination clause of the Fifth Amendment applied to the states via the due process clause, but at the same time it attempted to formulate a general rule governing the relationship of the Bill of Rights to the due process clause. Although the rights in the Bill of Rights did not apply to the states exactly as they applied to the national government, the Court concluded, the due process clause might embrace some rights similar to those in the Bill of Rights because they were essential to the concept of due process of law. The test was this: "Is it a fundamental principle of liberty and justice which inheres in the very idea of free government and is the inalienable right of a citizen of such a government?" The *Twining* case thus opened the door to the future application to the states of some rights at least similar to some of those in the Bill of Rights.

Despite the promise of the *Twining* case, the nationalization process nevertheless stalled for seventeen years. Then, in 1925, the Court reviewed Benjamin Gitlow's conviction in New York for advocating the violent overthrow of the government, which he claimed deprived him of freedom of expression under the due process clause of the Fourteenth Amendment. While the Court affirmed the conviction in *Gitlow v. New York* in 1925, it took a major step in the nationalization process by declaring that for "present purposes we may and do assume that freedom of speech and of the press—which are protected by the First Amendment from abridgement by Congress—are among the fundamental personal rights and 'liberties' protected by the due process clause of the Fourteenth Amendment from impairment by the states."

Whether the "assumption" in the *Gitlow* case was a reality remained unclear until 1931. In that year, the Court decided *Stromberg v. California* and *Near v. Minnesota* and ruled squarely that the due process clause guaranteed both freedom of speech (*Stromberg*) and freedom of the press (*Near*). "It is no longer open to doubt," Chief Justice Charles Evans Hughes wrote in the *Near* case, "that the liberty of the press and of speech is within the liberty safeguarded by the due process clause of the Fourteenth Amendment. It was found impossible to conclude that this essential liberty of the citizen was left unprotected by the general guaranty of fundamental rights of person and property."

Benjamin Gitlow

After the freedoms of speech and press had been nationalized, the question remained about other rights in the First Amendment. Did they come under the Court's definition in the *Twining* case, as fundamental principles of liberty and justice that inhere "in the very idea of free government" and that are "the inalienable right of a citizen of such a government"? The Court addressed these questions in short order. The right of assembly and petition, the free exercise of religion, and the prohibition of an establishment of religion were held to be applicable to the states via the due process clause in the Court's decisions in *DeJonge v. Oregon* (1937), *Cantwell v. Connecticut* (1940), and *Everson v. Board of Education* (1947). Thus, by 1947, the nationalization of the First Amendment was complete, with all of the rights in that amendment having been held to be applicable to the states via the due process clause.

Criminal Procedure

The third phase of the nationalization of the Bill of Rights paralleled the nationalization of the First Amendment and concerned the question of which criminal procedure protections like those in the Bill of Rights applied to the states. The Court first began to increase its attention to questions of criminal procedure under the due process clause in *Moore v. Dempsey* in 1923. At its most rudimentary level, due process had always required that the defendant receive adequate notice of the charges and a fair trial or hearing in criminal cases, but in *Moore v. Dempsey* the Court began to insist that state criminal trials must be fair in fact as well as form to meet the requirements of due process. If a defendant's trial met proper formal standards but the trial was mob-dominated, the Court held in *Moore,* the state had nevertheless violated due process of law.

Charles Evans Hughes

Following the fair trial rule that emerged from *Moore v. Dempsey,* the Supreme Court focused more closely on which elements were necessary to ensure a fair trial in fact as well as form. In *Powell v. Alabama,* decided in 1932, it ruled that uneducated, indigent black youths could not receive a fair trial in a capital case unless they were afforded the effective assistance of state-appointed counsel in their defense. In 1936, the Court similarly held in *Brown v. Mississippi* that the admission of a coerced confession as evidence against a state criminal defendant also violated the due process clause. In neither *Powell v. Alabama* nor *Brown v. Mississippi,* however, did the Court hold that the "assistance of counsel" clause of the Sixth Amendment or the Fifth Amendment's "self-incrimination" clause applied to state criminal trials under the due process clause. Rather, the Court was focusing on the question of whether fair trials had in fact been afforded the defendants in those cases, and it concluded that the lack of counsel in a capital case and the use of a coerced confession as evidence denied the right to a fair trial.

In the *Powell* and *Brown* cases, the Court was therefore following the rule of the *Twining* case, that the due process clause imposed upon the states in the conduct of criminal trials certain rights *similar* to some of those in the Bill of Rights, but if such rights did apply to the states, they were only similar and not identical to their counterparts in the Bill of Rights. The "fair trial" rule, involving the application to state criminal trials of rights similar but not identical to some of those in the Bill of Rights, became the Court's dominant approach to issues of criminal procedure under the due process clause until 1961.

Thus, by the late 1930s, the Court had not only begun the nationalization of the First Amendment, which it would complete in 1947, but it had also started tightening the meaning of due process in state criminal trials. The Court took the occasion of its decision in *Palko v. Connecticut* in 1937 to restate the general principles it was following in the nationalization of the Bill of Rights. Speaking for the Court in the *Palko* case, Justice Benjamin Cardozo at the outset rejected the argument that the due process clause applied all the rights in the Bill of Rights to the states. If some but not all of the rights in the Bill of Rights applied to the states, the question then became one of how the Court distinguished between those rights that did apply to the states and those that did not. The answer, Cardozo said, was that the due process clause imposed upon the states those rights that were "of the very essence of a scheme of ordered liberty," such as freedom of speech, as well as those rights of criminal procedure that were "essential to the substance of a hearing." The question of whether a state criminal trial violated the due process clause, Cardozo added, was whether it involved "a hardship so shocking that our polity will not endure it." Applying this test to the *Palko* case, he concluded that the Fifth Amendment's prohibition of double jeopardy was not applicable to the states, just as the right to be indicted by a grand jury, right against compulsory self-incrimination, and jury trials in criminal and civil cases were equally inapplicable to the states via the due process clause.

The decision in the *Palko* case expressed the consensus the Court had reached regarding the nationalization of the Bill of Rights at the end of the 1930s, but it left unclear whether the First Amendment rights that had been nationalized were *similar* or *identical* to those in the Bill of Rights. Was the freedom of speech and of the press, recognized in the *Stromberg* and *Near* cases in 1931, somehow different from the freedoms of speech and press guaranteed in the First Amendment? The Court soon provided the answers. By the early 1940s, the language used in its decisions involving First Amendment rights clearly indicated that it considered the First Amendment rights applicable to the states to be identical, not merely similar, to those in the First Amendment itself. The result was, however, considerable theoretical tension between the Court's treatment of First Amendment rights and its treatment of criminal procedure rights under the due process clause.

Despite the disparate treatment by the Court of nationalized First Amendment rights and rights of criminal procedure, its adherence to the fair trial rule did yield two important decisions in the field of criminal procedure during the 1940s. In a 1948 decision in *In re Oliver,* the Court stated that the due process clause required the states to hold public criminal trials, a requirement that was also a part of the Sixth Amendment. And in *Wolf v. Colorado,* decided in 1949, the Court declared that the due process clause embraced at least "the core" of the Fourth Amendment and therefore prohibited state officers from engaging in unreasonable searches and seizures. It further held, however, that the federal exclusionary rule, which barred from trial evidence seized in violation of the Fourth Amendment, did not apply to the states. So, after *Wolf v. Colorado,* state officers were prohibited from engaging in unlawful searches and seizures, but the evidence they obtained by such illegal measures could continue to be admitted as evidence in state criminal trials.

A 1947 case revealed that the consensus of the Court regarding the nationalization issue, expressed in *Palko,* had been shattered. In *Adamson v. California,* the majority of the Court once again rejected the proposition that the Fifth Amendment's self-incrimination clause applied to the states and reaffirmed the ruling in *Twining v. New Jersey* on that point. Justice Hugo Black dissented however, contending that a study of the historical evidence regarding the proposal and ratification of the Fourteenth Amendment had convinced him that the intent of the framers of the amendment was to apply all of the Bill of Rights to the states in the identical way in which it applied to the national government. He argued further that defining the meaning of the due process clause of the Fourteenth Amendment to embrace all of the rights in the Bill of Rights would prevent the Court from reading its own personal predilections into the due process clause.

Black's position favoring the "total incorporation" of the Bill of Rights into the due process clause had been anticipated by Justice John Marshall Harlan I during the nineteenth and early twentieth centuries, but Harlan had usually been in lonely dissent on that issue. Black's dissent in the *Adamson* case, however, attracted the support of three of his colleagues, Justices William O. Douglas, Wiley Rutledge, and Frank Murphy, so that the total incorporation position received the largest number of votes in the *Adamson* case than it had ever received before. The majority position was vigorously defended by Justice Felix Frankfurter in a concurring opinion in the *Adamson* case, and despite Black's challenge in his dissent, the *Twining* fair trial approach to the nationalization of criminal procedure rights remained dominant throughout the 1950s.

Total Incorporation?

John Marshall Harlan

Selective Incorporation

During the late 1950s, a new approach to the theory of nationalization, offered by Chief Justice Earl Warren and Justice William Brennan, began to emerge on the Court. The new theory came to be called "selective incorporation," since the theory rejected Black's argument that all of the rights in the Bill of Rights applied to the states via the Fourteenth Amendment. However, the selective incorporationists agreed that most of the rights in the Bill of Rights did apply to the states, and they agreed with Black on a crucial issue—that if a right in the Bill of Rights did apply to the states, it applied in

Earl Warren

the identical way as it applied to the national government.

The incorporationist theory of nationalization was stoutly resisted by Justice John Marshall Harlan II (grandson of the total incorporationist) throughout the 1960s. Harlan insisted that the Bill of Rights had not been intended historically to apply to the states at all. The due process clause of the Fourteenth Amendment, he conceded, did impose upon the states certain fundamental rights similar to those in the Bill of Rights, but the crucial point for Harlan was that those rights found in the due process clause had as their source the due process clause itself and were therefore only similar to but not identical to the rights in the Bill of Rights. Despite Harlan's eloquent defense of his position, he was increasingly isolated on the Court.

The breakthrough for the incorporationists came in *Mapp v. Ohio* in 1961, when a majority of the Court held that the full Fourth Amendment as well as the federal exclusionary rule, forbidding the use of illegally seized evidence in court, applied to the states via the due process clause. There followed a series of decisions in which the Court held that "cruel and unusual punishments" clause of the Eighth Amendment (*Robinson v. California,* 1962), "assistance of counsel" clause of the Sixth Amendment (*Gideon v. Wainwright,* 1963), self-incrimination clause of the Fifth Amendment (*Malloy v. Hogan,* 1964), the provisions in the Sixth Amendment guaranteeing defendants the right to confront and cross-examine prosecution witnesses (*Pointer v. Texas,* 1965), the right to a speedy trial (*Klopfer v. North Carolina,* 1967), the right to subpoena favorable witnesses (*Washington v. Texas,* 1967), and the right to a trial by jury (*Duncan v. Louisiana,* 1968), and, finally, the double jeopardy clause of the Fifth Amendment (*Benton v. Maryland,* 1969) were applicable to the states in the identical way in which they applied to the national government. With the completion of the nationalization process in the *Benton* decision in 1969, the only rights remaining in the Bill of Rights that had not been made applicable to the states were the Second and Third Amendments, the "grand jury indictment" clause of the Fifth Amendment, the Seventh Amendment's requirements of jury trials in civil cases, and the "excessive fines and bail" clause of the Eighth Amendment.

When he introduced in Congress his proposed amendments that would become the Bill of Rights, James Madison had included restrictions on state powers as well as those directed at the national government, but Congress ultimately rejected the proposed restrictions on state power. By the time the Supreme Court had concluded the nationalization of the Bill of Rights in the late 1960s, however, it had more than made up for Madison's failure to restrict the powers of the states in 1789. Indeed, the Court had through the nationalization process transformed the due process clause of the Fourteenth Amendment into a second bill of rights applicable to the states—a bill of rights far more salient to the liberty of the average American than the original authored by Madison and ratified by the states in 1791.

Richard C. Cortner is professor of political science at the Univerity of Arizona. He is the author of *The Supreme Court and the Second Bill of Rights* (1981) and *A Mob Intent on Death: The NAACP and the Phillips County Riot Case* (1988).

The Bill of Rights: Protector of Minorities and Dissenters

Norman Dorsen

The American political system is built upon two fundamental principles. The first is majority rule through electoral democracy. This precept is firmly established in our culture. The second fundamental tenet is less established, less understood, and much more fragile. This is the principle that even in a democracy the majority must be limited in order to assure individual liberty.

The Bill of Rights—the first ten amendments to the Constitution—is the primary source of the legal limits on what the majority, acting through the government, can do. Such limits guarantee rights to all but in practice they often serve to protect dissenters and unpopular minorities from official wrongdoing. This process is indispensable to a free society, which in turn is the highest purpose of organized government. As John Locke wrote, "However it may be mistaken, the end of law is not to abolish or restrain, but to preserve and enlarge freedom."

How the Bill of Rights came to be appended to the original Constitution is a fascinating tale. How over two centuries it came to mean what it does today is a complex story that is not over yet. In the words of Chief Justice John Marshall, the Constitution is a document "intended to endure for ages to come, and, consequently, to be adapted to the various crises of human affairs."

The original Constitution protected civil liberty but it did so incompletely. The principal means it employed was structural—the ingenious carving up of governmental power both vertically and horizontally, through the creation of a federal system and the separation of powers within the national government.

191

It is well known that the Constitution created a national government possessing only limited powers, leaving to the states all other powers over its inhabitants. Although state authority could not be exercised inconsistently with the Constitution or acts of Congress, this formula nevertheless left the states with dominant authority over the people's welfare.

The Constitution also created a tri-partite division of national authority by reposing separate spheres of power in the executive, legislative, and judicial branches. While the chambers are not airtight, they serve to fulfill the theory of our government, which (as the Supreme Court said in 1874) "is opposed to the deposit of unlimited power anywhere."

The original Constitution did not merely seek to enhance civil liberty by dividing the authority to rule. It also contained some explicit safeguards. It provided that the privilege of habeas corpus, which requires a judge to release an imprisoned person unless he is being lawfully detained, may not be suspended except in cases of rebellion or invasion. The ex post facto and bill of attainder clauses seek to guarantee legislative fairness by prohibiting laws that make new crimes out of conduct that has already occurred and by requiring laws to operate generally and not against particular people. Article III guarantees a jury trial in all federal criminal cases, defines treason narrowly, and imposes evidentiary requirements to assure that this most political of crimes will not be lightly charged. Article VI prohibits religious tests as a qualification for public office.

But these safeguards were not enough. In 1787, many people were displeased by the absence of an explicit Bill of Rights in the newly drafted Constitution, and some state conventions refused to ratify without a commitment, or at least a strong indication, that one would soon be introduced. The framers promptly made good on this commitment, and the Bill of Rights was ratified in 1791. Thus the new nation's novel and creative structure that simultaneously provided for majority rule and limitations on that rule was in place.

Two further ingredients were needed to make the system work. The first occurred in 1803, when the Supreme Court unanimously ruled in *Marbury v. Madison* that the federal courts could enforce the Constitution by invalidating statutes passed by Congress that were inconsistent with it. In the twentieth century, the Supreme Court put the final component in place by holding that almost all provisions of the Bill of Rights restrict unlawful actions by state and local officials as

BILL OF RIGHTS

FREEDOM of SPEECH

FREEDOM of ASSEMBLY

FREEDOM of RELIGION

FREEDOM of The PRESS

150 YEARS

Bill of Rights Sesquicentennial poster by Howard Chandler Christy

well as the national government.

The Bill of Rights protects all Americans, but it is of particular value to minorities and dissenters. Supreme Court Justice Hugo Black expressed this thought eloquently in 1940:

> Under our constitutional system, courts stand against any winds that blow as havens of refuge for those who might otherwise suffer because they are helpless, weak, outnumbered, or because they are non-conforming victims of prejudice and public excitement.

While the Supreme Court has not always been faithful to that trust, it has often used the Constitution to shield the powerless.

Free Expression
The First Amendment guarantees of free speech and free press serve an especially important function in this respect by prohibiting the government from forcing everyone to espouse officially sanctioned opinions. Early Supreme Court cases on free speech were not promising. During World War I, appellants had been prosecuted for opposing enlistment in the armed services and protesting American involvement in the war, extremely unpopular positions at that time. The convictions were all affirmed in 1919, and the defendants jailed, some for many years. However, by 1931 an enthusiastic displayer of a red flag and the publisher of a "scandalous and defamatory" newspaper won their free speech and free press cases, although they were equally unpopular to most Americans. Fittingly, public debate and private reflection had begun to lead informed opinion to appreciate the value of free expression in a free society. Justice Oliver Wendell Holmes, who wrote the opinion sustaining the first convictions for speech relying on a "clear and present danger" standard, voted to reverse the later convictions.

From the 1930s through the 1950s, free speech claims were pressed by Communist activists and radical labor union leaders and in the 1960s and 1970s by civil rights protestors, the Ku Klux Klan, and the American Nazi party. Although the results were mixed, in 1969 the Supreme Court enunciated the principle—broadly protective of free expression—that political expression cannot be punished unless it is directed to inciting or producing imminent lawless action and is likely to incite or produce such action.

The Court has not been as hospitable to claims under the First Amendment when "speech" and "nonspeech" elements are combined in the same course of conduct. The Court has protected the right of children to wear an armband to class to protest the Vietnam War and the right to burn or disfigure the American flag for the same purpose. But it sustained the conviction of a man for burning his draft card as a protest against the war. More recently, it rejected protests against the government's policies toward poor people that were expressed through the form of sleeping outdoors in a public park.

The framers of the First Amendment expected it to promote democratic self-government and facilitate orderly

Oliver Wendell Holmes and Louis D. Brandeis

social change through the medium of new and unfamiliar ideas; to check possible government corruption and excess; and to advance knowledge and reveal truth, especially in the arts and sciences. The framers recognized that some speech would be controversial, some even repugnant. But their belief in free speech rested upon the premise that censorship brought worse consequences. As Justice Brandeis wrote in 1927, "If there be time to expose through discussion the falsehood and fallacies, to avert the evil by the process of education, the remedy to be applied is more speech, not enforced silence."

A free society has confidence in its people to separate the wheat from the chaff. A wise and principled conservative, Justice John Marshall Harlan, recognized that "the constitutional right of free expression is powerful medicine in a society as diverse as ours." "It is designed," he said,

> ... to remove governmental restraints from public discussion, putting the decision as to what views shall be voiced largely into the hands of each of us, in the hope that use of such freedom will ultimately produce a more capable citizenry ... and in the belief that no other approach would comport with the premise of individual dignity and choice upon which our political system rests.

The desirability of protecting unpopular expression also rests on hard practical considerations. The government apparatus required to impose limitations on speech, by its very nature, tends toward administrative extremes. History has shown that the techniques of enforcement—chilling investigations, surveillance of lawful activity, secret informers, unauthorized searches of homes and offices—are often carried out by police or zealous officials without adequate concern for the consequences of their actions.

Religious Freedom   The First Amendment also contains two clauses providing for religious liberty: one guarantees the "free exercise of religion" and the other bars laws that put state power behind religion or entangle the state with religious activities. These clauses also have served to safeguard minorities. This protection seems particularly appropriate because many of our early settlers—Puritans, Roman Catholics, Huguenots, and others—fled religious persecution in Europe, where the dominant national churches were often intolerant and cruel to those who professed dissenting beliefs. At different times in American history, Christian sects, Jews, Mormons, and atheists all have relied on the First Amendment guarantee of religious liberty to protect their rights against official and private discrimination; more recently Moslems, Buddhists, and the Unification Church have also done so. Few constitutional provisions have proved more decisively that guarantees of liberty must be accorded to all or they will erode.

Additional provisions of the Bill of Rights protect unpopular individuals and groups from other kinds of state action. The Fourth Amendment guarantee that the people will be "secure in their persons, houses, papers, and effects, against unreasonable searches and seizures" can be traced to English history. In 1763, repeated abuses led William Pitt the Elder to defend in Parliament the sanctity of one's home:

Controlling State Action

> The poorest man may in his cottage bid defiance to all the force of the Crown. It may be frail—its roof may shake— the wind may blow through it—the storm may enter, the rain may enter—but the King of England cannot enter—all his force dares not cross the threshold of the ruined tenement!

In response to such protests, Parliament enacted new legal protections in England. But high-handed treatment by British governors was, in the words of the Supreme Court, "fresh in the memories of those who achieved our independence and established our form of government." The right of a person to privacy in his or her home became one of the essentials of our constitutional system.

The lessening of restraints on official misconduct would undermine the rights of all. Although private property is not always a refuge, police and other officials must secure a judicial warrant based on probable cause or they must justify a search on other grounds. The alternative to these safeguards is a regime where no citizen is safe from a dreaded knock on the door by officers who, unaccountable to law, may violate privacy at their discretion, the very evil the Fourth Amendment was designed to prevent.

Similarly, the right to counsel contained in the Sixth Amendment prevents the government from misusing its power by providing that citizens are entitled to legal advice when accused of crime. In the famous Scottsboro case (*Powell v. Alabama,* decided in 1932), the Supreme Court reversed the death sentence of black teenagers who were convicted of raping two white women in a trial in which they were denied lawyers.

Protest against the Vietnam War outside the Pentagon, 1967

A generation later, the Court held that the public must pay for lawyers if an accused lacks funds, recognizing that without the assistance of counsel it is virtually impossible for a defendant, guilty or innocent, to mount a creditable defense against a government charge.

Equal Treatment   Despite its broad reach, the Bill of Rights (like the Constitution itself) was incomplete because it did not address outright the issue of inequality or prohibit government discrimination. The original Constitution in several clauses countenanced slavery, and in most states the right to vote at the time of ratification was limited to property-holding white males. Although the Fourteenth Amendment attempted to erase disabilities against former slaves by prohibiting states from denying the "equal protection of the laws," the end of Reconstruction in the South after 1876 and unsympathetic Supreme Court decisions undercut the promise of equality for generations.

After a long campaign by civil rights groups, the Supreme Court in 1954 invalidated state-supported segregation in *Brown v. Board of Education,* and the movement toward equal treatment gathered momentum. Much public and private discrimination persists in the United States, but there have been enormous gains in recent decades as Congress, the executive branch, and the states, reinforced by judicial decisions, have provided increased protection for racial minorities, women, nonmarital children, and other vulnerable groups.

Judicial Guardians

The courts have also identified certain liberties not expressly enumerated in the Bill of Rights but well grounded in the constitutional structure, such as freedom of association and the rights to travel and sexual privacy. These rights tend to come under attack when individuals wish to exercise them in a way that offends the majority. Thus, Alabama sought to interfere with the associational rights of the National Association for the Advancement of Colored People, the federal government sought to deny Communists the right to travel abroad, and many states imposed restraints on abortion. The protection of these individual rights not only comports with the premises of a free society but is supported by the language of the Ninth Amendment, which provides that "The enumeration in the Constitution, of certain rights, shall not be construed to deny or disparage others retained by the people."

The Bill of Rights was not designed as an abstraction. If it were, the rights it contains would have no more value than the barren promises entombed in many totalitarian constitutions. To be real, rights must be exercised and respected. The political branches of government—legislators and executive officials—can be instrumental in protecting rights, but majoritarian pressures on elected representatives are great during times of crisis, when the stress on liberty is most acute. A nation threatened from without is rarely the best guardian of civil liberties within. As already noted, President Wilson presided over massive invasions of free speech during World War I. In addition, President Roosevelt approved the internment of Japanese-Americans during World War II, and McCarthyism, the virulent repression of dissent, was a product of the cold war of the late 1940s and early 1950s.

The vulnerability of politically accountable officials to popular pressure teaches that freedom is most secure when protected by life-tenured judges insulated from electoral retribution. The doctrine of judicial review, which gives the courts

"SURE I'M A STRONG DEFENDER OF THE FIRST AMENDMENT AND ALL ITS RAMIFICATIONS, BUT IT'S VERY CLEAR THAT IF HE CALLED US A 'BUNCH OF JERKS,' THAT'S LIBEL."

final authority to define constitutional rights, is the most important original contribution of the American political system to civil liberty. James Madison summed it up when he said in proposing a bill of rights, "Independent tribunals of justice will consider themselves in a peculiar manner the guardians of those rights; they will be an impenetrable bulwark against every assumption of power in the Legislative or Executive." Thus, judicial review reinforces the central premise of the Bill of Rights that even in a democracy the majority must be subject to limits.

*   *   *   *

While the principles of the Bill of Rights are timeless, experience teaches that civil liberties are never secure but must be defended again and again in each generation. Examples of frequently repetitive violations of the Bill of Rights include police misconduct, school book censorship, and interference with free speech and assembly. Thus, the American Civil Liberties Union found it necessary to assert the right of peaceful demonstration when that right was threatened by Mayor Frank Hague's ban of labor organizers in New Jersey in the 1930s, by Sheriff Bull Connor's violence to civil rights demonstrators in Alabama in the 1960s, by the government's efforts to stop antiwar demonstrators in Washington in the 1970s, and by the legal barriers erected by the city of Skokie, Ill., in 1977-1978 to prevent American Nazis from parading.

The defense of the rights of Americans is often thankless. Strong opponents have invoked both necessity and patriotism while subverting liberty and dominating the weak, the unorthodox, and the despised. Government efficiency, international influence, domestic order, and economic needs are all important in a complex world. But none is more important than the principles of civil liberty and human dignity embodied in the Constitution and Bill of Rights, our proudest heritage.

Norman Dorsen is Stokes Professor of Law, New York University and the president of the American Civil Liberties Union. He is also a member of the Bicentennial Committees of the United States Court of Appeals for the Second Circuit and the Association of the Bar of the City of New York.

Religion and the Constitution

A. James Reichley

Shortly after the adjournment of the Constitutional Convention in 1787, Alexander Hamilton encountered on the street in Philadelphia a professor from nearby Princeton College who told him that the Princeton faculty were "greatly grieved that the Constitution has no recognition of God or the Christian religion." Hamilton replied: "I declare, we forgot it!"

Hamilton's dodge was among the first in a long series of efforts by American statesmen to reconcile broad social support for religion with cultural pluralism and belief in the rights of individual conscience. In our own time, differences over the role of religion in public life have fueled important political issues and given rise to both fear and resentment among major social groups. It is, therefore, worthwhile to reexamine the constitutional framework for relations between religion and civil society that the founders eventually worked out through the First Amendment, and to trace the evolving interpretations through which this structure has since been applied.

Religious enthusiasm, buffeted by the winds of the Enlightenment, was at a relatively low ebb in America in 1787. The effects of the Great Awakening of the 1740s, which had remained strong at the time of the Revolution, had receded, and the beginning of the Second Great Awakening was still more than a decade in the future. Nevertheless, about 75 percent of Americans had their roots in some form of Calvinism, and most of the rest belonged to Anglican, Baptist, Quaker, Catholic, or Lutheran traditions. A few Jewish congregations had gathered in places like Newport, R.I., and Charleston, S.C. The reason the framers of the Constitution avoided the topic of religion, except for the prohibition of a religious test for national public office in Article VI, was neither hostility nor indifference, but that they had not yet developed a conceptual means for relating religion to public life in a free society.

203

Enactment of the First Amendment

Most of the founders were not particularly pious men. Some, like Thomas Jefferson and Benjamin Franklin, were personally religious in only a very broad and loosely defined sense. But practically all were convinced that republican government rests on moral values that spring ultimately from religion. They shared George Washington's view, that "of all the dispositions and habits which lead to political prosperity, religion and morality are indispensable supports." Even Jefferson, despite his personal skepticism, held that religion should be regarded as "a supplement to law in the government of men," and as "the alpha and omega of the moral law."

Belief in the socially beneficial effects of religion led some of the founders, including Washington, John Adams, Patrick Henry, and John Marshall, to favor maintenance of established churches, directly supported by public funds, in their own states. Others, notably Jefferson and James Madison, argued that government should play no role whatever in direct sponsorship of religion. All agreed that there could be no established national church in a country already so culturally various and intellectually diverse as the new United States.

Their common objective was to secure the moral guidance and support of religion for the republic, while escaping the political repression and social conflict with which religion had often been associated throughout history, and specifically in the public life of the former colonies. Since no scheme of generally accepted constitutional doctrine to achieve this end was available, the framers of the original Constitution ducked the subject almost entirely.

The need to define the relationship of religion to civil society, however, would not go away. In the bitter battle over ratification of the Constitution in the states, some opponents attacked the proposed federal charter's failure to include a guarantee of the free exercise of religion. Several of the state ratifying conventions, including those in Virginia and New York, passed resolutions calling for an amendment declaring the "unalienable right to the free exercise of religion according to the dictates of conscience," and assuring that "no particular religious sect or society" would be "favored or established by Law in preference to others."

When the first Congress met in 1789, James Madison, who a few years before had led the fight for passage of Jefferson's bill for religious liberty in Virginia, quickly moved in the House of Representatives that the Constitution be amended to incorporate a Bill of Rights, including prohibitions against establishment of a national religion or infringement on "full and equal rights of conscience" by either the federal government or the states. When Madison's bill came to the floor of the House for debate, several members of Congress objected that it might be interpreted to undermine religion. The clause dealing with establishment, Peter Sylvester of New York warned, "might be thought to have a tendency to abolish religion altogether." Benjamin Huntingdon of Connecticut, one of the five states that still maintained an established church, asked if the amendment could be construed to prohibit state "support of ministers or building of places of worship?" Huntingdon said he favored an amendment "to secure the rights of conscience," but not one that would "patronise those who profess no religion at all." At Madison's suggestion, the bill was reworded to make clear that the prohibition against establishment applied only to the federal government. The entire Bill of Rights was then approved by the House without major change.

The First Prayer in Congress by T. H. Matteson. Carpenters Hall, Philadelphia, September 1774

In the Senate, the ban against infringement on rights of conscience by the states was dropped, presumably reflecting the Senate's particular concern for upholding the authority of the state governments, and the religion clauses aimed at the federal level were combined in a single amendment with provisions for freedom of speech and a free press. The language of the religious clauses was considerably watered down, requiring only that Congress "make no law establishing articles of faith, or a mode of worship, or prohibiting the free exercise of religion." Under this formulation, even the national government would be permitted to give direct financial support to the churches and would be excluded only from meddling in matters of theology or ritual.

A conference committee between the House and the Senate, which Madison is generally believed to have dominated, kept the Senate's textual framework combining the religion clauses with the free speech and free press clauses but toughened the religion clauses to read, "Congress shall make no law respecting an establishment of religion or prohibiting the free exercise thereof." This formulation was approved by two-thirds majorities in both houses of Congress and later was ratified by the required three-fourths of the state legislatures— giving us the First Amendment as we have it today.

What Did the Fourteenth Amendment Do?

The first thing to be said about the First Amendment is that when enacted it clearly applied only to the federal government. Madison's proposed amendment to prohibit infringement by the state on individual rights of conscience would have done nothing to upset the established churches still supported by some of the states. (The last of the state religious establishments was finally terminated when Massachusetts disestablished the Congregational church in 1833.) But Congress did not approve even this modest prohibition. During the first half of the nineteenth century, the Supreme Court issued a series of decisions specifically placing the state governments outside the authority of the First Amendment.

At the end of the Civil War, Congress proposed and the states ratified the Fourteenth Amendment, prohibiting the states from abridging "the privileges or immunities of citizens of the United States," or depriving "any person of life, liberty, or property without due process of law," or denying any person "equal protection of the laws." The chief purpose of the Fourteenth Amendment, everyone agreed, was to extend full rights of citizenship to the former slaves who had been freed under the Emancipation Proclamation or the Thirteenth Amendment. Beyond that, some of the principal sponsors of the amendment spoke vaguely of giving the federal government power to enforce "the personal rights guaranteed and secured by the first eight amendments to the Constitution." But the idea that the entire Bill of Rights might be extended to cover the states by the due process clause or the privileges or immunities clause of the Fourteenth Amendment played no significant part in the debates over the amendment in Congress or the state legislatures.

For some years thereafter, neither the Supreme Court nor the governmental community at large showed any signs of believing that the states were now subject to the Bill of Rights. In 1876, the Grant administration sought enactment of a constitutional amendment that would have specifically prohibited the states from aiding church-related schools. Neither supporters nor opponents of the proposed amendment (which passed the House and failed in the Senate by only two votes) suggested that such aid might already be unconstitutional. When some imaginative jurists in the 1890s began to argue that the Fourteenth Amendment prohibited infringement by the states on some of the rights set forth in the first eight amendments, the majority of the Court at first rejected this claim.

Beginning in the 1920s, however, the Supreme Court gradually discovered a growing portion of the Bill of Rights in the due process clause of the Fourteenth Amendment. In 1925, the Court ruled in *Gitlow v. New York* that the free speech and free press clauses of the First Amendment applied to the states. (Gitlow was the author of a left-wing publication that had been suppressed by the state of New York. He did not himself benefit from the new interpretation, since the Court held that his book was an active "incitement" to violence, and therefore not shielded by the First Amendment.)

In 1940, the free exercise clause and the establishment clause were at last extended to cover the states. The Court decided in *Cantwell v. Connecticut* that the First Amendment prohibited the state from prosecuting a member of the Jehovah's Witnesses sect for breaching the peace by playing a recorded diatribe against the Catholic religion on a streetcorner in a neighborhood of New Haven heavily populated by Catholics. From the legacy of *Cantwell* has sprung the large body of decisions through which the Court has defined and generally broadened the rights of citizens against infringement on religious liberty or establishment of religion by either the federal government or the states.

The line of decisions based on the free exercise clause, though often controversial, has produced a reasonably clear and consistent set of guidelines on how far religious liberty goes, and where other social values, such as public safety, the rights of children to education in basic skills and citizenship,

Baptist Meeting House, Providence, R.I., 1789

and the need for discipline in the armed forces, must take precedence.

In contrast to the decisions on "free exercise," the Court's rulings based on the establishment clause—including the 1948 decision prohibiting the use of public school facilities for religious instruction, the 1962 decision banning organized prayer in the public schools, and the great tangle of decisions that forbid some but not all forms of public aid to students in parochial schools—have produced a disconcerting muddle. "We are divided among ourselves," Justice Byron White ruefully conceded in 1981, "perhaps reflecting the different views on this subject of the people in this country." A part of the reason for the Court's intellectual disarray on establishment clause issues may be the inherent difficulty of finding the prohibition of religious establishment in the Fourteenth Amendment's protection against deprivation of "liberty."

The Meaning of "Establishment"

Recently, some conservative scholars and public figures have suggested that the Court may have erred in the whole line of decisions descending from *Gitlow*. Some have even proposed returning authority over most First Amendment issues to the states. It is extremely unlikely that any foreseeable Court would abandon federal protections against infringement by government at any level on basic freedoms of speech, press, or religion. There is some possibility that a future Supreme Court might modify the current reach of the establishment clause. But civil libertarians argue that limiting the coverage of the establishment clause could encourage some states, such as Utah, where Mormons constitute about two-thirds of the population, actually to establish a church. Improbable though this result may be, the claim provides an effective last-ditch defense against limiting even the establishment clause to the federal government.

In any case, even if the states were exempted from the reach of the establishment clause, many important church-state issues, such as federal aid to students in parochial schools and the many symbolic relationships that continue to exist between religion and the federal government, would still have to be decided at the federal level. From a practical standpoint, the most important question regarding the establishment clause now is not the extent of its coverage but what "establishment" means in the context of the First Amendment.

Some interpreters argue that the founders intended that the prohibition against establishment should do nothing more than prevent the government from singling out a particular church for support or recognition, as most of the colonies had done before the Revolution, and as many European governments still do today. (Whether the "intentions" of the founders should have any bearing on current interpretation is a question that I will turn to shortly.) In this view, the establishment clause presents no impediment against government giving support, financial or otherwise, to religious institutions, so long as such aid is distributed impartially among the several churches, or among churches and secular institutions supplying similar services.

One trouble with this interpretation is that it does not go beyond what would have been permitted under the First Amendment in the form originally passed by the Senate in 1789. Since the establishment clause as finally enacted contains tighter language, it is reasonable to assume that Congress meant to require something more strict. Furthermore, as Freeman Butts has pointed out, the founders had before them examples of religious establishments in states like Maryland and South Carolina under which public support was authorized for a number of different denominations (all Protestant). Their understanding of establishment, therefore, must have included more than favoring a particular church.

At the opposite extreme of interpretation are those who would apply literally Jefferson's phrase calling for a "wall of separation between church and state." (Jefferson's remark appeared in a letter written more than ten years after the adoption of the First Amendment, but it has been cited so often in Court opinions that many Americans have come to regard it almost as part of the Constitution.)

According to these strict separationists, the establishment clause requires absolute neutrality by government, not only among religions but also between religion and irreligion, and prescribes keeping all activities of government, including conduct of the public schools, sealed as tightly as possible against any hint of religious influence or contact. "Neither a state nor the Federal Government," Justice Hugo Black wrote in 1947, in an opinion still approvingly quoted by separationists, "can pass laws which aid one religion, aid all religions, or prefer one religion over another. . . . No tax in any amount, large or small, can be levied to support any religious activities or institutions, whatever they may be called, or whatever form they may adopt, to teach or practice religion." The Supreme Court has carried this line of reasoning to the point of prohibiting display

CHURCH AND STATE—NO UNION UPON ANY TERMS.

Cartoon by Thomas Nast, Harper's Weekly, February 25, 1871

of the Ten Commandments in the hallways of public schools, though the Court itself sits beneath a frieze depicting promulgation of the Ten Commandments, and of forbidding use of public school teachers to give remedial instruction to mentally handicapped children in parochial schools.

It is difficult indeed to find mandate for such relentless exclusion of religion from publicly supported activities in the intent of the founders. The first Congress that enacted the First Amendment also appointed chaplains in both houses and adopted as part of the ordinance governing the Northwest Territory the directive, "Religion, morality, and knowledge, being necessary to good government and the happiness of mankind, schools and the means of learning shall forever be encouraged." Presidents Washington, Adams, and Madison, though not Jefferson, issued proclamations establishing national days of prayer and thanksgiving. Washington began the custom, continued by all his successors, of adding the phrase, "so help me God," to the presidential oath of office.

A Positive Freedom

Congress's decision to include the religious clauses in a single amendment with the free speech clause and the free press clause provides a useful indicator of intention. Clearly, Congress did not regard freedom of speech or of the press merely as privileges for the enjoyment of individuals. Both of these freedoms were justified, not only as personal rights but also as essential supports for the conduct of a free society and republican government. There is every reason to believe that the founders saw the free exercise of religion in the same light: both as a guaranteed liberty to the individual and, in Washington's words, as an "indispensable" support for "political prosperity." Free exercise of religion, that is, was not merely to be permitted, like such unspecified general rights as travel or recreation, but positively to be encouraged, like the free expression of ideas, as a vital contributor to the public good.

Of course, the First Amendment includes no parallels to the establishment clause in the areas of speech or the press. Government, beside encouraging free discussion and a free exchange of ideas, may also, under the First Amendment, enter the marketplace of ideas with substantive arguments and policy proposals of its own. It has no such right in the area of religion. The founders recognized the dangers to social harmony, personal freedom, and religion itself if government attempts to sponsor its own versions of religious practice or belief. To counteract these dangers, they enacted the establishment clause. They specifically rejected any public religion—or civil religion, as it is now sometimes called—for the United States. By prohibiting establishment of religion, they intended that government should give no direct support or sponsorship to any church, or any group of churches, or even to the cause of religion in general. But they did not intend that prohibition of establishment should extend to preventing symbolic acknowledgment of the dependence of civil government, as of all life, on transcendent direction, or to impeding normal functions of government in areas like education and health care that might indirectly benefit church-related institutions.

The founders sought to maintain a society in which civil government would receive moral support and guidance from transcendent values. To help promote continuing renewal of the source for recognition of these values, they enacted the free exercise clause. To assure that the source would not be polluted by the narrow political interests of either government or the institutional churches, they added the establishment clause.

Georgetown Convent School, circa 1900

Judicial Activism

In recent times, a school of legal philosophers known generally as judicial activists, or among legal scholars as "noninterpretivists" (because they do not believe the courts should be limited to interpreting the text of the Constitution), has held that the intentions of the framers of the Constitution are to a great extent unknowable, and in any case should have little bearing on current understanding of basic law. Lawrence Friedman, professor of law at Stanford, has argued that in the modern United States part of the function of the courts should be to act as "brooms," sweeping out legal anachronisms that "cannot now be repealed" because of political blockages. In performing this clean-up function, Friedman suggests, the courts should draw on a general sense of where society currently stands: "The measuring rods are very vague, very broad principles. These are attached loosely to phrases in the Constitution. They are connected more organically to the general culture."

The question of what is meant by "general culture" as a standard for judicial interpretation is particularly problematic with regard to establishment clause issues. If general culture is equated with public opinion, many of the Court's decisions in the 1960s and 1970s on establishment clause cases were without ground. National opinion polls have consistently shown a large majority of the public favoring return of organized prayer to the public schools, for example. By general culture, Friedman may mean public opinion if the public were as well informed as Supreme Court justices, or opinion at the more refined levels of culture, or opinion elevated by judicial vision. There is something to be said for all of these as partial sources for judicial reasoning, but all hold obvious perils as standards to be relied on by the courts in a political democracy.

The activists surely are right when they argue that the

"FRANKLY, I SOMETIMES FORGET WHICH IS AN AMENDMENT AND WHICH IS A COMMANDMENT."

Constitution should not be employed as a judicial cookbook, in which legal recipes can be found to apply to particular cases. As Laurence Tribe, a leading proponent of noninterpretivism, says, the courts should search out "the principles behind the words" in the written Constitution. But in doing so, they must, if their decisions are to be accepted as objectively valid, seek the principles that moved the authors of the Constitution and its amendments rather than impose standards derived from a vaguely conceived contemporary "general culture." Tribe concedes, "The Justices may not follow a policy of 'anything goes' so long as it helps put an end to what they personally consider to be injustice."

During the 1960s and the 1970s, some of the Supreme Court's strict separationist decisions, perhaps reacting against an earlier period of excessive passivity, went well beyond any principles that can credibly be ascribed to the enactors of the First or Fourteenth Amendments. To claim otherwise is like suggesting that the enactors of the Fourteenth Amendment had a secret plan to reimpose slavery.

More recently, the Court has appeared to move back toward more traditional interpretations. In 1983, the Court upheld the constitutionality of the Nebraska legislature's employment of a chaplain and approved a scheme through which Minnesota permits parents to take a state income tax deduction for part of the costs of educating their children in parochial schools. In 1984, the Court found no implication of establishment in maintenance by the city government of Pawtucket, R.I., of a nativity scene during Christmas season. And in 1986 the Court let stand on precedural grounds a policy instituted by the public schools in Williamsport, Pa., of making school facilities available for use by volunteer prayer groups on the same basis as other extracurricular clubs.

Return to Accommodationism

The Court's apparent trend toward a more accommodationist stance has by no means been undeviating. In 1985, the Court ruled unconstitutional an Alabama statute authorizing a one-minute period of silence in the public schools "for meditation or voluntary prayer"—though a concurring opinion by Justice Sandra Day O'Connor suggested that state laws calling for moments of silence without specific mention of prayer might "not necessarily manifest the same infirmity." Also in 1985 the Court issued the prohibition against use of public school teachers to give remedial instruction to handicapped children in parochial schools mentioned above.

Many of the Court's recent establishment clause decisions have been closely divided. To the extent that prediction is possible, it seems likely that the accommodationist trend will continue, though not nearly back to the point at which the previous trend toward strict separationism began in the 1940s. The principle of institutional separation between church and state will surely be maintained, though the line of separation is likely to be regarded more as a fence through which church and state carry on mutually beneficial interactions than as a grimly impenetrable barrier or wall. In any case, the question of what the Constitution intends for the relationship between religion and civil government will no doubt continue to cause much controversy—a tribute, after all, to the unquenchable vitality of religion in American national life.

SUGGESTED ADDITIONAL READING

Robert N. Bellah and Phillip E. Hammond, *Varieties of Civil Religion* (1980).

Walter Berns, *The First Amendment and the Future of American Democracy* (1985).

R. Freeman Butts, *The American Tradition in Religion and Education* (1950).

Leo Pfeffer, *God, Caesar, and the Constitution* (1975).

Laurence H. Tribe, *God Save This Honorable Court* (1985).

A. James Reichley is a senior fellow in governmental studies at the Brookings Institution.

Race and the Constitution: The Case of the Japanese-American Internment

Peter Irons

More than four decades have passed since the forced exodus of Japanese-Americans from the West Coast in 1942. Herded from their homes by Army orders, more than 110,000 members of this racial minority spent the wartime years behind the barbed wire fences of detention camps guarded by armed troops. For an average of nine hundred days each, Americans of Japanese ancestry were imprisoned, held without charge, without counsel, and without trial. With an excess of candor, Assistant Secretary of War John J. McCloy, the official most responsible for this assault on the Constitution, later attributed the mass incarceration to "retribution" for the Japanese attack on Pearl Harbor.

All three branches of the federal government shared responsibility in the evacuation and internment of Japanese-Americans. Acting on the advice of War Department officials, President Franklin D. Roosevelt signed Executive Order 9066 on February 19, 1942, authorizing the exclusion by military order of "any or all persons" from areas designated by these officials. One month later, both houses of Congress enacted without any recorded opposition a law that made violation of any military order a federal crime, punishable by imprisonment for one year. Finally, the Supreme Court ruled in 1943 and 1944 that the military curfew and exclusion orders did not violate the constitutional rights of those few Japanese-Americans who had risked a criminal record to challenge the orders.

The wartime internment of Japanese-Americans, and the Supreme Court decisions that upheld Roosevelt's order, have generated an almost unanimous condemnation by legal scholars and historians. As early as 1945, Eugene V. Rostow of the Yale School faculty blasted the Court's opinions as a judicial

217

"disaster" for allowing imprisonment without charge or trial on the basis of ancestry alone. One of the government prosecutors in the internment cases later denounced the program as "the greatest deprivation of civil liberties in this country since slavery." More recently, a blue-ribbon federal commission reported to Congress in 1982 that a "grave injustice" had been done to the Japanese-Americans who suffered the loss of their liberties.

Few decisions of the Supreme Court have been so thoroughly repudiated as those that upheld the military orders that forced Japanese-Americans from their homes. Only the *Dred Scott* decision in 1857, ruling that black Americans were not citizens, and the *Plessy* decision in 1896 that established the "separate but equal" doctrine of racial segregation, match the internment decisions as "self-inflicted wounds" on the Court's reputation. Significantly, all these discredited decisions involved the "American dilemma" of race. But the corrective processes of constitutional amendment and congressional enactment have erased *Dred Scott* and *Plessy* from the law, while the internment decisions have not received explicit reversal as judicial precedent.

The widespread criticism of these Supreme Court opinions raises several fundamental questions. Stated most simply, how could the Court allow such a judicial disaster to happen? Answering this question requires a close look beneath the surface of the internment cases and behind the closed door of the Court's conference room. How the Court defined the constitutional issues in these cases, and applied the "facts" presented by the opposing lawyers in their briefs and arguments, becomes an exercise in historical dissection, much as a coroner performs an autopsy.

A Tide of Intolerance   Our examination of the internment cases begins in the hectic weeks that followed the shock of the Pearl Harbor attack on December 7, 1941. Widespread fear of a follow-up invasion of the West Coast provoked a resurgence of the "Yellow Peril" campaign that infected the public in earlier decades. Editorial calls for tolerance of Japanese-Americans gave way to a crusade for their removal in late January 1942, spurred by headlines that charged Hawaiians of Japanese ancestry with aiding the Pearl Harbor attackers through espionage and sabotage. These charges, made by a presidential commission headed by Supreme Court Justice Owen Roberts, were disclaimed by military officials after the war. But the wave of hostility that followed these headlines did its damage before the belated retraction of the disloyalty charges.

The tide of intolerance toward Japanese-Americans had its greatest impact on Gen. John L. DeWitt, the elderly and indecisive commander of Army troops on the West Coast. Before the publication of the Roberts commission report, DeWitt resisted pressure to order the "wholesale internment" of Japanese-Americans and assured a fellow general that the Army could "weed the disloyal out of the loyal and lock them up if necessary." DeWitt knew the Army lacked power, without presidential approval, to impose restrictions on American citizens of any ancestry. Although Congress had barred persons born in Japan from citizenship in 1924, two-thirds of those with Japanese ancestry were native-born Americans and held full citizenship under the Constitution. "An American citizen, after all, is an American citizen," DeWitt reminded an advocate of mass internment in the last week of 1941.

John L. DeWitt

DeWitt's initial reluctance to ask for authority to uproot the Japanese-Americans crumbled quickly under political pressure. After meeting with California governor Culbert Olson and Attorney General Earl Warren in late January 1942, DeWitt reported "a tremendous volume of public opinion now developing against the Japanese" that included pressure from "the best people of California." The majority of Japanese-Americans lived in California, and visitors to DeWitt's headquarters in San Francisco "feel that they are living in the midst of a lot of enemies," the general told his subordinate, Col. Karl R. Bendetsen.

Bendetsen was a Stanford Law School graduate who played a key role in the internment decision as liaison between DeWitt and John J. McCloy, the assistant secretary of war who assumed responsibility for deciding the fate of Japanese-Americans. Caught between pressure from West Coast politicians who demanded immediate evacuation and the qualms of Secretary of War Henry L. Stimson, who feared that the forcible removal of American citizens would tear "a tremendous hole in our constitutional system," McCloy delegated Bendetsen to assist DeWitt in preparing a "final recommendation" on the treatment of Japanese-Americans.

In approaching his assignment from McCloy, Bendetsen knew as a lawyer that authority to force citizens to leave their homes depended on a showing that "military necessity" required such an extreme move. In cases that stemmed back to the Civil War, the Supreme Court had restrained the military from control over civilians, absent a formal declaration of martial law or proof that civilians posed a real threat to military security. General DeWitt had received many reports, both from Army units and civilians, that Japanese-Americans had committed acts of espionage and sabotage, from cutting power lines to making short-wave radio transmissions to Japanese submarines lurking off the coastline. Bendetsen also knew, from the reports of intelligence officials who investigated these charges, that not a single claim of espionage or sabotage had been substantiated. Every such charge had been investigated and traced to mistaken reports, from thinking erroneously that a radio station in Japan was transmitting from California to concluding that interference from cows rubbing their backs on power lines meant sabotage.

Faced with intelligence reports that dismissed claims of espionage and sabotage, Bendetsen responded to calls for internment by warning that "no one has justified fully the sheer military necessity for such action." But the mounting tide of political pressure finally took its toll. After meeting in Washington with insistent members of the West Coast congressional delegation, Bendetsen prepared a "final recommendation" to the secretary of war that labeled Japanese-Americans as members of "an enemy race" whose loyalty to the United States was inherently suspect. Arguing that Japanese "racial strains are undiluted" even among those born and educated in America, Bendetsen recommended on behalf of General DeWitt the "mass internment" of Japanese-Americans as a step in their removal from the West Coast.

Armed with DeWitt's signature on the report that Bendetsen prepared, McCloy subdued the last opponents of internment. Secretary of War Stimson reluctantly accepted Bendetsen's argument that "their racial characteristics are such that we cannot understand or trust even the citizen Japanese." Attorney General Francis Biddle, who initially opposed internment because DeWitt had not proved its military necessity, finally bowed to Stimson and abandoned his objections in a dramatic showdown with McCloy and Bendetsen on February 17, 1942. At this crucial meeting, held in Biddle's living room, tempers flared over McCloy's dismissal of the constitutional objections raised by two of Biddle's assistants, Edward Ennis and James Rowe. One observer, Army general Allen Gullion, quoted McCloy as responding that "to a Wall Street lawyer, the Constitution is just a scrap of paper." Although Biddle later expressed regret at his action, he failed at this meeting to back up Ennis and Rowe and deferred to the War Department. Two days later, President Roosevelt signed the executive order that Biddle and McCloy had jointly approved.

General DeWitt wasted no time in implementing the authority conferred on him by Roosevelt. He first appointed Colonel Bendetsen, the architect of internment, to "provide for

Evacuees at the Santa Fe train station waiting to be taken to relocation camp, April 1942

the evacuation of all persons of Japanese ancestry" from the West Coast. Bendetsen recommended that a curfew be imposed on Japanese-Americans as a first step, and DeWitt signed an order that forced members of this monority to remain indoors between 8 p.m. and 6 a.m. Dewitt accompanied the curfew order with the first of more than one hundred "exclusion orders." These military edicts, applied to Japanese-Americans up and down the West Coast, required that they dispose of their property on a week's notice, leave their homes and businesses, and report to "assembly centers" in race tracks and fairgrounds with only those possessions they could carry in their arms. From these temporary quarters, they were dispatched under armed guard to permanent "relocation centers" located in barren deserts and swamps from California to Arkansas. Confronted with the choice between barbed-wire fences or prison bars, it is hardly surprising that all but a handful of law-abiding Japanese-Americans chose to obey the orders and "relocate" with family and friends.

Three Challenges   Only three young men accepted the risk of a criminal record in deciding to challenge DeWitt's curfew and exclusion orders. The first challenger was Min Yasui, a lawyer and Army reserve officer who resigned his job with the Japanese consulate in Chicago the day after Pearl Harbor to volunteer for military service in Portland, Ore. Turned away on account of his race, Yasui decided that DeWitt's curfew order "infringed on my rights as a citizen" because it made "distinctions between citizens on the basis of ancestry." Yasui turned himself in for curfew violation and was sentenced after conviction to a maximum term of one year in prison.

The second challenger to DeWitt's orders was a University of Washington senior, Gordon Hirabayashi, a Quaker pacifist who opposed both the curfew and exclusion orders on religious grounds. "I must maintain my Christian principles," Hirabayashi wrote in a statement to the FBI. "I consider it my duty to maintain the democratic principles for which this nation lives. Therefore, I must refuse this order for evacuation." Tried before a judge who ordered the jury to find him guilty, Hirabayashi was convicted of violating both the curfew and exclusion orders and was sentenced to three-month terms for each offense.

The final criminal defendant among the internment challengers was Fred Korematsu, a shipyard welder who had been rejected on medical grounds after volunteering for military

service. Korematsu went to the extreme of plastic surgery to
change his appearance, hoping to remain with his Caucasian
fiancee and to escape the internment camps. Picked up by the
police on a street corner, Korematsu offered himself as a test
case to the American Civil Liberties Union in San Francisco
and demanded on behalf of all Japanese-Americans "a fair
trial in order that they may defend their loyalty at court." But
the federal judge who presided at Korematsu's trial for
violation of the exclusion order ignored the prosecutor's concession that he was loyal. After pronouncing Korematsu guilty,
the judge imposed a five-year probationary sentence and
imprisonment in an internment camp.

All three of these criminal convictions reached the Supreme Court early in 1943, passed on by the Court of Appeals
in San Francisco without decision. Each of the criminal
defendants based his appeal on claims that the "due process"
clause of the Fifth Amendment prohibited discrimination
founded solely on racial factors. Because the right of Fred
Korematsu to appeal his probationary sentence remained
unclear, the Supreme Court remanded his case to the lower
appellate court and deferred decision on the lawfulness of the
exclusion orders. Lawyers for Gordon Hirabayashi and Min
Yasui focused their arguments before the Supreme Court on
claims that racial antagonism—and not military necessity—
had motivated General DeWitt. They cited DeWitt's statement
to a congressional panel that "a Jap's a Jap" and the government's failure to present evidence of espionage and sabotage as
arguments against the convictions.

Responding to these arguments on behalf of the government, Solicitor General Charles Fahy defended DeWitt's
orders as reasonable responses to the "serious threat" of
Japanese attack on the West Coast. Fahy also warned the
Court that the Japanese-American population included "a
number of persons who might assist the enemy" in case of
attack or invasion. The Supreme Court adopted Fahy's argument in its unanimous opinion in the Hirabayashi case, issued
in June 1943. The Court also sustained Yasui's conviction
without dissent, although it found flaws in the trial judge's
opinion and sent the case back for resentencing.

Writing for the Court in *Hirabayashi,* Chief Justice
Harlan Fiske Stone admitted that legal distinctions "between
citizens solely because of their ancestry are by their very nature
odious to a free people whose institutions are founded upon the
doctrine of equality." Stone had proclaimed in a 1938 decision

the proposition that racial discriminations were presumptively unconstitutional and required "more searching" judicial scrutiny than ordinary laws. But the chief justice held in *Hirabayashi* that the government might in wartime "place citizens of one ancestry in a different category from others." The relevant factors, Stone wrote, were those that might hinder the assimilation of Japanese-Americans "as an integral part of the white population" and thus make them "a greater source of danger than those of a different ancestry." Along with those tainted assumptions, Fahy's undocumented claims that there were "disloyal members" of the Japanese-American population who could not be "precisely and quickly" identified persuaded the Supreme Court to uphold DeWitt's curfew order.

The Supreme Court consciously evaded decision in *Hirabayashi* on the exclusion orders and the legality of continued detention of Japanese-Americans. The appeal of Fred Korematsu, which returned to the Court in late 1944, raised the first issue, while the case of Mitsuye Endo posed the second question. Unlike the three criminal defendants, Endo was a young woman who first reported for internment and then filed a challenge to her detention through a habeas corpus petition. The denial of her petition for release by lower courts came before the Supreme Court at the same time as the *Korematsu* case. Between them, these two cases confronted the justices with the most troubling aspects of the internment program, exclusion and temporary detention in *Korematsu* and indefinite detention in *Endo*.

Solicitor General Fahy returned to the Supreme Court in October 1944 to argue for the government in the second pair of internment cases. He was prepared for defeat in the *Endo* case, since he conceded that Congress had not authorized the indefinite detention of admittedly loyal citizens. Along with most federal officials, Fahy was willing at this time—with an Allied victory over the Axis within sight—to allow the Court to open the internment camps. But Fahy also supported the argument that General DeWitt was justified in ordering Fred Korematsu and other Japanese-Americans to undergo a temporary period of detention while their loyalty was investigated. Fahy considered this issue as a matter of principle, since he strongly believed in expanded military powers during wartime.

Korematsu's lawyers based their attack on his conviction on the claim that the only alternative to "remaining in" his home town, the legal charge against him, was temporary detention in an assembly center. Since the record showed that

Santa Anita reception center, Los Angeles, Calif., April 1942

virtually all the Japanese-Americans who reported to assembly centers were later shipped to internment camps, Korematsu's lawyers argued strenuously that compliance with the exclusion order would have subjected him to indefinite detention. Fahy confronted an agonizing dilemma in countering this argument. Justice Department lawyers who dug into the facts of the internment program had presented Fahy with powerful evidence that Korematsu could not have escaped transfer to an internment camp. Over their heated protest, Fahy ignored this evidence and assured the Court that Korematsu had no basis for claiming that "he would ever have found himself in a relocation center" if he had obeyed the exclusion order.

Another issue in the *Korematsu* case raised doubts about the claims of "military necessity" on which General DeWitt's exclusion orders rested. DeWitt had submitted an official report to Secretary of War Stimson that made explicit charges of espionage against Japanese-Americans to support the orders. Two of the Justice Department lawyers assigned to prepare the Supreme Court brief in *Korematsu* had become suspicious about DeWitt's charges. These young lawyers, Edward Ennis and John Burling, convinced Attorney General Biddle to order an investigation of the espionage charges by the FBI and other intelligence agencies. Reports from these agencies convinced Ennis and Burling that DeWitt had included "lies" and "intentional falsehoods" in his report.

A Crucial Footnote   Appalled by evidence of DeWitt's deliberate fabrications, Ennis and Burling drafted a crucial footnote in their brief that alerted the Court to the "contrariety of evidence" on the Army's espionage charges. This footnote stated that the Justice Department had evidence that disputed these charges and was intended to wave a red flag in front of the Court on the issue of DeWitt's veracity. Before the brief reached the Court, however, Assistant Secretary of War McCloy prevailed on Fahy to dilute the wording and to remove any hint that the DeWitt report had lied about the espionage charges. When they argued to the Supreme Court, Korematsu's lawyers stressed the lack of evidence in the public record to support DeWitt's charges and suggested that the revised footnote constituted a confession by the government on this issue.

Stung by suggestions that he did not stand behind "the truth of every recitation" in the disputed report of General DeWitt, Fahy assured the Court that "there is not a single line, a single word, or a single syllable in that report" that cast any doubt on the "military necessity" of DeWitt's exclusion orders. Fahy responded to critical questions from the bench about the factual basis of DeWitt's report with an assurance that it constituted "a complete justification and explanation of the reasons which led to his judgment." Although the Solicitor General had been warned by Ennis and Burling that reliance on the DeWitt report would compromise the government's integrity, Fahy told the Court that he stood "four square and indivisible in support of this conviction."

When the justices returned to their conference room to discuss the *Korematsu* case behind closed doors, the unanimity of the previous year turned to discord. Four members of the Court voted to reverse Korematsu's conviction. Justice Wiley Rutledge, the junior member and the last to vote at the conference, expressed his "anguish" over the case. "Nothing but necessity would justify it because of Hirabayashi and so I vote to affirm," Rutledge told his colleagues with resignation in his voice. Fahy's unbending defense of General DeWitt's "military necessity" had swayed the deciding vote on the Supreme Court.

Before the Court announced its opinion in *Korematsu,* Justice William O. Douglas shifted his vote to the majority in order to placate Hugo Black, who wrote the Court's opinion. Black first deferred to the principle that "all legal restrictions which curtail the civil rights of a single racial group are immediately suspect" and are subject to "the most rigid scrutiny" by the Court. Despite this shifting of the burden of proof to the government, Black echoed Fahy in concluding that "evidence of disloyalty" among the Japanese-Americans overcame the concession that Fred Korematsu was a loyal American citizen who posed no threat of espionage or sabotage. This concept of racial guilt prompted Justice Frank Murphy, the most vehement of the three dissenters, to blast his colleagues for approving "this legalization of racism." Another dissenter, Justice Robert Jackson, noted "the sharp controversy as to the credibility of the DeWitt report." With no "real evidence before it," Jackson complained, the Court had "no choice but to accept General DeWitt's own unsworn, self-serving statement, untested by any cross-examination, that what he did was reasonable."

The Court's bitter division over the *Korematsu* case did not extend to the *Endo* case. Justice Douglas wrote for a unanimous Court in granting the habeas corpus petition; advance word of the decision prompted the War Department to announce that Japanese-Americans cleared as "loyal" could leave the internment camps in January 1945. But the *Endo* decision was hardly a victory, since the Court evaded the constitutional question of detention without charge and simply held that Congress had failed to sanction the indefinite detention program. The proper legislative action, Douglas hinted, would have permitted the internment to continue.

Vindication

The three young men whose challenges to internment were rebuffed by the Supreme Court lived for four decades with criminal records and neared retirement before the dramatic revival of their cases. The judicial principle of finality, holding that a Supreme Court decision brings an end to every case, would normally bar any later review. But the release in 1981 of Justice Department files in these cases, under the Freedom of Information Act, allowed the defendants to ask the courts for vindication.

With the help of third-generation Japanese-American lawyers, whose parents had endured the wartime internment camps, the three original challengers filed similar suits in 1983 in the federal courts in San Francisco, Portland, and Seattle. These suits rested on an obscure provision of federal law that allows criminal defendants who have completed their sentences to argue that acts of "prosecutorial misconduct" had violated their constitutional right to due process of law. The acts of misconduct charged in the suits came from the recently opened Justice Department files, which revealed that government lawyers had accused Solicitor General Fahy of "suppression of evidence" in the *Hirabayashi* and *Yasui* cases and with failing to alert the Supreme Court to the "lies" in the internment report of General DeWitt.

The first suit to be heard was that filed by Fred Korematsu in San Francisco. Government lawyers agreed to the vacation of his conviction and labeled the wartime internment as an "unfortunate episode" in our history. They refused, however, to admit to any claims of prosecutorial misconduct and asked Federal Judge Marilyn Hall Patel of the Federal District Court to dismiss the suit. Judge Patel listened to the legal arguments by the lawyers on both sides at a hearing in October 1983. After the lawyers concluded, she asked Fred

Examining baggage of Japanese-Americans as they arrived at Santa Anita reception center, April 1942

Korematsu to address the court. Speaking in a quiet but firm voice, before an audience filled with former residents of the internment camps, Korematsu recalled the time in 1942 he had been led in handcuffs and at gunpoint into the courtroom. "I knew I was an American, and I knew I hadn't done anything wrong," he told the hushed audience.

Many in the courtroom shed joyful tears when Judge Patel told Fred Korematsu that she would vacate his conviction and erase his criminal record. In a later written opinion, the judge dismissed the government's response as "tantamount to a confession of error" and went on to find "substantial support in the record that the government deliberately omitted relevant information" before the Supreme Court. Citing the disputed footnote in the original *Korematsu* brief, Judge Patel upheld the misconduct charges and wrote that "the judicial process is seriously impaired when the government's law enforcement officers violate their ethical obligations to the court."

Stung by this judicial rebuke, government lawyers changed course in defending the two remaining suits. Federal District Court Judge Robert Belloni gave the government a sympathetic hearing in the suit filed by Min Yasui in Portland, Ore. Granting the government's motion to vacate the conviction, Judge Belloni ruled that Yasui had no right to judicial review of the misconduct charges in his suit. After this ruling in February 1984, Yasui asked the Ninth Circuit Court of Appeals to reverse Judge Belloni and return his suit for a full hearing. As of October 1986, Yasui still was awaiting a decision on his appeal.

The most dramatic, and potentially the most significant, hearing in the internment suits took place in Seattle in June 1985. Federal District Court Judge Donald Voorhees listened for two weeks to witnesses on both sides of the suit filed by Gordon Hirabayashi. Voorhees scheduled the full-scale hearing over the government's objections, ruling that Hirabayashi had the right to seek "vindication of his honor" through a review of his misconduct charges. In an unprecedented turnaround, Hirabayashi's lawyers called as their chief witness Edward Ennis, who had defended his conviction four decades earlier. Ennis told Judge Voorhees that crucial evidence had been withheld from the Supreme Court in 1943 by Solicitor General Fahy, and that War Department officials had altered a key military report in order to mislead the Court.

The government's lawyers in the Seattle hearing tried to convince Judge Voorhees that the misconduct charges Ennis had substantiated were "ridiculous." To counter these charges, they called witnesses who claimed that decoded Japanese wartime cables showed evidence of a "massive espionage network" on the West Coast that included Americans of Japanese ancestry. Fears of widespread espionage, government lawyers told Judge Voorhees, justified the internment program. The need for wartime secrecy, they added, required that evidence of espionage be withheld from the Supreme Court. A former military officer called by the government echoed General DeWitt's "a Jap's a Jap" statement in testifying that Japanese-Americans were the most likely "friends of the enemy" on the West Coast. Under cross-examination by Hirabayashi's lawyers, none of the government's witnesses could identify a single instance of wartime espionage or sabotage by Japanese-Americans.

After both sides submitted final arguments in written form, Judge Voorhees handed down his decision on February 10, 1986. The judge struck down Hirabayashi's conviction for refusing to obey the military exclusion order that required him to report for detention in a barbed-wire compound, an issue that the Supreme Court had evaded in its 1943 decision. Judge Voorhees based his thirty-five-page opinion on the initial version of General DeWitt's official evacuation report, which War Department officials had withheld from Justice Department lawyers and the Supreme Court in 1943. This version claimed that lack of time to conduct individual loyalty hearings had not been a factor in ordering mass evacuation, since DeWitt considered it "impossible" to separate the loyal and disloyal among the Japanese-Americans. "There isn't such a thing as a loyal Japanese," DeWitt had stated.

Keeping this report from the Supreme Court and Hirabayashi's lawyers, Voorhees concluded, "was an error of the most fundamental character" because it directly contradicted the government's argument that lack of time to conduct loyalty hearings had forced the evacuation. Hirabayashi won a legal victory, and belated vindication, on the most serious charge against him, although Judge Voorhees declined to reverse the curfew conviction, finding the curfew a "relatively mild" burden as opposed to exclusion from one's home. Significantly, Voorhees completely ignored the government's espionage charges in his opinion, indicating he considered all the testimony on this issue irrelevant to the misconduct charges raised by Hirabayashi.

There is an obvious drama to the outcome of the wartime

internment cases. First of all, three men who lived with criminal records for more than four decades have finally won their vindication. Second, judicial review of the Korematsu and Hirabayashi cases has exposed the racist underpinnings of the government's "military necessity" claims and has cleared all the Japanese-Americans who endured the internment as suspects in a spy plot that rested only on suspicion. Finally, the recent judicial decisions have undermined the value of the wartime Supreme Court opinions as legal precedent. "Only two of this Court's modern cases have held the use of racial classifications to be constitutional," Justice Lewis Powell wrote in a 1980 decision that cited the *Korematsu* and *Hirabayashi* opinions.

What lessons can we learn from this account of these historic cases? Judge Patel stated one lesson in her opinion, a moral that is easy to grasp but hard to implement: the wartime conviction of Fred Korematsu "stands as a caution that in times of international hostility and antagonism our institutions, legislative, executive and judicial, must be prepared to protect all citizens from the petty fears and prejudices that are so easily aroused." Japanese-Americans became the victims of fear and prejudice in the aftermath of Pearl Harbor, but the members of any racial or ethnic group can be held hostage to the actions of their country of ancestry if we do not guard against prejudice.

Another obvious lesson is that any form of racial discrimination must be subject, as Justice Stone argued in 1938, to the most stringent test of judicial scrutiny. The courts had failed to apply this test in the internment cases. Over the protest that General DeWitt's espionage charges had never been subjected to cross-examination, the Supreme Court adopted the "military necessity" claims that Solicitor General Fahy echoed to the justices. Forty years later, when the government raised the same charges at the hearing before Judge Voorhees, they were demolished by cross-examination and judicial scrutiny.

Finally, we have learned from the recent hearings in the internment cases a truth that goes back more than a century to the Civil War cases. In denying to the military the power to punish civilians, the Supreme Court in 1867 denounced the "pernicious doctrine" that America has one Constitution for peacetime and another in wartime. More than a century has passed since the Court proclaimed this profound truth. If the Constitution cannot restrain the excesses of wartime passions, we cannot protect any group of citizens from hostility and racial prejudice. If the nation had heeded this lesson four decades ago, we might have avoided the "grave injustice" that we imposed on Americans of Japanese ancestry.

SUGGESTED ADDITIONAL READING

Commission on Wartime Relocation and Internment of Civilians, *Personal Justice Denied* (1982).

Peter Irons, *Justice at War: The Story of the Japanese-American Internment Cases* (1983).

Peter Irons, *Justice Delayed* (1986).

Jacobus tenBroek, Edward N. Barnhart, and Floyd W. Matson, *Prejudice, War, and the Constitution: Causes and Consequences of the Evacuation of the Japanese-Americans in World War II* (1954).

Peter Irons is professor of political science and director of the Law and Society Program at the University of California, San Diego. He received a Ph.D. from Boston University and a J.D. from Harvard Law School. A member of state and federal bars, he served as counsel to Fred Korematsu in the reopening of his case.

The Supreme Court and the Evolution of Women's Rights

Earlean M. McCarrick

First introduced in Congress at the behest of the National Woman's party in 1923, the Equal Rights Amendment (ERA) boldly proclaimed "Men and Women shall have equal rights throughout the United States and every place subject to its jurisdiction." It never got out of the Judiciary Committee in either house. A more subdued version—"Equality of rights under the law shall not be denied or abridged by the United States or any state on account of sex"—cleared Congress in March 1972, with only twenty-three House members and eight senators in opposition. Roughly two-thirds of the populace—then and now—supported the ERA. State legislatures responded enthusiastically. By the end of the year, twenty-two states had ratified. Adoption seemed certain; but the euphoria of supporters was short-lived. By mid-1973, opponents were organized. The ratification process slowed; only thirteen more states ratified before the expiration date, three short of the necessary thirty-eight. Four states voted to rescind. The proposed amendment died in June 1982 when the deadline, though extended beyond the originally specified period of seven years, passed without ratification by the requisite number of states. Although reintroduced in Congress in 1983, the Equal Rights Amendment is no longer a prominent item on the nation's agenda.

Rejection of pleas for sexual equality is one of our oldest traditions, predating the Constitution itself, upheld by women as well as men. Changes in the status of women have been slow and arduous, wrought chiefly by legislation, belatedly by constitutional interpretation, rarely by constitutional amendment.

Formal constitutional amendment is deliberately difficult, requiring a two-thirds vote in both houses of Congress and ratification by three-fourths of the states. The difficulty has

233

been surmounted only twenty-six times—only sixteen if we exclude the first ten amendments, usually considered to be a part of the original Constitution. This small number does not, of course, mean that the Constitution has changed only sixteen or twenty-six times. To the contrary, this eighteenth-century document serves the twentieth century primarily because it adapts to contemporary conditions by other means. In some instance, of course, the Constitution can be changed only by formal amendment; to substitute a six-year presidential term for a four-year term would necessitate a formal amendment because the Constitution is quite explicit about the length of a presidential term. For the most part, the constitutional amendment process has been reserved for changing this kind of explicit provision—thus, the Twentieth Amendment changed the presidential inauguration date from March to January.

Not all important constitutional provisions are so explicit that an amendment is necessary to change their meaning. Many significant constitutional provisions are so broad that they accommodate varing interpretations. For example, from the late nineteenth century to the 1930s, the Supreme Court's interpretation of the Constitution led to the invalidation of many state and national laws regulating various aspects of the socioeconomic order such as wages and hours. In the late 1930s, the Court capitulated to popular political demands by construing the same provisions of the Constitution to permit extensive governmental regulation, thus legitimizing the New Deal and the social welfare state. Similarly, the civil rights revolution of the 1960s is partly attributable to the Court's changed construction of the Constitution—whereas it had earlier permitted legally prescribed racial segregation, for example, in the 1950s it began to forbid such official discrimination. The Court is, in Woodrow Wilson's words, "a continuing constitutional convention." It "amends" the Constitution through changed interpretation.

On the matter of sex discrimination, there is no explicit provision in the Constitution that requires distinctions on the basis of gender *or* that prevents egalitarian policy. The problem is thus, not that the Constitution discriminates against women; it is that the Constitution does not by explicit terms protect against the historic disabilities imposed upon women. There is a general provision against discrimination in the Fourteenth Amendment that the Court could interpret as prohibiting all distinctions based upon sex, but it has not done so.

The legal denigration of women is a part of our common law heritage, most vividly exemplified by the ancient doctrine of "coverture," which suspended a woman's legal identity upon marriage. "Dead in the law," a married woman could not own property, make contracts, conduct her own business, enter a profession, sue or be sued. Whether married or single, eighteenth-century standards prevented women from serving on juries, voting, speaking in public, seeking public office, or

Common Law Roots

Woman suffrage in Wyoming territory

acquiring the education necessary to earn a living or perform the duties of citizenship in a republic.

It was against this prescribed inferior status that Abigail Adams protested in her famous 1776 letter in which she pleaded with her husband, John, to "remember the ladies" in the "new code of laws." It was to protest the persistence of the denial of rights and to demand removal of gender as a barrier to individual participation in the social, economic, cultural, religious, and political life of nineteenth-century America that feminists gathered at Seneca Falls, N.Y., in 1848.

Nineteenth-century state legislatures responded grudgingly to the demands of feminists. Still, by the end of the century, state laws granted married women many of the same rights of single women to own property, to control their earnings, to enter into contracts, and to sue and be sued. No state legislature, however, guaranteed to women the same legal status that men enjoyed.

During the reform fervor of the immediate post-Civil War era, feminists targeted Congress as the instrument for the redress of their grievances. Taking advantage of the momentum toward constitutional change they argued for protection against sex discrimination in the new amendments prohibiting racial discrimination. Congress refused.

Turning to the Supreme Court in the early 1870s, feminists were rebuffed again. The Court declined to apply to women the new Fourteenth Amendment requirement of "equal protection of the law." Specifically, the Court held that the right to practice law and the right to vote were not "privileges and immunities" of national citizenship protected against state denial. The Supreme Court opinions so narrowly construed the rights protected against state deprivation that it seemed clear that the states could continue to make distinctions based on gender without fear that the Court or the Constitution would deny them the power to do so.

The Nineteenth Amendment

Faced with an unsympathetic Court, women turned away from the judiciary and the existing Constitution as vehicles for change. Convinced that nothing short of access to the political process would enable them to eradicate unjust laws, activist women began to focus their energies upon acquiring the right to vote.

Suffrage, of course, had long been an item on the feminist agenda—political equality was among the demands made by the women at Seneca Falls in 1848; a woman suffrage amendment had been introduced in Congress six months before the introduction of the Fifteenth Amendment prohibiting race as a barrier to voting. The right to vote took on a new urgency, however, with the formation of two major organizations in 1869. The National Woman Suffrage Association (NWSA) pushed for an amendment to the national Constitution. The American Woman Suffrage Association (AWSA) opted for a state-by-state approach.

By 1878, the "Anthony Amendment," which prohibited the states from denying the right to vote on the basis of sex, had gained the allegiance of large numbers of women. Middle and upper class women with the leisure to devote to public affairs became its particular champions, making it a serious issue on the public policy agenda. By the 1890s, when the two suffrage organizations merged to form the National American Woman Suffrage Association (NAWSA), the idea of women voting—at least if those women were educated and middle-class—was no longer alien. But the movement suffered from ideological and organizational disarray. Reflecting the middle- and upper-class conservatism, biases, and bigotry of many of their leaders and members, the woman suffrage organizations largely disassociated themselves from the aspirations of the working class, the burgeoning immigrant population, and the political reform movements of their day. The Anthony Amendment continued to be introduced perfunctorily in nearly every Congress, but it was not again reported out of committee for debate on the floor of either House until 1913.

Vigor returned with the rise of the progressive movement, the arrival in 1910 of the militant Alice Paul fresh from the trenches of the woman suffrage fight in England, and the revitalization and expansion of NAWSA under the leadership of Carrie Chapman Catt. Burning with the kind of passion for justice long absent from the woman's movement, Alice Paul led her National Woman's party into the streets and into partisan politics. Using such direct action tactics as picketing, arrests, and hunger strikes, as well as the more conventional means of congressional lobbying, pressure on political parties and presidential and congressional candidates, the suffragists got the Anthony Amendment out of committee and onto the floor of both houses for debate—and defeat—in 1914. Strengthened by the mass movement of women into the labor force and into positions of responsibility in the public and private sectors during World War I, feminists marshalled their political talents for the final assault upon the male bastions of power.

Carrie Chapman Catt

With President Wilson's emphasis upon making the world "safe for democracy" as a major war aim, denial of the right to vote to one-half of America's adult population—the half that supplied the civilian war effort—became an embarrassment. By the spring of 1919, the suffragists garnered the votes of two-thirds of the House and Senate. Turning their skills to the state level where they had achieved some small success by winning a few state voting referenda, they won ratification by three-fourths of the states by 1920.

The Nineteenth Amendment was a milestone in the quest for sexual equality; 133 years after the Philadelphia Convention, disenfranchised women forced their politicians to alter the nation's fundamental law to include a second reference to gender. The first such reference in the Constitution—in the never-enforced provision of the Fourteenth Amendment that a state's representation in Congress would be reduced if it denied qualified "males" the right to vote—made it clear that the voting was a male prerogative. Without the right to vote, women could not function as full citizens. With it, they could achieve political and legal equality.

Women's potential political clout was reflected in the new deference accorded them by political parties, by presidents, and by Congress. Both major parties made room for women in their organizational hierarchy. Presidents of both parties appointed women to prominent positions. Congress passed legislation of particular concern to women such as that designed to reduce maternal and infant mortality. A woman's bureau was established in the Labor Department to protect the interests of working women.

Survival of Discrimination

The Amendment, however, directly produced little immediate change in the day-to-day lives of most women; economically, politically, and legally, they continued to be man's inferior. If women entered the work force, their wages rarely exceeded half of that of men. Cultural expectations and legal restrictions conspired to keep women in lower-paid, less prestigious jobs. Some legislation designed to protect women—limitations on hours, night work, and lifting heavy objects, for example—had the unintended effect of reducing women's employment opportunities. A woman's legal right to property acquired during marriage was limited; in most jurisdictions, the husband owned what was acquired with his earnings. Civic duties, too, continued to be different for men and women. Fewer women than men served on juries either because women were by law ineligible or because gender-based qualifications made it unlikely; women defendants continued to be judged by male jurors in many states.

Survival of sexual discrimination is not a reproach to the achievements of the woman suffrage movement, nor is it surprising. The social, economic, political, and legal relevance of gender was too pervasive to be radically altered by one constitutional change. The complacency of the jazz age, of the era of the flapper, of prosperity, and of "normalcy" proved inhospitable to further attempts at change.

Former suffragists, perhaps assuming that the egalitarian battle had been won, turned their attention to other matters. The group founded by Susan B. Anthony, for example, became the League of Women Voters, an organization devoted to good government and an informed electorate. The woman's movement disintegrated. Until the 1960s, only a small group of women continued an organized effort on behalf of sexual equality. The Equal Rights Amendment was introduced in every Congress; sometimes it was favorably reported by a committee to the floor of one house, occasionally it was accepted by a majority of the Senate although not by the two-thirds required to propose a constitutional amendment, but for the most part it was ignored. In the 1940s, as women entered the work force in unprecedented numbers in response to the needs of World War II, legislation was introduced to mandate equal pay for equal work, but the proposal failed.

The Supreme Court continued to dismiss the notion that the Constitution commands a gender-neutral public policy. Only once did the Court bestow constitutional equality on women: without specifically overruling an earlier case upholding maximum hour legislation for women only (*Muller v. Oregon,* 1908), the Court in 1923 invalidated a minimum wage law designed to protect women workers (*Adkins v. Children's Hospital*). Because the "ancient inequality of the sexes" was diminishing, said the Court, women's constitutional right to contract freely with employers could not be infringed by governmental efforts to assure women a living wage. Indeed, the Court turned the Nineteenth Amendment against women; with the addition of that Amendment, women were now, said the Court, equal to men. What this "equality" meant in practice was that women now enjoyed an even greater constitutional right than men to be underpaid.

With this problematic exception, when the Court confronted gender-based legislation, it simply reaffirmed a state's

The laundry of Curt Muller, the plaintiff in *Muller v. Oregon*. In this 1908 landmark case, the Supreme Court upheld laws regulating hours of work for women.

authority to classify on the basis of sex. In the 1940s, a Michigan woman who wanted to work as a bartender challenged the constitutionality of a state law that prohibited the occupation to women except for wives or daughters of bar owners. The Court rejected her plea (*Goesaert v. Cleary,* 1948). The Court held that nothing in the Constitution prohibited a state "from drawing a sharp line between the sexes"; the Equal Protection Clause of the Fourteenth Amendment—"No state shall ... deny to any person within its jurisdiction the equal protection of the law"—did not mean that a state had to treat men and women similarly. To the Court it was reasonable for a state to decide that the occupation of bartending was inconsistent with the proper role of women, and to forbid women from entering that and, presumably, any other inappropriate occupation. When a Florida woman in the 1960s sought reversal of her conviction for beating her husband to death with a baseball bat, the Court rejected her challenge to the all-male composition of her jury; it held that the state's decision to relieve women of the duty of serving on juries was reasonable (*Hoyt v. Florida,* 1961). Throughout the 1960s, the Court was unreceptive to demands for sexual equality.

During the 1960s, however, events occurred outside the Court that produced changes in the legal status of women within a decade. In February 1963, a new book appeared that spoke to the frustration of college-educated, middle-class women who were dissatisfied with their socially assigned roles: *The Feminine Mystique* by Betty Friedan let these women know they were not alone in wanting access to the world outside their homes. Also in 1963, in June, Congress passed the first federal law that addressed sex discrimination in private employment; a new provision of the Fair Labor Standards Act, the Equal Pay Act prohibited discrimination in wage rates based upon sex. Then, in October, the President's Commission on the Status of Women, appointed by John F. Kennedy in 1961, issued its final report, documenting the inferior legal, economic, and social position of women. The following year, Congress made a pivotal move. Title VII of the Civil Rights Act forbade discrimination on the basis of sex in hiring, firing, pay, and other conditions of employment. In 1967, President Lyndon Johnson required federal departments to insist upon sexually nondiscriminatory employment policies by federal contractors. By the end of the 1960s, gender had become an illegitimate employment criterion. In 1972, Congress not only adopted the ERA and sent it to the states, it also forbade sex discrimination in federally funded educational programs. The Equal Credit Act of 1974 prohibited discrimination in credit on the basis of sex and marital status.

Women, having participated in the civil rights movement in the 1960s, much as their nineteenth-century counterparts had engaged in the abolitionist movement, followed the precedent of earlier feminists by moving into the political arena on their own behalf. The second women's rights movement was launched with the formation of the National Organization for Women (NOW) in 1966, the Women's Equity Action League (WEAL) in 1968, and the National Women's Political Caucus (NWPC) in 1971. Unlike such traditional women's organizations as the League of Women Voters or the American Association of University Women (AAUW), which shied away

A New Women's Movement

from identifying too closely with purely women's interests, these new organizations were explicitly feminist.

This new-found political power inspired changes in the law at the state as well as the national level. Equal rights amendments were added to the constitutions of fourteen states. Some of the states made changes in their laws that would not be commanded even by the ERA—reform of rape laws and marital property laws, for example. In 1970, four states legalized abortion—three years before the Supreme Court decision in *Roe v. Wade* (1973), which severely limited the authority of the state to regulation abortion.

The Supreme Court, too, reflected the new awareness of the unequal status of women. Whereas the pre-1970s' Court considered legal distinctions on the basis of sex to be reasonable in almost all cases, the Court of the 1970s began to question the legitimacy of such distinctions. In 1971, the Court for the first time invalidated a state law on the grounds that it denied to women the equal protection of the law guaranteed by the Fourteenth Amendment provision.

The controversy that led to such a momentous, though limited, holding was an otherwise inconsequential dispute—a quarrel between an estranged husband and wife over the administration of their deceased son's $1,000 estate. An Idaho probate court appointed Cecil Reed rather than Sally Reed as administration of their son's money; the case assumed constitutional proportions because a state law gave absolute preference to a father over a mother as administrator of a minor offspring's estate. Mrs. Reed charged that this gender distinction violated the equal protection clause. She argued that classifications on the basis of gender, like classifications on the basis of race, were "suspect"—constitutional only if the state can demonstrate that the objective the classification is designed to achieve is "compelling" and cannot be achieved by any other means; because the interest advanced by the classification was not compelling, the classification was unconstitutional.

The Court accepted Mrs. Reed's conclusion—that the legislation was unconstitutional—but not her reasoning. The Court held that classifications on the basis of sex did give rise to legitimate equal protection questions but that they were not necessarily "suspect," that the equal protection clause forbids arbitrary distinctions but it permits "reasonable" ones and that requires that similarly situated individuals be treated similarly; in short, the state has to have a good reason—though not a compelling one—to justify gender classifications. Finding no good reasons for preferring a father over a mother as an administrator of a child's estate, the Court concluded that the classification was the very kind of arbitrary distinction that the equal protection clause was designed to prevent.

The Court's opinion was cautious. It simply reaffirmed the traditional equal protection standard—usually referred to as the "rationality" test to distinguish it from the stricter "compelling interest" test—a classification "must be reasonable, not arbitrary, and must rest upon some ground of difference having a fair and substantial relation to the object of the legislation, so that all persons similarly situated shall be treated alike." What was new was that the Court applied that standard to a gender classification for the first time; it questioned the reasonableness of the relationship between a gender classification and the achievement of a legitimate state objective. The mere fact that the Court invalidated sexually discriminatory legislation constituted an invitation to contest other sexually discriminatory laws. From this modest beginning in the *Reed* case, the Court began its role as an instrument of constitutional change for women as two decades earlier it had become a forum for the redress of the grievances of black Americans.

Following in Sally Reed's footsteps, subsequent litigants pressed the Court to adopt the stricter "compelling interest" standard to judge sex-based legislation. The Court refused to do so. It did, however, develop a distinct guideline to judge the constitutionality of legislation that classifies on the basis of sex—not as strict as the compelling interest test but more stringent than the test used in the *Reed* Case. In a 1976 case—*Craig v. Boren*—the court enunciated an intermediate standard when it invalidated an Oklahoma law that permitted females between eighteen and twenty-one to buy beer but prohibited males of the same age from doing so. It held that in order for gender-based legal classifications to pass constitutional muster, the government would have to prove that the gender classification "substantially advanced an important governmental objective." Oklahoma sought to defend the constitutionality of its law by arguing that the purpose of the legislation was important (to reduce the slaughter on its highways) and that gender was related to that purpose (young males were more prone to drunk driving than were young females). Conceding that the purpose was important, the Court concluded that the state had not proved that the incidence of male drunk driving was significantly greater than the incidence of female drunk driving; the gender classification did not therefore substantially advance achievement of the state's objective.

Since 1971, the Supreme Court has invalidated most state and national legislation challenged on the grounds that it discriminated against women. Thus, it struck down a national law that made servicemen automatically eligible for certain spousal benefits but denied such benefits to servicewomen unless their husbands were in fact dependent upon them (*Frontiero v. Richardson,* 1973); it overturned a state law that specified a lower age of majority for females than for males (*Stanton v. Stanton,* 1975); and it nullified a state law that declared husbands to be the "head and master" of the household and thus authorized to dispose unilaterally of jointly-owned property (*Kirchberg v. Feenstra,* 1981).

However, in 1974, the Court allowed California to deny benefits for pregnancy-related disabilities of its employees because it concluded that denial of benefits on the basis of pregnancy did not discriminate against women because of their sex (*Geduldig v. Aiello,* 1974). In response, Congress passed the Pregnancy Discrimination Act, prohibiting the action the Court had allowed.

The Court has also invalidated most legislation challenged on the grounds that it discriminated against men; thus it prohibited government from denying a man admission to a women's nursing school (*Mississippi University for Women v. Hogan,* 1982), from conferring social security benefits upon widows, but not widowers, with dependent children (*Weinberger v. Wiesenfeld,* 1975), and from authorizing alimony to wives only (*Orr v. Orr,* 1979). The Court has, however, upheld some gender-based legislation that burdened men more than women; it permitted government to confer a tax exemption upon widows but not on widowers (*Kahn v. Shevin,* 1974), to punish males but not females for statutory rape (*Michael M. v. Superior Court,* 1981), and to limit draft registration to men (*Rostker v. Goldberg,* 1981).

The Court's invalidation in the last decade of most gender-specific legislation is significant in light of the defeat of the ERA. Until recently, the Court refused to use its formidable power to realize the historic pleas for sexual equality; to the contrary, it openly conferred upon the state the authority to treat men and women differently. The principle of equality embodied in the Fourteenth Amendment's equal protection clause, however, is sufficiently flexible to permit the Court to interpret it to require gender equality. If the Court views most admittedly sexually discriminatory laws as illegitimate—and it

Elizabeth Cady Stanton and Susan B. Anthony

seems now to have reached that point—the Constitution may now afford protection against most overt forms of governmental discrimination against women. All the egalitarian eggs are not, thus, in the ERA basket. The Court is serving as an instrument for achieving sexual equality in much the same way that it has served as an instrument for achieving racial equality.

The fact that the judiciary, along with Congress, the president, and the states, moved against sex discrimination in the 1960s and 1970s does not, of course, necessarily mean that it will continue to do so until sexual equality has been achieved. However, having construed the provisions of the Fourteenth Amendment to prohibit most challenged forms of sex discrimination for over a decade, the Court would find it as difficult to return to the pre-1970s interpretation permitting government to draw a sharp line between the sexes as it would to return to the pre-1950s interpretation permitting government to make racial distinctions.

There is no indication that the Rehnquist Court will reverse course. Although the Burger Court was perceived to be more conservative than the Warren Court (and a reconstituted Court appointed by President Reagan, it is widely assumed, would be even more conservative), it was the Burger Court, not the Warren Court, that effectively included women in the Constitution. Even the most conservative members of the present Court agree that the Fourteenth Amendment forbids most sexually discriminatory laws.

Whatever the fate of the ERA or whatever the changes on the Court, the Constitution has changed. The legal status of women has changed. The nation's legislative, executive, and judicial policy makers in the 1960s and the 1970s did "remember the ladies." This is not to say that the aims of Abigail Adams, of the women of Seneca Falls, of the suffragists, or of contemporary feminists have been totally achieved; gender continues to be relevant in determining an individual's social, political, and economic status. Nonetheless, national constitutional and statutory law now furnish the ammunition for destruction of officially sanctioned sex discrimination.

SUGGESTED ADDITIONAL READING

Eleanor Flexner, *Century of Struggle: The Women's Rights Movement in the United States,* rev. ed. (1975).

Barbara Sinclair Deckard, *The Women's Movement: Political, Socioeconomic and Psychological Issues,* 2d ed. (1979).

Susan Cary Nicholas, Alice Price, Rachel Rubin, *Rights and Wrongs: Women's Struggle for Legal Equality,* 2d ed. (1983).

Janet Boles, *The Politics of the Equal Rights Amendment* (1979).

Earlean M. McCarrick, assistant professor of government and politics at the University of Maryland, College Park campus, teaches courses in constitutional law and the legal status of women. She is the editor of *The U.S. Constitution: Guide to Information Sources* (1980).

Call a Second Convention?

Paul J. Weber

Through two hundred remarkable years the Constitution has both grown in stature and become surrounded by myths and truisms that are rarely questioned. The Bicentennial provides an excellent opportunity to examine our roots and challenge our assumptions. One truism is that calling a second convention to amend the Constitution would be a dangerous step, since a convention might "run away" and either repeal parts of the Bill of Rights or add a number of controversial clauses.

This essay challenges that assumption. It argues that whatever one thinks about the value of any particular amendment, the convention method of amending the Constitution would be a safe political procedure. Indeed, the framers adopted the convention alternative as a means of protecting the rights and liberties of the people against a potentially oppressive Congress. While a convention may not be the preferred method of resolving major policy problems, neither would it be the "constitutional catastrophe" envisioned by some commentators.

The arguments *against* calling a second convention fall into three categories: first, fear of the unknown. We have never had a convention called under Article V and no legally established procedures exist for convening and conducting a meeting. Second, opponents appeal to the framers, contending that because they objected to a second convention in 1788, they would therefore oppose ever having another convention. In other words, even a call for a convention betrays the founders. Finally, some oppose a convention call because they dislike the proposed amendment. For example, Common Cause's position paper on the call for a balanced budget amendment lists six arguments, most of them against the amendment, not the convention.

The present article considers not whether a particular amendment is wise but only whether calling a convention is a safe political procedure. My argument proceeds in two stages, first pointing out that those who create and exploit fears of a convention make a fundamental mistake in their assumptions about the American political system, and then spelling out step by step the political safeguards inherent in the process of calling and conducting a constitutional convention.

The System as Safeguard

Over the years a number of eminent constitutional scholars have warned of the dangers inherent in calling a convention, emphasizing the many unknowns in the convention process. They list many questions: "What constitutes a valid petition of Congress?" "When must Congress act?" "What happens if Congress refuses to act?" "What is the role of the Supreme Court?" "Who sets the rules for the convention when it is in session?" "What happens if the convention delegates refuse to obey the rules?" Since the states have never called a constitutional convention under Article V of the U.S. Constitution, no definitive precedents exist. Opponents of a convention then move easily to the next step, a list of hypothetical horribles that could happen if a convention were to meet.

We find a hidden assumption here—namely, that unsettled law is unsafe law. That assumption is valid only if the institutions and procedures necessary for settling questions of law are not in place or are not functioning. But we do have such institutions and procedures, and they are healthy. Congress, the courts, state legislatures, and both federal and state bureaucracies deal with unsettled law on a regular basis. Opponents of a convention ignore these precedents. Professor Laurence Tribe of Harvard Law School, for example, argues that calling a convention risks "confrontation" between political institutions. But confrontation—an emotionally charged word—takes place whenever Congress passes a law that supercedes state laws or whenever the Supreme Court declares an act of Congress unconstitutional. We have no reason to expect Congress or a state legislature to refuse to accept a clear ruling of the Supreme Court on the subject of a constitutional convention. In brief, the assumption that unsettled law is unsafe law lacks foundation. It is not supported by American experience.

A related argument observes that there are currently no legal constraints on the convention process. Although true, this problem can be easily remedied. The Senate Judiciary Committee has reported several bills to establish rights, responsibilities, duties, and procedures for the call and conduct of a

constitutional convention. So bills establishing the necessary legal constraints exist if and when they are needed. Even without them, the federal courts are capable of making the necessary decisions to settle law in this area.

The second argument against a constitutional convention—the appeal to the framers—holds even less water than the safety argument. James Madison led the fight against a second convention in 1788 for a very specific reason: the call was a rear guard action by Anti-Federalists, led by Patrick Henry, to undo several of the basic compromises reached at the first convention before the Constitution was even ratified. Madison argued successfully that the Constitution should be implemented and be given a chance to work before changes were made. He added no warning about conventions in the future. Thomas Jefferson in fact advocated them.

Occasionally opponents argue that the first convention "ran away" and a second might do the same. While I do not agree that the first convention ran away (the founders very consciously established their legitimacy, seeking the approval of the Congress), two hundred years of experience, the establishment of an aggressive national print and electronic press, a powerful, functioning Supreme Court, and a well-established, effective Congress make the present situation radically different from that facing the first convention. No convention could run away under such scrutiny.

Even if a second convention were a risky venture, that uncertainty itself would not necessarily warrant dismissing it out of hand. In deciding to undertake any action, we weigh the risk itself, that is, the likelihood of a negative consequence of acting; we weigh the *comparative* risk of *not* acting versus the risk of acting (the risk of a runaway convention for example, compared to the risk of a runaway deficit); and, finally, we consider the possibility of reaching one's objectives through alternative, less risky means.

The fact that some risk exists, in an absolute sense of that word, does not mean that a constitutional convention is a politically unsafe event. Professor Tribe uses a wonderfully seductive phrase when he writes of the "unanswered and unanswerable questions" about a convention, a rhetorical sleight-of-hand. Professor Tribe is of course correct that such questions exist. But we can predict with some confidence the outcomes of actions based on past experience. In other words, a particular outcome can be uncertain in principle but highly predictable in practice. In the world of politics, business, and even the law, high predictability, not certainty, is the best humans can do. Those who argue that a constitutional convention would be unsafe make a fundamental error. They ignore the basis for predictability; that is, the political safeguards built into the constitutional convention process.

The Process as Safeguard

Article V of the federal Constitution provides that:

The Congress, whenever two-thirds of both Houses shall deem it necessary, shall propose amendments to this Constitution, or, on the Application of the Legislatures of two-thirds of the several States, shall call a Convention for proposing Amendments, which, in either Case, shall be valid to all Intents and Purposes, as Part of this Constitution, when ratified by the Legislatures of three-fourths of the several States, or by Conventions in three-fourths thereof, as the one or the other mode of Ratification may be proposed by the Congress. . . .

From a political perspective the process of calling and conducting a convention must take place in six distinct stages: application by the states, call by Congress, election of delegates, the convention itself, submission of the amendment to Congress, and ratification. Each stage provides a variety of political safeguards that have been given too little attention by those concerned with the uncertainties of the convention process.

Stage one: Applications made to Congress by legislatures of two-thirds of the states. Since the federal constitution was adopted in 1789 there have been *more than four hundred applications* for calling a convention, including at least one from every state. None has ever succeeded, chiefly because it is more efficient in terms of time, effort, and money to have Congress propose amendments. When state legislatures agree on the need for an amendment, Congress usually responds, a precedent set by the passage of the first ten amendments under the guidance of James Madison.

Most scholars think it unlikely that a convention will be called in the foreseeable future for two reasons: with calls for a convention approaching the required number, legislatures in the remaining states have become cautious, sending petitions to Congress only after considerable debate, public hearings, and intense lobbying. Equally important, even a reluctant Congress will likely prefer to pass the desired amendment rather than leave its wording in the hands of a constitutional convention. Under current proposed legislation, each congressional district will elect delegates to the national convention, with two delegates chosen from each state on an at-large basis. No delegates may come from the ranks of current federal office holders. Sitting members of Congress will want to avoid setting up a political event that will allow a potential future competitor to gain name recognition, to build up a following, and to receive important news coverage. At this stage both state legislatures and Congress act as restraints. As a result, the application process itself serves as a major defense against unwise or hasty calls for a convention.

Stage two: Calling the convention. No convention has yet taken place under Article V, so we can only speculate about the final five steps in the process. Congress is required to call a convention when the requisite number of petitions is received from the states, but numerous safety factors operate here: Congress determines the validity of petitions; Congress passes the laws spelling out the procedures a convention must follow and the limits on its actions; and court challenges will test whatever Congress does. Finally, one must include as another safeguard the attention that will be focused on the event by political parties, the president, interest groups, and media. All the players will not only be pursuing their own agendas but watching the others as well.

Stage three: Election of delegates. Constitutional scholars remain reticent about this aspect of the process yet this stage provides a safety feature of major proportions, the nature of the American electoral system. Successful political campaigns on congressional districtwide levels involve major expense, requiring those who run successfully to have either independent wealth or support of a political party and major interest groups. Parties and major interest groups rarely back unstable candidates or those perceived as extremists; candidates who are backed by controversial interest groups trigger vigorous opposition. Moreover, candidates campaigning for election to the convention will repeatedly and publicly be asked to declare themselves on two questions: where they stand on the issue of the convention call (for example, whether they will vote in favor of or against a balanced budget amendment), and whether, if elected, they will abide by the rules Congress established to limit the convention to a single issue. Successful candidates comprise those who can appeal to the broadest range of individual citizens and groups. Candidates perceived as too extremist or too controversial will have little chance of winning election to serve as delegates to the convention.

Some raise the objection that, except for presidential elections, Americans often vote at a very low rate. Therefore, the argument goes, if voter turnout for convention delegates lags, zealots or those intent on overturning the Bill of Rights will have a good chance of winning. In response, one must first question the assumption. An unprecedented historic event given enormous media coverage such as a convention will likely stimulate heavy turnout. But if not, party regulars who vote for party regulars tend to be the traditional voters in such circumstances, not outsiders with special interests.

Who then will be the delegates to a convention? Our electoral experience suggests that the delegates will look very much like current elected officials: in other words, a variety of relatively well-known, experienced politicians—hardly the sort of people to pursue a radical agenda.

Stage four: The convention is the heart of the process. Scholars who wring their hands over the lack of legal con-

STATE OF ALASKA

THE LEGISLATURE

1982

Source

Legislative
Resolve No.

HJR 17 am S

1

Relating to an amendment to the Constitution of the United
States which would require that total federal appropriations
not exceed total estimated federal revenues in a fiscal year
in the absence of a national emergency.

———————

BE IT RESOLVED BY THE LEGISLATURE OF THE STATE OF ALASKA:

WHEREAS annually the United States moves more deeply into
debt as its expenditures exceed its available revenues and the
public debt now exceeds hundreds of billions of dollars; and

WHEREAS annually the federal budget demonstrates the
unwillingness or inability of the federal government to spend
in conformity with available revenues; and

WHEREAS proper planning, fiscal prudence, and plain good
sense require that the federal budget be in balance absent
national emergency; and

WHEREAS a continuously unbalanced federal budget except
in a national emergency causes continuous and damaging inflation and consequently a severe threat to the political and
economic stability of the United States; and

WHEREAS, under Article V of the Constitution of the
United States, amendments to the Constitution may be proposed
by Congress or, on the application of the legislatures of
two-thirds of the states, Congress shall call a constitutional
convention for the purpose of proposing amendments;

BE IT RESOLVED by the Alaska State Legislature that the
Congress of the United States is requested to propose and
submit to the states an amendment to the Constitution of the
United States which would require that within four years after
its ratification by the various states, in the absence of a
national emergency, the total of all appropriations made by
Congress for a fiscal year shall not exceed the total of all
estimated federal revenues for that fiscal year; and be it

, this body makes
s of the United
exclusive purpose of
n of the United
bsence of a national
s made by Congress
tal of all estimated
d be it

oposes such an amend-
shall no longer be

on and request shall
e convention is not
d by this resolution.

ent to the Secretary
f the United States
e Ted Stevens and the
, and the Honorable
of the Alaska delega-

LR 1
-2-

Alaska's call for a balanced budget constitutional amendment straints in the convention hall turn their heads from the very ample protections provided by the founders—political constraints. At least six such constraints will operate within the convention itself: the composition of the delegates, the public campaign statements and promises of the delegates (and the media attention that will be given to discrepancies between words and actions), the number of delegates and divisions within the convention (which would make it extraordinarily difficult for one faction or radical position to prevail), the constant awareness that whatever the Convention proposes must pass through a Congress unlikely to forward to the states any proposals that go beyond the convention mandate, the knowledge that the Supreme Court can declare unconstitutional any proposals that go beyond the purpose for which the convention gathered, and most important of all, the delegates' constant awareness of the need to get their proposed amendments ratified by thirty-eight states. One can hardly imagine more effective constraints on a constitutional convention.

Before moving to the next stage, three further questions merit consideration. Can a convention be confined to a particular, limited amendment, or must the convention necessarily stand "wide open"? If it can be confined, will the delegates gather simply to vote "yea" or "nay" on a specifically worded amendment? First, every one of the currently relevant calls for a convention for the purpose of proposing a balanced budget amendment specifies a convention limited to that topic. Second, since every bill proposing rules for a convention has included provisions limiting the convention to the topic that stimulated the call, certainly Congress can propose such limits. Would the Supreme Court uphold such limitations? While one cannot predict what a particular court will do with absolute certainty, one can predict with a high degree of probability, based on past experience and on the constitutional foundation on which the Court supports its decisions. Since Article V is silent on the issue of "limitedness" and since the states and presumably Congress would have called for a limited convention, one may predict that the Supreme Court would uphold the limitation.

Granted a limited convention, would delegates be restricted to simple positive or negative votes? In one sense the very question betrays a lack of understanding of the democratic political process. First, suppose that a clear majority of the delegates elected either favored or opposed the proposed amendment. They would still have important functions to perform: they would need to formalize the majority position through a vote, to legitimize their position through appropriate ritual (thereby attempting to win acceptance of their position from the nation), and, in the case of supporting an amendment, they would have to organize a strategy for getting the amendment ratified. In performing these functions, a constitutional convention would play a role very similar to presidential conventions when the party's candidate has already been chosen.

Suppose, on the other hand, that no clear majority has been elected—it is quite conceivable that some districts might elect uncommitted or "favorite son" delegates or delegates committed to differing versions of an amendment. Added to the tasks of formalizing, legitimizing, and organizing a strategy would be the quintessential political act of *compromising.* While a deadlocked convention is certainly a possibility— which would simply mean that no amendment could be forwarded before the convention disbanded—the more likely scenario projects a compromise amendment. Anyone familiar with the first American constitutional convention will recognize how significant was the process of compromising. In brief, even in a convention limited to the consideration of a specific amendment, delegates would have very important political functions to perform.

Throughout delegates would have to take note of the role of the press—could a convention enforce a rule of secrecy such as the first convention did? Would it try? Under current proposals the convention would have 535 delegates, and it is hardly conceivable that a rule of secrecy could stop strategic leaks. Whether the convention was opened to the press or closed, the news media would undoubtedly play a major watchdog role.

Stage five: Submitting a proposed amendment to Congress. Article V designates Congress as the institution to determine whether ratification shall be by state legislatures or ratifying conventions. Stage five thus provides yet another safety feature. Congress may conceivably refuse to submit to the states any amendment(s) that it deems to have gone beyond the convention mandate. Members of Congress would consider voter sentiment in their states and districts; the positions and intensity of interest of the various groups, especially those that provide support for the members and those that feel particularly threatened; the views of media outlets in their own districts; the potential gains or losses of the possible stances;

and, of course, the merits of any amendment offered.

Suppose Congress did refuse to forward an amendment. Would such a refusal be constitutional? The Supreme Court stands both accustomed to and capable of providing an answer to that type of question. The procedures for taking the issue before the Court are well established, and two hundred years of constitutional history provide a firm foundation for predicting that Congress would obey a court decision to send an amendment on.

Contemporary political considerations also come into play. If the proposed amendment proves popular, members would risk political defeat by taking the extraordinary step of disobeying the Court and leaving themselves open to the charge of betraying their oath of office. If the proposed amendment provokes a negative reaction, members of Congress can forward it with impunity, since the amendment will suffer certain defeat anyway. If an amendment triggers passionate, but evenly divided, support and opposition, the politically safe step for members of Congress to take is a vote to obey the Court ruling and send the amendment to the states (claiming the necessity to do so under the oath of office), then work to defeat the amendment during the state ratification process. As shall be seen in stage six, such an amendment would face certain defeat.

Just as important at this stage are the political constraints outside of Congress. The product of a convention will be known and analyzed, and interested groups will form to press or oppose ratification. There will be no sneak attacks on the Constitution, no surgical strikes against the Bill of Rights, no commando raids against unprepared defenders. Opponents of the proposed amendment will have ample time to organize groups, develop strategies, and prepare arguments in their own favor. Most important, as we shall see in the final stage, they need persuade only a minority of citizens in a minority of states in order to stymie ratification.

Stage six: Ratification. After the nation's experience with the Equal Rights Amendment, one need not labor the point that both Congress and constitutional conventions can only *propose* amendments; states must *ratify* them. The number of states required to ratify is thirty-eight, and both houses of each state legislature must vote favorably. In other words, the process of sending an amendment through the convention process must persuade more people than it dissuades. One can say with confidence that no amendment can pass unless it represents a consensus of the nation. One can hardly imagine a more formidable safety device than ratification.

This article began by criticizing the unwarranted assumption of those who oppose a convention on the basis of its risk for the country, namely that unsettled law is unsafe law. So as long as the institutions and processes for settling law are established, a constitutional convention poses few risks. Further, as our discussion has shown, the convention process *adds* a number of safety features not available in the more traditional mode of proposing amendments.

The convention mode of proposing amendments favors the status quo until a unique circumstance arises: a majority of voters, maintained over time, pushing for a constitutional change opposed by a majority of Congress. It was precisely for just such a limited circumstance that the founders created the convention mode of proposing amendments. It remains a safe, political option.

SUGGESTED ADDITIONAL READING

American Bar Association, *Amendment of the Constitution by the Convention Method under Article V* (1974).

Wilbur Edel, *A Constitutional Convention: Threat or Challenge?* (1983).

Kermit Hall, Harold Hyman, Leon Siegal, *The Constitutional Convention as an Amending Device* (1981).

Paul J. Weber is professor of political science at the University of Louisville and the author of numerous articles on constitutional issues.

The Constitution of the United States

The Preamble

We the People of the United States, in Order to form a more perfect Union, establish Justice, insure domestic Tranquility, provide for the common defence, promote the general Welfare, and secure the Blessings of Liberty to ourselves and our Posterity, do ordain and establish this Constitution for the United States of America.

Article I

Section 1

All legislative Powers herein granted shall be vested in a Congress of the United States, which shall consist of a Senate and House of Representatives.

Section 2

1. The House of Representatives shall be composed of Members chosen every second Year by the People of the several States, and the Electors in each State shall have the Qualifications requisite for Electors of the most numerous Branch of the State Legislature.

2. No Person shall be a Representative who shall not have attained to the age of twenty five Years, and been seven Years a Citizen of the United States, and who shall not, when elected, be an Inhabitant of that State in which he shall be chosen.

3. [Representatives and direct Taxes shall be apportioned among the several States which may be included within this Union, according to their respective Numbers, which shall be determined by adding to the whole Number of free Persons, including those bound to Service for a Term of Years, and excluding Indians not taxed, three fifths of all other Persons.] [1] The actual Enumeration shall be made within three Years after the first Meeting of the Congress of the United States, and within every subsequent Term of ten Years, in such Manner as they shall by Law direct. The Number of Representatives shall not exceed one for every thirty Thousand, but each State shall have at Least one Representative; and until such enumeration shall be made, the State of New Hampshire shall be entitled to chuse three, Massachusetts eight, Rhode-Island and Providence Plantations one, Connecticut five, New-York six, New Jersey

four, Pennsylvania eight, Delaware one, Maryland six, Virginia ten, North Carolina five, South Carolina five, and Georgia three.

4. When vacancies happen in the Representation from any State, the Executive Authority thereof shall issue Writs of Election to fill such Vacancies.

5. The House of Representatives shall chuse their Speaker and other Officers; and shall have the sole Power of Impeachment.

Section 3

1. The Senate of the United States shall be composed of two Senators from each State, [chosen by the Legislature thereof,][2] for six Years; and each Senator shall have one Vote.

2. Immediately after they shall be assembled in Consequence of the first Election, they shall be divided as equally as may be into three Classes. The Seats of the Senators of the first Class shall be vacated at the Expiration of the second Year, of the second Class at the Expiration of the fourth Year, and of the third Class at the Expiration of the sixth Year, so that one third may be chosen every second Year; [and if Vacancies happen by Resignation, or otherwise, during the Recess of the Legislature of any State, the Executive thereof may make temporary Appointments until the next Meeting of the Legislature, which shall then fill such Vacancies].[3]

3. No Person shall be a Senator who shall not have attained to the Age of thirty Years, and been nine Years a Citizen of the United States, and who shall not, when elected, be an Inhabitant of that State for which he shall be chosen.

4. The Vice President of the United States shall be President of the Senate, but shall have no Vote, unless they be equally divided.

5. The Senate shall chuse their other Officers, and also a President pro tempore, in the Absence of the Vice President, or when he shall exercise the Office of President of the United States.

6. The Senate shall have the sole Power to try all Impeachments. When sitting for that Purpose, they shall be on Oath or Affirmation. When the President of the United States is tried the Chief Justice shall preside: And no Person shall be convicted without the Concurrence of two thirds of the Members present.

7. Judgment in Cases of Impeachment shall not extend further than to removal from Office, and disqualification to hold and enjoy any Office of honor, Trust or Profit under the United States: but the Party convicted shall nevertheless be liable and subject to Indictment, Trial, Judgment and Punishment, according to Law.

Section 4

1. The Times, Places and Manner of holding Elections for Senators

and Representatives, shall be prescribed in each State by the Legislature thereof; but the Congress may at any time by Law make or alter such Regulations, except as to the Places of chusing Senators.

2. The Congress shall assemble at least once in every Year, and such Meeting shall [be on the first Monday in December],[4] unless they shall by Law appoint a different Day.

Section 5

1. Each House shall be the Judge of the Elections, Returns and Qualifications of its own Members, and a Majority of each shall constitute a Quorum to do Business; but a smaller Number may adjourn from day to day, and may be authorized to compel the Attendance of absent Members, in such Manner, and under such Penalties as each House may provide.

2. Each House may determine the Rules of its Proceedings, punish its Members for disorderly Behaviour, and, with the Concurrence of two thirds, expel a Member.

3. Each House shall keep a Journal of its Proceedings, and from time to time publish the same, excepting such Parts as may in their Judgment require Secrecy; and the Yeas and Nays of the Members of either House on any question shall, at the Desire of one fifth of those Present, be entered on the Journal.

4. Neither House, during the Session of Congress, shall, without the Consent of the other, adjourn for more than three days, nor to any other Place than that in which the two Houses shall be sitting.

Section 6

1. The Senators and Representatives shall receive a Compensation for their Services, to be ascertained by Law, and paid out of the Treasury of the United States. They shall in all Cases, except Treason, Felony and Breach of the Peace, be privileged from Arrest during their Attendance at the Session of their respective Houses, and in going to and returning from the same; and for any Speech or Debate in either House, they shall not be questioned in any other Place.

2. No Senator or Representative shall, during the Time for which he was elected, be appointed to any civil Office under the Authority of the United States, which shall have been created, or the Emoluments whereof shall have been encreased during such time; and no Person holding any Office under the United States, shall be a Member of either House during his Continuance in Office.

Section 7

1. All Bills for raising Revenue shall originate in the House of

Representatives; but the Senate may propose or concur with amendments as on other Bills.

2. Every Bill which shall have passed the House of Representatives and the Senate, shall, before it become a Law, be presented to the President of the United States; If he approve he shall sign it, but if not he shall return it, with his Objections to that House in which it shall have originated, who shall enter the Objections at large on their Journal, and proceed to reconsider it. If after such Reconsideration two thirds of that House shall agree to pass the Bill, it shall be sent, together with the Objections, to the other House, by which it shall likewise be reconsidered, and if approved by two thirds of that House, it shall become a Law. But in all such Cases the Votes of both Houses shall be determined by yeas and Nays, and the Names of the Persons voting for and against the Bill shall be entered on the Journal of each House respectively. If any Bill shall not be returned by the President within ten Days (Sunday excepted) after it shall have been presented to him, the Same shall be a Law, in like Manner as if he had signed it, unless the Congress by their Adjournment prevent its Return, in which Case it shall not be a Law.

3. Every Order, Resolution, or Vote to which the Concurrence of the Senate and House of Representatives may be necessary (except on a question of Adjournment) shall be presented to the President of the United States; and before the Same shall take Effect, shall be approved by him, or being disapproved by him, shall be repassed by two thirds of the Senate and House of Representatives, according to the Rules and Limitations prescribed in the Case of a Bill.

Section 8

1. The Congress shall have Power To lay and collect Taxes, Duties, Imposts and Excises, to pay the Debts and provide for the common Defence and general Welfare of the United States; but all Duties, Imposts and Excises shall be uniform throughout the United States;

2. To borrow Money on the credit of the United States;

3. To regulate Commerce with foreign Nations, and among the several States, and with the Indian Tribes;

4. To establish an uniform Rule of Naturalization, and uniform Laws on the subject of Bankruptcies throughout the United States;

5. To coin Money, regulate the Value thereof, and of foreign Coin, and fix the Standard of Weights and Measures;

6. To provide for the Punishment of counterfeiting the Securities and current Coin of the United States;

7. To establish Post Offices and post Roads;

8. To promote the Progress of Science and useful Arts, by securing for limited Times to Authors and Inventors the exclusive Right to their respective Writings and Discoveries;

9. To constitute Tribunals inferior to the supreme Court;

10. To define and punish Piracies and Felonies commited on the high Seas, and Offences against the Law of Nations;

11. To declare War, grant Letters of Marque and Reprisal, and make Rules concerning Captures on Land and Water;

12. To raise and support Armies, but no Appropriation of Money to that Use shall be for a longer Term than two Years;

13. To provide and maintain a Navy;

14. To make Rules for the Government and Regulation of the land and naval Forces;

15. To provide for calling forth the Militia to execute the Laws of the Union, suppress Insurrections and repel Invasions;

16. To provide for organizing, arming, and disciplining, the Militia, and for governing such Part of them as may be employed in the Service of the United States, reserving to the States respectively, the Appointment of the Officers, and the Authority of training the Militia according to the discipline prescribed by Congress;

17. To exercise exclusive Legislation in all Cases whatsoever, over such District (not exceeding ten Miles square) as may, by Cession of Particular States, and the Acceptance of Congress, become the Seat of the Government of the United States, and to exercise like Authority over all Places purchased by the Consent of the Legislature of the State in which the Same shall be, for the Erection of Forts, Magazines, Arsenals, dock-Yards, and other needful Buildings; — And

18. To make all Laws which shall be necessary and proper for carrying into Execution the foregoing Powers, and all other Powers vested by this Constitution in the Government of the United States, or in any Department or Officer thereof.

Section 9

1. The Migration or Importation of such Persons as any of the States now existing shall think proper to admit, shall not be prohibited by the Congress prior to the Year one thousand eight hundred and eight, but a Tax or duty may be imposed on such Importation, not exceeding ten dollars for each Person.

2. The Privilege of the Writ of Habeas Corpus shall not be suspended, unless when in Cases of Rebellion or Invasion the public Safety may require it.

3. No Bill of Attainder or ex post facto Law shall be passed.

4. No capitation, or other direct, Tax shall be laid, unless in Proportion to the Census of Enumeration herein before directed to be taken.[5]

5. No Tax or Duty shall be laid on Articles exported from any State.

6. No Preference shall be given by any Regulation of Commerce or

Revenue to the Ports of one State over those of another; nor shall Vessels bound to, or from, one State, be obliged to enter, clear or pay Duties in another.

7. No Money shall be drawn from the Treasury, but in Consequence of Appropriations made by Law; and a regular Statement and Account of the Receipts and Expenditures of all public Money shall be published from time to time.

8. No Title of Nobility shall be granted by the United States: And no Person holding any Office of Profit or Trust under them, shall, without the Consent of the Congress, accept of any present, Emolument, Office, or Title, of any kind whatever, from any King, Prince or foreign State.

Section 10

1. No State shall enter into any Treaty, Alliance, or Confederation; grant Letters of Marque and Reprisal; coin Money; emit Bills of Credit; make any Thing but gold and silver Coin a Tender in Payment of Debts; pass any Bill of Attainder, ex post facto Law, or Law impairing the Obligation of Contracts, or grant any Title of Nobility.

2. No State shall, without the Consent of the Congress, lay any Imposts or Duties on Imports or Exports, except what may be absolutely necessary for executing it's inspection Laws: and the net Produce of all Duties and Imposts, laid by any State on Imports or Exports, shall be for the Use of the Treasury of the United States; and all such Laws shall be subject to the Revision and Controul of the Congress.

3. No State shall, without the Consent of Congress, lay any Duty of Tonnage, keep Troops, or Ships of War in time of Peace, enter into any Agreement or Compact with another State, or with a foreign Power, or engage in War, unless actually invaded, or in such imminent Danger as will not admit of delay.

Article II

Section 1

1. The executive Power shall be vested in a President of the United States of America. He shall hold his Office during the Term of four Years, and, together with the Vice President, chosen for the same Term, be elected, as follows.

2. Each State shall appoint, in such Manner as the Legislature thereof may direct, a Number of Electors, equal to the whole Number of Senators and Representatives to which the State may be entitled in the Congress: but no Senator or Representative, or Person holding an Office of Trust or Profit under the United States, shall be appointed an Elector.

3. [The Electors shall meet in their respective States, and vote by Ballot for two Persons, of whom one at least shall not be an Inhabitant of the same State with themselves. And they shall make a List of all the Per-

sons voted for, and of the Number of Votes for each; which List they shall sign and certify, and transmit sealed to the Seat of the Government of the United States, directed to the President of the Senate. The President of the Senate shall, in the Presence of the Senate and House of Representatives, open all the Certificates, and the Votes shall then be counted. The Person having the greatest Number of Votes shall be the President, if such Number be a Majority of the whole Number of Electors appointed; and if there be more than one who have such Majority, and have an equal Number of Votes, then the House of Representatives shall immediately chuse by Ballot one of them for President; and if no Person have a Majority, then from the five highest on the list the said House shall in like Manner chuse the President. But in chusing the President, the Votes shall be taken by States, the Representation from each State having one Vote; a quorum for this Purpose shall consist of a Member or Members from two thirds of the States, and a Majority of all the States shall be necessary to a Choice. In every Case, after the Choice of the President, the Person having the greatest Number of Votes of the Electors shall be the Vice President. But if there should remain two or more who have equal Votes, the Senate shall chuse from them by Ballot the Vice President.] [6]

4. The Congress may determine the Time of chusing the Electors, and the Day on which they shall give their Votes; which Day shall be the same throughout the United States.

5. No Person except a natural born Citizen, or a Citizen of the United States, at the time of the Adoption of this Constitution, shall be eligible to the Office of President; neither shall any Person be eligible to that Office who shall not have attained to the Age of thirty five Years, and been fourteen Years a Resident within the United States.

6. In Case of the Removal of the President from Office, or of his Death, Resignation, or Inability to discharge the Powers and Duties of the said Office,[7] the Same shall devolve on the Vice President, and the Congress may by Law provide for the Case of Removal, Death, Resignation or Inability, both of the President and Vice President, declaring what Officer shall then act as President, and such Officer shall act accordingly, until the Disability be removed, or a President shall be elected.

7. The President shall, at stated Times, receive for his Services, a Compensation, which shall neither be encreased nor diminished during the Period for which he shall have been elected, and he shall not receive within that Period any other Emolument from the United States, or any of them.

8. Before he enter on the Execution of his Office, he shall take the following Oath or Affirmation: — "I do solemnly swear (or affirm) that I will faithfully execute the Office of President of the United States, and

will to the best of my Ability, preserve, protect and defend the Constitution of the United States."

Section 2

1. The President shall be Commander in Chief of the Army and Navy of the United States, and of the Militia of the several States, when called into the actual Service of the United States; he may require the Opinion, in writing, of the principal Officer in each of the executive Departments, upon any Subject relating to the Duties of their respective Offices, and he shall have Power to grant Reprieves and Pardons for Offenses against the United States, except in Cases of Impeachment.

2. He shall have Power, by and with the Advice and Consent of the Senate, to make Treaties, provided two thirds of the Senators present concur; and he shall nominate, and by and with the Advice and Consent of the Senate, shall appoint Ambassadors, other public Ministers and Consuls, Judges of the supreme Court, and all other Officers of the United States, whose Appointments are not herein otherwise provided for, and which shall be established by Law: but the Congress may by Law vest the Appointment of such inferior Officers, as they think proper, in the President alone, in the Courts of Law, or in the Heads of Departments.

3. The President shall have Power to fill up all Vacancies that may happen during the Recess of the Senate, by granting Commissions which shall expire at the End of their next Session.

Section 3

He shall from time to time give to the Congress Information of the State of the Union, and recommend to their Consideration such Measures as he shall judge necessary and expedient; he may, on extraordinary Occasions, convene both Houses, or either of them, and in Case of Disagreement between them, with Respect to the Time of Adjournment, he may adjourn them to such Time as he shall think proper; he shall receive Ambassadors and other public Ministers; he shall take Care that the Laws be faithfully executed, and shall Commission all the Officers of the United States.

Section 4

The President, Vice President and all Civil Officers of the United States, shall be removed from office on Impeachment for, and Conviction of, Treason, Bribery, or other high Crimes and Misdemeanors.

Article III

Section 1

The judicial Power of the United States, shall be vested in one supreme Court, and in such inferior Courts as the Congress may from time to time ordain and establish. The Judges, both of the supreme and inferior Courts, shall hold their Offices during good Behaviour, and shall, at stated Times, receive for their Services, a Compensation, which shall not be diminished during their Continuance in Office.

Section 2

1. The judicial Power shall extend to all Cases, in Law and Equity, arising under this Constitution, the Laws of the United States, and Treaties made, or which shall be made, under their Authority; — to all Cases affecting Ambassadors, other public Ministers and Consuls; — to all Cases of admiralty and maritime Jurisdiction; — to Controversies to which the United States shall be a Party; — to Controversies between two or more States; — between a State and Citizens of another State;[8] — between Citizens of different States; — between Citizens of the same State claiming Lands under Grants of different States, and between a State, or the Citizens thereof, and foreign States, Citizens or Subjects.[8]

2. In all Cases affecting Ambassadors, other public Ministers and Consuls, and those in which a State shall be Party, the supreme Court shall have original Jurisdiction. In all the other Cases before mentioned, the supreme Court shall have appellate Jurisdiction, both as to Law and Fact, with such Exceptions, and under such Regulations as the Congress shall make.

3. The Trial of all Crimes, except in cases of Impeachment, shall be by Jury; and such Trial shall be held in the State where the said Crimes shall have been committed; but when not committed within any State, the Trial shall be at such Place or Places as the Congress may by Law have directed.

Section 3

1. Treason against the United States, shall consist only in levying War against them, or in adhering to their Enemies, giving them Aid and Comfort. No Person shall be convicted of Treason unless on the Testimony of two Witnesses to the same overt Act, or on Confession in open Court.

2. The Congress shall have Power to declare the Punishment of Treason, but no Attainder of Treason shall work Corruption of Blood, or Forfeiture except during the Life of the Person attainted.

Article IV

Section 1

Full Faith and Credit shall be given in each State to the public Acts, Records, and judicial Proceedings of every other State. And the Congress may by general Laws prescribe the Manner in which such Acts, Records and Proceedings shall be proved, and the Effect thereof.

Section 2

1. The Citizens of each State shall be entitled to all Privileges and Immunities of Citizens in the several States.

2. A Person charged in any State with Treason, Felony, or other Crime, who shall flee from Justice, and be found in another State, shall on Demand of the executive Authority of the State from which he fled, be delivered up, to be removed to the State having Jurisdiction of the Crime.

3. [No Person held to Service or Labour in one State, under the Laws thereof, escaping into another, shall, in Consequence of any Law or Regulation therein, be discharged from such Service or Labour, but shall be delivered up on Claim of the Party to whom such Service or Labour may be due.][9]

Section 3

1. New States may be admitted by the Congress into this Union; but no new State shall be formed or erected within the Jurisdiction of any other State; nor any State be formed by the Junction of two or more States, or Parts of States, without the Consent of the Legislatures of the States concerned as well as of the Congress.

2. The Congress shall have Power to dispose of and make all needful Rules and Regulations respecting the Territory or other Property belonging to the United States; and nothing in this Constitution shall be so construed as to Prejudice any Claims of the United States, or of any particular State.

Section 4

The United States shall guarantee to every State in this Union a Republican Form of Government, and shall protect each of them against Invasion; and on Application of the Legislature, or of the Executive (when the Legislature cannot be convened) against domestic Violence.

Article V

The Congress, whenever two thirds of both Houses shall deem it necessary, shall propose Amendments to this Constitution, or, on the Application of the Legislatures of two thirds of the several States, shall call a Convention for proposing Amendments, which, in either Case, shall be valid to all Intents and Purposes, as Part of this Constitution, when ratified by the Legislatures of three fourths of the several States, or by Conventions in three fourths thereof, as the one or the other Mode of Ratification may be proposed by the Congress; Provided [that no Amendment which may be made prior to the Year One thousand eight hundred and eight shall in any Manner affect the first and fourth Clauses in the Ninth Section of the first Article; and][10] that no State, without its Consent, shall be deprived of its equal Suffrage in the Senate.

Article VI

1. All Debts contracted and Engagements entered into, before the Adoption of this Constitution, shall be as valid against the United States under this Constitution, as under the Confederation.

2. This Constitution, and the Laws of the United States which shall be made in Pursuance thereof; and all Treaties made, or which shall be made, under the Authority of the United States, shall be the supreme Law of the Land; and the Judges in every State shall be bound thereby, any Thing in the Constitution or Laws of any State to the Contrary notwithstanding.

3. The Senators and Representatives before mentioned, and the Members of the several State Legislatures, and all executive and judicial Officers, both of the United States and of the several States, shall be bound by Oath or Affirmation, to support this Constitution; but no religious Test shall ever be required as a Qualification to any Office or public Trust under the United States.

Article VII

The Ratification of the Conventions of nine States, shall be sufficient for the Establishment of this Constitution between the States so ratifying the Same. Done in Convention by the Unanimous Consent of the States present the Seventeenth Day of September in the Year of our Lord one thousand seven hundred and Eighty seven and of the Independence of the United States of America the Twelfth' In witness whereof We have hereunto subscribed our Names, George Washington, President and deputy from Virginia.

New Hampshire:	John Langdon, Nicholas Gilman.
Massachusetts:	Nathaniel Gorham, Rufus King.
Connecticut:	William Samuel Johnson, Roger Sherman.
New York:	Alexander Hamilton
New Jersey:	William Livingston, David Brearley, William Paterson, Jonathan Dayton.
Pennsylvania:	Benjamin Franklin, Thomas Mifflin, Robert Morris, George Clymer,

Thomas FitzSimons,
Jared Ingersoll,
James Wilson,
Gouverneur Morris.

Delaware:

George Read,
Gunning Bedford Jr.,
John Dickinson,
Richard Bassett,
Jacob Broom.

Maryland:

James McHenry,
Daniel of St. Thomas Jenifer,
Daniel Carroll.

Virginia:

John Blair,
James Madison Jr.

North Carolina:

William Blount,
Richard Dobbs Spaight,
Hugh Williamson.

South Carolina:

John Rutledge,
Charles Cotesworth Pinckney,
Charles Pinckney,
Pierce Butler.

Georgia:

William Few,
Abraham Baldwin.

[The language of the original Constitution, not including the Amendments, was adopted by a convention of the states on September 17, 1787, and was subsequently ratified by the states on the following dates: Delaware, December 7, 1787; Pennsylvania, December 12, 1787; New Jersey, December 18, 1787; Georgia, January 2, 1788; Connecticut, January 9, 1788; Massachusetts, February 6, 1788; Maryland, April 28, 1788; South Carolina, May 23, 1788; New Hampshire, June 21, 1788.

Ratification was completed on June 21, 1788.

The Constitution subsequently was ratified by Virginia, June 25, 1788; New York, July 26, 1788; North Carolina, November 21, 1789; Rhode Island, May 29, 1790; and Vermont, January 10, 1791.]

The Amendments

Amendment I

*(First ten amendments
ratified December 15, 1791.)*

Congress shall make no law respecting an establishment of religion, or prohibiting the free exercise thereof; or abridging the freedom of speech, or of the press; or the right of the people peaceably to assemble, and to petition the Government for a redress of grievances.

Amendment II

A well regulated Militia, being necessary to the security of a free State, the right of the people to keep and bear Arms, shall not be infringed.

Amendment III

No Soldier shall, in time of peace be quartered in any house, without the consent of the Owner, nor in time of war, but in a manner to be prescribed by law.

Amendment IV

The right of the people to be secure in their persons, houses, papers, and effects, against unreasonable searches and seizures, shall not be violated, and no Warrants shall issue, but upon probable cause, supported by Oath or affirmation, and particularly describing the place to be searched, and the persons or things to be seized.

Amendment V

No person shall be held to answer for a capital, or otherwise infamous crime, unless on a presentment or indictment of a Grand Jury, except in cases arising in the land or naval forces, or in the Militia, when in actual service in time of War or public danger; nor shall any person be subject for the same offence to be twice put in jeopardy of life or limb; nor shall be compelled in any criminal case to be a witness against himself, nor be deprived of life, liberty, or property, without due process of law; nor shall private property be taken for public use, without just compensation.

Amendment VI

In all criminal prosecutions, the accused shall enjoy the right to a speedy and public trial, by an impartial jury of the State and district wherein the crime shall have been committed, which district shall have been previously ascertained by law, and to be informed of the nature and cause of the accusation; to be confronted with the witnesses against him; to have compulsory process for obtaining witnesses in his favor, and to have the Assistance of Counsel for his defence.

Amendment VII

In Suits at common law, where the value in controversy shall exceed twenty dollars, the right of trial by jury shall be preserved, and no fact tried by a jury, shall be otherwise re-examined in any Court of the United States, than according to the rules of the common law.

Amendment VIII

Excessive bail shall not be required, nor excessive fines imposed, nor cruel and unusual punishments inflicted.

Amendment IX

The enumeration in the Constitution, of certain rights, shall not be construed to deny or disparage others retained by the people.

Amendment X

The powers not delegated to the United States by the Constitution, nor prohibited by it to the States, are reserved to the States respectively, or to the people.

Amendment XI

(Ratified February 7, 1795)

The Judicial power of the United States shall not be construed to extend to any suit in law or equity, commenced or prosecuted against one of the United States by Citizens of another State, or by Citizens or Subjects of any Foreign State.

Amendment XII

(Ratified June 15, 1804)

The Electors shall meet in their respective states and vote by ballot for President and Vice-President, one of whom, at least, shall not be an inhabitant of the same state with themselves; they shall name in their ballots the person voted for as President, and in distinct ballots the person voted for as Vice-President, and they shall make distinct lists of all persons voted for as President, and of all persons voted for as Vice-President, and of the number of votes for each, which lists they shall sign and certify, and transmit sealed to the seat of the government of the United States, directed to the President of the Senate; — The President of the Senate shall, in the presence of the Senate and House of Representatives, open all the certificates and the votes shall then be counted; — The person having the greatest number of votes for President, shall be the President, if such number be a majority of the whole number of Electors appointed; and if no person have such majority, then from the persons having the highest numbers not exceeding three on the list of those voted for as President, the House of Representatives shall choose immediately, by ballot, the President. But in choosing the President, the votes shall be taken by states, the representation from each state having one vote; a quorum for this purpose shall consist of a member or members from two-thirds of the states, and a majority of all the states shall be necessary to a choice. [And if the House of Representatives shall not choose a President whenever the right of choice shall devolve upon them, before the fourth day of March next following, then the Vice-President shall act as President, as in the case of the death or other constitutional disability of the President —][11] The person having the greatest number of votes as Vice-President, shall be the Vice-President, if such number be a majority of the whole number of Electors appointed, and if no person have a majority, then from the two highest numbers on the list, the Senate shall choose the Vice-President; a quorum for the purpose shall consist of two-thirds of the whole number of Senators, and a majority of the whole number shall be necessary to a choice. But no person constitutionally ineligible to the office of President shall be eligible to that of Vice-President of the United States.

Amendment XIII

(Ratified December 6, 1865)

Section 1

Neither slavery nor involuntary servitude, except as a punishment for crime whereof the party shall have been duly convicted, shall exist within the United States, or any place subject to their jurisdiction.

Section 2

Congress shall have power to enforce this article by appropriate legislation.

Amendment XIV

(Ratified July 9, 1868)

Section 1

All persons born or naturalized in the United States and subject to the jurisdiction thereof, are citizens of the United States and of the State wherein they reside. No State shall make or enforce any law which shall abridge the privileges or immunities of citizens of the United States; nor shall any State deprive any person of life, liberty, or property, without due process of law; nor deny to any person within its jurisdiction the equal protection of the laws.

Section 2

Representatives shall be apportioned among the several States according to their respective numbers, counting the whole number of persons in each State, excluding Indians not taxed. But when the right to vote at any election for the choice of electors for President and Vice President of the United States, Representatives in Congress, the Executive and Judicial officers of a State, or the members of the Legislature thereof, is denied to any of the male inhabitants of such State, being twenty-one years of age,[12] and citizens of the United States, or in any way abridged, except for participation in rebellion, or other crime, the basis of representation therein shall be reduced in the proportion which the number of such male citizens shall bear to the whole number of male citizens twenty-one years of age in such State.

Section 3

No person shall be a Senator or Representative in Congress, or elector of President and Vice President, or hold any office, civil or military, under the United States, or under any State, who, having previously taken an oath, as a member of Congress, or as an officer of the United States, or as a member of any State legislature, or as an executive or judicial officer of any State, to support the Constitution of the United States, shall have engaged in insurrection or rebellion against the same, or given aid or comfort to the enemies thereof. But Congress may by a vote of two-thirds of each House, remove such disability.

Section 4

The validity of the public debt of the United States, authorized by law, including debts incurred for payment of pensions and bounties for services in suppressing insurrection or rebellion, shall not be questioned. But neither the United States nor any State shall assume or pay any debt or obligation incurred in aid of insurrection or rebellion against the United States, or any claim for the loss or emancipation of any slave; but all such debts, obligations and claims shall be held illegal and void.

Section 5

The Congress shall have power to enforce, by appropriate legislation, the provisions of this article.

Amendment XV

(Ratified February 3, 1870)

Section 1

The right of citizens of the United States to vote shall not be denied or abridged by the United States or by any State on account of race, color, or previous condition of servitude.

Section 2
The Congress shall have power to enforce this article by appropriate legislation.

Amendment XVI
(Ratified February 3, 1913)
The Congress shall have power to lay and collect taxes on incomes, from whatever source derived, without apportionment among the several States, and without regard to any census or enumeration.

Amendment XVII
(Ratified April 8, 1913)
The Senate of the United States shall be composed of two Senators from each State, elected by the people thereof, for six years; and each Senator shall have one vote. The electors in each State shall have the qualifications requisite for electors of the most numerous branch of the State legislatures.

When vacancies happen in the representation of any State in the Senate, the executive authority of such State shall issue writs of election to fill such vacancies: *Provided,* That the legislature of any State may empower the executive thereof to make temporary appointments until the people fill the vacancies by election as the legislature may direct.

This amendment shall not be so construed as to affect the election or term of any Senator chosen before it becomes valid as part of the Constitution.

Amendment XVIII
(Ratified January 16, 1919)
Section 1
After one year from the ratification of this article the manufacture, sale, or transportation of intoxicating liquors within, the importation thereof into, or the exportation thereof from the United States and all territory subject to the jurisdiction thereof for beverage purposes is hereby prohibited.

Section 2
The Congress and the several States shall have concurrent power to enforce this article by appropriate legislation.

Section 3
This article shall be inoperative unless it shall have been ratified as

an amendment to the Constitution by the legislatures of the several States, as provided in the Constitution, within seven years from the date of the submission hereof to the States by the Congress.][13]

Amendment XIX
(Ratified August 18, 1920)

The right of citizens of the United States to vote shall not be denied or abridged by the United States or by any State on account of sex.

Congress shall have power to enforce this article by appropriate legislation.

Amendment XX
(Ratified January 23, 1933)

Section 1

The terms of the President and Vice President shall end at noon on the 20th day of January, and the terms of Senators and Representatives at noon on the 3d day of January, of the years in which such terms would have ended if this article had not been ratified; and the terms of their successors shall then begin.

Section 2

The Congress shall assemble at least once in every year, and such meeting shall begin at noon on the 3d day of January, unless they shall by law appoint a different day.

Section 3[14]

If, at the time fixed for the beginning of the term of the President, the President elect shall have died, the Vice President elect shall become President. If a President shall not have been chosen before the time fixed for the beginning of his term, or if the President elect shall have failed to qualify, then the Vice President elect shall act as President until a President shall have qualified; and the Congress may by law provide for the case wherein neither a President elect nor a Vice President elect shall have qualified, declaring who shall then act as President, or the manner in which one who is to act shall be selected, and such person shall act accordingly until a President or Vice President shall have qualified.

Section 4

The Congress may by law provide for the case of the death of any of the persons from whom the House of Representatives may choose a President whenever the right of choice shall have devolved upon them, and for the case of the death of any of the persons from whom the Senate may choose a Vice President whenever the right of choice shall have devolved upon them.

Section 5

Sections 1 and 2 shall take effect on the 15th day of October following the ratification of this article.

Section 6

This article shall be inoperative unless it shall have been ratified as an amendment to the Constitution by the legislatures of three-fourths of the several States within seven years from the date of its submission.

Amendment XXI

(Ratified December 5, 1933)

Section 1

The eighteenth article of amendment to the Constitution of the United States is hereby repealed.

Section 2

The transportation or importation into any State, Territory or possession of the United States for delivery or use therein of intoxicating liquors, in violation of the laws thereof, is hereby prohibited.

Section 3

This article shall be inoperative unless it shall have been ratified as an amendment to the Constitution by conventions in the several States, as provided in the Constitution, within seven years from the date of the submission hereof to the States by the Congress.

Amendment XXII

(Ratified February 27, 1951)

Section 1

No person shall be elected to the office of the President more than twice, and no person who has held the office of President, or acted as President, for more than two years of a term to which some other person was elected President shall be elected to the office of the President more than once. But this Article shall not apply to any person holding the office of President when this Article was proposed by the Congress, and shall not prevent any person who may be holding the office of President, or acting as President, during the term within which this Article become operative from holding the office of President or acting as President during the remainder of such term.

Section 2

This Article shall be inoperative unless it shall have been ratified as an amendment to the Constitution by the legislatures of three-fourths of the several States within seven years from the date of its submission to the States by the Congress.

Amendment XXIII

(Ratified March 29, 1961)

Section 1

The District constituting the seat of Government of the United States shall appoint in such manner as the Congress may direct:

A number of electors of President and Vice President equal to the whole number of Senators and Representatives in Congress to which the District would be entitled if it were a State, but in no event more than the least populous State; they shall be in addition to those appointed by the States, but they shall be considered, for the purposes of the election of President and Vice President, to be electors appointed by a State; and they shall meet in the District and perform such duties as provided by the twelfth article of amendment.

Section 2

The Congress shall have power to enforce this article by appropriate legislation.

Amendment XXIV

(Ratified January 23, 1964)

Section 1

The right of citizens of the United States to vote in any primary or other election for President or Vice President, for electors for President or Vice President, or for Senator or Representative in Congress, shall not be denied or abridged by the United States or any State by reason of failure to pay any poll tax or other tax.

Section 2

The Congress shall have power to enforce this article by appropriate legislation.

Amendment XXV

(Ratified February 10, 1967)

Section 1

In case of the removal of the President from office or of his death or resignation, the Vice President shall become President.

Section 2

Whenever there is a vacancy in the office of the Vice President, the President shall nominate a Vice President who shall take office upon confirmation by a majority vote of both Houses of Congress.

Section 3

Whenever the President transmits to the President pro tempore of the Senate and the Speaker of the House of Representatives his written declaration that he is unable to discharge the powers and duties of his office, and until he transmits to them a written declaration to the contrary, such powers and duties shall be discharged by the Vice President as Acting President.

Section 4

Whenever the Vice President and a majority of either the principal officers of the executive departments or of such other body as Congress may by law provide, transmit to the President pro tempore of the Senate and the Speaker of the House of Representatives their written declaration that the President is unable to discharge the powers and duties of his office, the Vice President shall immediately assume the powers and duties of the office as Acting President.

Thereafter, when the President transmits to the President pro tempore of the Senate and the Speaker of the House of Representatives his written declaration that no inability exists, he shall resume the powers and duties of his office unless the Vice President and a majority of either the principal officers of the executive department or of such other body as Congress may by law provide, transmit within four days to the President pro tempore of the Senate and the Speaker of the House of Representatives their written declaration that the President is unable to discharge the powers and duties of his office. Thereupon Congress shall decide the issue, assembling within forty-eight hours for that purpose if not in session. If the Congress, within twenty-one days after receipt of the latter written declaration, or, if Congress is not in session, within twenty-one days after Congress is required to assemble, determines by two-thirds vote of both houses that the President is unable to discharge the powers and duties of his office, the Vice President shall continue to discharge the same as Acting President; otherwise, the President shall resume the powers and duties of his office.

Amendment XXVI

(Ratified July 1, 1971)

Section 1

The right of citizens of the United States, who are eighteen years of age or older, to vote shall not be denied or abridged by the United States or by any State on account of age.

Section 2

The Congress shall have power to enforce this article by appropriate legislation.

Notes

1. The part in brackets was changed by section 2 of the Fourteenth Amendment.
2. The part in brackets was changed by section 1 of the Seventeenth Amendment.
3. The part in brackets was changed by the second paragraph of the Seventeenth Amendment.
4. The part in brackets was changed by section 2 of the Twentieth Amendment.
5. The Sixteenth Amendment gave Congress the power to tax incomes.
6. The material in brackets has been superseded by the Twelfth Amendment.
7. This provision has been affected by the Twenty-fifth Amendment.
8. These clauses were affected by the Eleventh Amendment.
9. This paragraph has been superseded by the Thirteenth Amendment.
10. Obsolete.
11. The part in brackets has been superseded by section 3 of the Twentieth Amendment.
12. See the Twenty-sixth Amendment.
13. This Amendment was repealed by section 1 of the Twenty-first Amendment.
14. See the Twenty-fifth Amendment.

Source: U.S. Congress, House, Committee on the Judiciary, *The Constitution of the United States of America, As Amended Through July 1971,* H. Doc. 93-215, 93rd Cong., 2nd sess., 1974.

Bicentennial Presentations

The following list, prepared in late 1987, includes television programs, video cassettes, films, filmstrips, radio programs, audio cassettes, scripts, and other presentations designed for the Bicentennial of the Constitution. The *Educational Film Video Locator* (1986) provides information on additional films and video programs. Lists of related materials can also be obtained from the Commission on the Bicentennial of the United States Constitution, 736 Jackson Place, Washington, D.C. 20503, and from *The U.S. Constitution Bicentennial: A WE THE PEOPLE Resource Book,* published by the American Bar Association and the American Library Association.

Scripts
After the Revolution, a play about ratification in New Hampshire. Contact New Hampshire Commission on the Bicentennial of the United States Constitution, Middletown Road, Wolfeboro, N.H. 03894.

Alexander Hamilton, a three-act play about the political rivalry between Hamilton and Aaron Burr. Contact Daniel Fernandez, 601 W. 176th Street, New York, N.Y. 10033.

The Constitution, 110 scripts with corresponding quizzes. Contact National Association of Broadcasters, 1771 N Street N.W., Washington, D.C. 20036.

The Constitution: Little Short of a Miracle, one-act drama, which takes place on September 17, 1787, written by George T. Blume for middle and high schools. Contact the American Legion, P.O. Box 1055, Indianapolis, Ind. 46206.

The Constitution of the United States, script, props, and activities for elementary school children, written and illustrated by Janice Howes. A thirty-five-page story book is also available. Contact Teachers Publishing House, P.O. Box 9358, Canton, Ohio 44711-9358.

The Constitutional Dialogues, three dialogues among members of the founding generation about constitutional issues, by Ferdinand Alexi Hilenski. Contact Academic Development Office, SDEV-106, Fayetteville, Ark. 72701.

Decision at Richmond: June 1788, a three-act play on the ratification battle in Virginia, by Robert O. Byrd. Contact World without War Publications, 421 S. Wabash, Chicago, Ill. 60605.

Father Anonymous, a three-act play, based in Massachusetts, that takes place from the Boston Massacre until the ratification of the Constitution. Contact Robert Blecker, 15 Bayberry Ridge, Roslyn, N.Y. 11576.

Mercy, a one-act play reenacting the life of Mercy Otis Warren (1782-1814), by Francine Ringold, 3215 S. Yorktown, Tulsa, Okla. 74105.

A More Perfect Union, a play by William K. Paynter about the Annapolis Convention, for adult audiences. Contact Maryland Office for the Bicentennial of the U.S. Constitution, Maryland State Archives, Box 828, Annapolis, Md. 21404.

Noah Webster's Words with Music, one-hour musical play about Noah Webster and the ratification, by Wade Barnes, 3A-20 Beekman Place, New York, N.Y. 10022.

Patriots and Thieves: A Musical Tale of 1787, by Ken Stone and Jan Powell, for ages 12+. Contact Ken Stone, 513 South Pacific Avenue, #2, Glendale, Calif. 91204.

The Sun is Rising; The Eagle Soars; 1787, a multimedia docudrama set in 1787 as the founders create the Constitution. Contact John A. Wiegand, 3455 Doris Road, Cleveland, Ohio 44111.

The United States Constitution: A Nontrivial Pursuit, fifty-two two-minute radio scripts telling the story of the Constitutional Convention, by Walter Mead, 1279 Grizzly Peak Boulevard, Berkeley, Calif. 94708.

We All Are a Part of It: USA 1776-1840, by Jean Lutterman. Musical play for elementary school students. Contact Norwood School, 8821 River Road, Box L, Bethesda, Md. 20817.

Touring Plays

Four Little Pages, a play about the founders. Tours the national parks—all ages. Produced by Franklin S. Roberts Associates, Philadelphia, Pa. Contact Division of Interpretation, Recreation and Visitor Services, National Park Service, 1100 Ohio Drive S.W., Washington, D.C. 20242.

The Public Happiness: Thomas Jefferson's Crusade against Ignorance. Contact East Lynne Company, 281 Lincoln Avenue, Secaucus, N.J. 07094.

Slide Shows

The Black American and the Bicentennial of the U.S. Constitution: A Mass Media Perspective, a traveling exhibit consisting of 175 items of print, paintings, documents, posters, postcards, newspapers, and magazines from the 1700s to the 1960s, with a slide show lecture. Contact Charles E. Simmons, P.O. Box 2235, Washington, D.C. 20013-2235.

Blessing of Liberty, sixteen-minute sound/slide show. Contact the National Audiovisual Center, 8700 Edgewater Drive, Capital Heights, Md. 20743-3701.

Films, Filmstrips, Television, Video Cassettes

An Abridgement of Hope: The Story of John Punch, a documentary about an indentured servant in colonial Virginia, preceded by an introduction dealing with the roots of freedom in the colonial period. Produced by Past America, 12100 N.E. 16th Avenue, Miami, Fla. 33161.

America: Colonization to Constitution, five sound filmstrips for grades 5-12. No. 03719. Other filmstrips available on American government. Contact National Geographic Society, Educational Services, Dept. 87, Washington, D.C. 20036.

American Forum: Madison, Jefferson, and Hamilton and Their Relationship to the Constitution. Three half-hours. Produced by World News Institute, P.O. Box 484, Great Falls, Va. 22066. Also available from the Southeastern Education Committee Association, P.O. Box 5966, 2628 Millwood Avenue, Columbia, S.C. 29250.

The Blessings of Liberty, ABC News Special on the Philadelphia Convention. Peter Jennings, David Brinkley, and Ted Koppel, hosts. Aired September 16, 1987. A sixteen-minute video is available. Contact Mail Order Department, Eastern National Parks and Monuments, 313 Walnut Street, Philadelphia, Pa. 19106.

A Celebration of Citizenship, live broadcast on ABC of events September 16, 1987, at the Capitol, including presentations by President Reagan and retired chief justice Warren Burger. Contact ABC, 1330 Avenue of the Americas, New York, N.Y. 10019.

The Constitution, one-minute video/audio spots of comments by spouses of members of Congress. Contact National Association of Broadcasters, 1771 N Street N.W., Washington, D.C. 20036.

The Constitution: A Framework to Govern the Nation. High school students question Washington law professor Edward Bruce about the importance of the Constitution in the 1980s. Originally produced for telecast over C-SPAN. Close Up Foundation. Contact Social Studies School Service, 10200 Jefferson Boulevard, Room R-2, P.O. Box 802, Culver City, Calif. 90232-0802.

The Constitution—A Living Document, a six-part filmstrip that explores the dynamic nature of the Constitution and encourages students to comment on interpretations of its meaning. #07968-920. Contact GA

Guidance Associates, Communications Park, Box 3000, Mount Kisco, N.Y. 10549-9989.

The Constitution at 200: Why Does It Still Work? Four parts, Teacher's Guide, Library Kit. #31330-920. The evolution of the Constitution, from the historic political theories on which it is founded, to today's modern interpretations. Video or sound filmstrips. Contact GA Guidance Associates, Communications Park, Box 3000, Mount Kisco, N.Y. 10549-9989, or Sales Department, Prentice Hall Media, Box 1050, Mount Kisco, N.Y. 10549.

The Constitution: Foundation of Our Government examines the seven constitutional articles; outlines the principles of republicanism, federalism, separation of powers, and checks and balances; and explains the amendment process, congressional elaboration, and judicial review. Includes three filmstrips with cassettes, a library kit, and a Teacher's Guide. Also filmstrips (GU-6140); or video cassette (GU-6140V). Contact Opportunities for Learning, 20417 Nordof Street, Dept. VR, Chatsworth, Calif. 91311.

Constitution Minutes, twenty-six one-minute spots on the Constitution. Remarks by historians, actors, and dignitaries. Contact Lou Reda Productions, Box 68, 44 North Second Street, Easton, Pa. 18042.

Constitution of the United States, a nineteen-minute look at the Constitutional Convention as seen through the eyes of James Madison. Available in VHS. Contact Encyclopaedia Britannica Education Corp., 425 N. Michigan Avenue, Chicago, Ill. 60611.

The Constitution Project, a nonprofit educational corporation, is developing a seven-part series for public television. The first two programs are *The Ghosts of '87* and *The Road to Runnymede.* Additional programs will address freedom of speech and religion, minority rights, and criminal justice. Contact Matthew E. Simek, 1126 S.W. 13th Avenue, Portland, Ore. 67205.

The Constitution: That Delicate Balance. Thirteen-part series (one hour each) presented by the Public Broadcasting Service and produced by Columbia University Seminars on Media and Society. Judges, scholars, lawyers, public officials, and journalists discuss constitutional issues. First aired in January 1983. Contact the Annenberg/CPB Collection, 1231 Wilmette Avenue, Wilmette, Ill. 60091.

The Constitution: We Live It Every Day, an hour-long program hosted by David Hartman on ABC, aired September 8, 1987. Four stories about personal freedom. Contact ABC, 1330 Avenue of the Americas, New York, N.Y. 10019.

Constitutional Law in Action. NYT851C-V6. Four filmstrips—"Search and Seizure," "Due Process, Right to Counsel," and "State Action"—dramatize actual cases, involving rights granted by the Constitution. The class is invited to interpret the case before hearing the actual Supreme Court verdict. Four color filmstrips, four cassettes, guide. Contact Social Studies School Service, 10200 Jefferson Boulevard, Room R-2, P.O. Box 802, Culver City, Calif. 90232-0802.

A Design for Liberty: The American Constitution, a twenty-eight-minute program on liberty from the American Revolution to the Constitution. Contact Modern Talking Pictures, 5000 Park Street North, St. Petersburg, Fla. 33709.

John Dickinson, sixty-minute film produced by the Delaware Heritage Commission, Carvel State Office Building, 820 N. French Street, Wilmington, Del. 19801.

Echoes of Freedom, a thirty-second public service television announcement recorded in January 1987 at Independence Hall by the Army Reserve program. Contact Office Chief, Army Reserve, Attention: DAAR-PA, Room 434, 2461 Eisenhower Avenue, Alexandria, Va. 22331.

Edmund Ross. Black-and-white. The Kansas senator blocks the impeachment of Andrew Johnson, basing his vote on the trial evidence instead of the dictates of his party's leaders. Part of the television series *Profiles in Courage.* Fifty minutes. Contact Social Studies School Service, 10200 Jefferson Boulevard, Room R-2, P.O. Box 802, Culver City, Calif. 90232-0802.

The 1879 Trial of Ponca Chief Standing Bear, a ninety-minute docudrama of the 1879 legal case that established that native Americans were recognized under the Constitution. Cassette available. Nonbroadcast use only. Contact Nebraska ETV Network, P.O. Box 83111, Lincoln, Neb. 68501.

Equal Justice under the Law, six half-hour dramas that cover the career of the first Supreme Court chief justice, John Marshall, through his most important decisions (in cases such as *Marbury v. Madison, Gibbons v. Odgen, McCulloch v. Maryland,* and the trial of Aaron Burr). Produced by WQED Pittsburgh and the Judicial Conference of the United States. Contact Social Studies School Service, 10200 Jefferson Boulevard, Room R-2, P.O. Box 802, Culver City, Calif. 90232-0802.

The Fifth Amendment. SED107C-V6. The evolution and application of the controversial protection against self-incrimination, discussing the impact of the McCarthy hearings in the 1950s and the Miranda decision. Two color filmstrips, two cassettes, eight reproducible pages, guide. Contact Social Studies School Service, 10200 Jefferson Boulevard, Room B-2, P.O. Box 802, Culver City, Calif. 90232-0802.

The First Amendment: That Radical Document examines the First Amendment from the perspective of current issues. Produced by WHYY-Philadelphia, 150 North Sixth Street, Philadelphia, Pa. 19106.

The First Freedom, a documentary examining religious freedom through the Virginia statute that served as the basis for the First Amendment. Contact Film America, 1832 Biltmore Street N.W., Washington, D.C. 20009.

Government as It Is: The Executive, Legislative, and Judicial Branches. Two versions available on government branches—thirty-minute tapes and one-hour tapes on all three branches or individual branches. Available only to organizations and educational institutions. Not for TV rebroadcast. Contact Pyramid Film & Video, Box 1048, Santa Monica, Calif. 90406.

A Grand Experiment: Bringing the U.S. Constitution into the Classroom, two interactive satellite teleconferences for secondary school teachers to discuss teaching resources. Hosted by John A. Moore, Jr. Contact Distance Learning Center, California State Polytechnic University, 3801 W. Temple Avenue, Pomona, Calif. 91768.

Inside the Constitution, a weekly series that appeared on C-SPAN from January to December 1987. The series included interviews that examine the historical development of the Constitution. C-SPAN also aired a variety of special events during 1987, including a conference of the governors of the original thirteen states in May in Philadelphia and the Philadelphia celebration on September 17. Contact C-SPAN, 444 North Capitol Street N.W., Suite 412, Washington, D.C. 20001.

Inventing a Nation, a twenty-minute tape from the "America: A Personal History of the United States" series. Available only to organizations and educational institutions. Not for TV rebroadcast. Contact Time-Life Films, 100 Eisenhower Drive, Paramus, N.J. 07652.

Korematsu v. United States, a sixty-minute docudrama that addresses the constitutional issues relating to the internment of Japanese-Americans during World War II. Contact Past America, 12100 N.E. 16th Avenue, Miami, Fla. 33161.

A Little Rebellion Now and Then: Prologue to the Constitution, a thirty-minute program on the years after the Revolution, culminating in Shays's Rebellion and leading to the Constitutional Convention. Available only to organizations and educational institutions. Not for TV rebroadcast. Contact Churchill Films, 662 N. Robertson Boulevard, Los Angeles, Calif. 90069.

Main Street, a series of five youth-oriented programs discussing the Constitution. Produced by NBC and hosted by Bryant Gumble. Contact NBC Washington, 4001 Nebraska Avenue N.W., Washington, D.C. 20016.

The Making of the American Constitution, a forty-four-minute video docudrama on the Convention of 1787. Volume one of three. Cable networks and educational use. Contact American Study Center/Radio America, 499 South Capitol Street S.W., Suite 404,

Washington, D.C. 20003.

Miracle at Philadelphia, an ABC production of Catherine Drinker Bowen's book. Funded by General Motors. Contact ABC, 1330 Avenue of the Americas, New York, N.Y. 10019.

A More Perfect Union: The Constitution at 200, a twenty-two-week television series, which aired from April to September 1987, of two-minute vignettes, produced by Cable News Network (CNN). Daily segments ran six times a day examining specific sections of the Constitution, Bill of Rights, and landmark Supreme Court decisions. CNN also produced eleven half-hour programs of a similar nature. Contact CNN, 100 International Boulevard, Atlanta, Ga. 30348. Also available as a series of eight forty-minute videotapes on the framers, the Constitutional Convention, and major Supreme Court decisions. Contact Britannica Films, 425 N. Michigan Avenue, Chicago, Ill. 60611.

Moyers: In Search of the Constitution, a series of ten one-hour conversations between Bill Moyers and philosophers, Supreme Court justices, judges, scholars, and historians. Aired from April to June 1987. Funded by General Motors; presented by WNET-New York and WTVS-Detroit. Contact WNET-New York, 356 West 58th Street, New York, N.Y. 10019.

Moyers: Report from Philadelphia, a series of ninety three-minute historical perspective commentaries by Bill Moyers on the Constitutional Convention, which aired from May to September 1987. Contact WNET-New York, 356 West 58th Street, New York, N.Y. 10019.

Musical Salute to the Constitution, a forty-three-minute musical salute as seen through the eyes of children. Contact Young Citizens for America, 310 Constitution Avenue N.E., Washington, D.C. 20002.

New Tests of the First Amendment. NYT122C-V6. A teacher's guide with discussion questions and a reproducible worksheet. New York Times 1980. Contact Social Studies School Service, 10200 Jefferson Boulevard, Room R-2, P.O. Box 802, Culver City, Calif. 90232-0802.

Our Living Constitution, two sound filmstrips for grades 5-12, seventeen minutes each: "The Constitution and the Bill of Rights" and "Amendments 11 though 26." No. 04060. Other filmstrips available on the U.S. government. Contact National Geographic Society, Educational Services, Dept. 87, Washington, D.C. 20036.

Portrait of a Daughter, a thirty-minute slide show with script on the evolution of documents from the Mayflower compact to the present. Available in slides with script. Contact Daughters of the American Revolution, 1776 D Street N.W., Washington, D.C. 20006

Presidents in Crisis, a four-part PBS series. Produced by WGBY-TV, 44 Hampden Street, Springfield, Mass. 01103.

The Presidency and the Constitution explores the domestic and foreign policy issues facing the modern presidency in eight one-hour programs. Tapes available. Contact Media and Society Seminars, Columbia University School of Journalism, New York, N.Y. 10027.

Rainbow's End, a half-hour PBS television program, entitled "Rules, Laws, and the U.S. Constitution," for deaf children, 8-12 years of age. Produced by D.E.A.F. Media, 2600 Tenth Street, Berkeley, Calif. 94710.

Searching for Justice: Three American Stories, an examination of three Supreme Court cases, one dealing with capital punishment, one with abortion, and one about racial discrimination. Includes commentary by Associate Justice Thurgood Marshall. Carl Rowan, moderator. Aired September 1987. Contact Gannett Broadcasting Group, 1611 W. Peachtree Street N.E., Atlanta, Ga. 30309.

Signers of the Constitution, a set featuring thirty-nine one-minute spots on the signers and a six-minute, forty-second piece on George Washington. Remarks by Secretary of the Army John O. Marsh, Jr. Contact U.S. Army, Command Info. Unit, Electronic Media Branch, Building 160/2, 2nd & M Streets S.E., Washington, D.C. 20315-0300.

Simple Justice: The Story of Brown v. Topeka Board of Education *(1954) Supreme Court Decision,* a four-hour mini-series. Produced by New Images Productions, 919 Euclid Avenue, Berkeley, Calif. 94708.

Supreme Court Decisions That Changed the Nation. Marbury v. Madison; McCulloch v. Maryland; the *Dred Scott* decision; *Plessy v. Ferguson; Brown v. Board of Education; Gideon v. Wainwright;* and *Miranda v. Arizona.* Each filmstrip is accompanied by a teacher's guide and a library kit. Contact GA Guidance Associates, Communications Park, Box 3000, Mount Kisco, N.Y. 10549-9989.

This Constitution: A History. Five thirty-minute television programs: the Federal City, South Carolina and the United States, Prayer in the Classroom, the Pursuit of Equality, and the Rise and Fall of Prohibition. Videocassettes available. Produced by the International University Consortium (IUC) and Maryland Public Television, in cooperation with Project '87. Contact Maryland Public TV, Maryland Center for Public Broadcasting, 11767 Bonita Avenue, Owings Mills, Md. 21117.

This Honorable Court, two one-hour programs examining the history and function of the Supreme Court. Produced by WETA; hosted by Paul Duke. Contact WETA, P.O. Box 2626, Washington, D.C. 20013.

This Precious Heritage: Civil Rights in the United States. Anti-Defamation League. AD144C-V6. Color filmstrip, cassette, guide. Contact Social Studies School Service, 10200 Jefferson Boulevard, Room R-2, P.O. Box 802, Culver City, Calif. 90232-0802.

To Form a More Perfect Union, a thirty-one-minute program depicting the Federalists' and Anti-Federalists' struggle in ratifying the Constitution. Produced by National Geographic Society, 17th and M Streets N.W., Washington, D.C. 20036.

The U.S. Constitution, six thirty-minute programs, hosted by Bill Moyers, on limited government, federalism, separation of powers, free speech, equal protection, and the economy. Contact Agency for Instructional Technology, Box A, Bloomington, Ind. 47402.

The United States Constitution: A Document for Democracy. This video and sound filmstrip production, narrated by newscaster Bill Kurtis, explores the Constitution as a living framework for government and introduces the framers. Available on VHS cassette and filmstrip. Grades 5-9. Contact SVE, 1342 W. Diversey Avenue, Chicago, Ill. 60614.

The U.S. Constitution in Action: Creating a Federal Union. Four fifteen-minute filmstrips. Educational use only. Contact Random House, Educational Enrichment Materials, Dept. 9261, 400 Haan Road, Westminister, Md. 21157.

The U.S. Constitution in Action: The Living Document. Four fifteen-minute filmstrips. Educational use only. Contact Random House, Educational Enrichment Materials, Dept. 9261, 400 Haan Road, Westminister, Md. 21157.

The U.S. Constitution: Origins in Classical Greece. A thirteen-minute videotape that discusses the Greek influence on the Philadelphia Convention, the Constitution, and architecture in America. VHS cassette, 16 mm film available. Produced by American Hellenic Alliance, 1700 North Moore Street, Suite 927, Arlington, Va. 22209.

Visions of the Constitution, a series of five programs that examines the Constitution and how it functions. Produced by WQED and Metropolian Pittsburgh Public Broadcasting. Hosted by Judy Woodruff and Tom Gerety. Contact WQED, 4802 Fifth Avenue, Pittsburgh, Pa. 15213.

We the People, four one-hour public affairs programs, produced by the American Bar Association and KQED-TV, San Francisco. Peter Jennings, host. Eight thirty-minute videocassettes available with study guide. Contact Films for the Humanities, P.O. Box 2053, Princeton, N.J. 08543.

We the People 200: The Celebration of the Bicentennial of the Constitution of the United States. Live coverage of the events in Philadelphia on September 17, 1987, by CBS. Contact CBS, 51 West 52nd Street, New York, N.Y. 10019.

The Work of Peace: The Treaty of Paris, 1783, film and curriculum materials pertaining to the Treaty of Paris, which ended the American War of Independence. Contact Office of Telecommunications,

Natural History Building, Room C22B, Smithsonian Institution, Washington, D.C. 20560.

Radio, Records, Audio Cassettes

Bill of Rights Radio Education Project, a series of thirteen half-hour radio documentaries on controversial issues (for example, the insanity defense, abortion, gun control, sex education, prayer in the public schools). Audio cassettes. Produced by the American Civil Liberties Union and Pacifica Foundation. Contact Pacifica Radio Archives, 5316 Venice Boulevard, Los Angeles, Calif. 90019.

Children's Guide to the Constitution, audio tape. Audio cassette available. Contact American Study Center, 499 South Capitol Street S.W., Suite 404, Washington, D.C. 20003.

A Choral Reading of Our Enduring Constitution. LP record or cassette. Contact Heritage Enterprises, 325 N. 13th Street, Philadelphia, Pa. 19107-1118.

The Constitutional Convention, twenty-four one-minute radio messages recorded by actor Gregory Peck that focus on the delegates and issues of the Constitutional Convention held at Philadelphia in 1787. Produced by the Constitutional Rights Foundation and the Los Angeles County Bar Association. The recorded messages will be distributed free of charge to radio stations nationwide through the cooperation of the National Association of Broadcasters. They will also be made available on cassette and in printed form for distribution to schools in Los Angeles County. Contact National Association of Broadcasters, 1771 N Street N.W., Washington, D.C. 20036.

Dateline 1787, National Radio Theatre of Chicago. Thirteen half-hour weekly programs. Available free to public radio stations. Contact NRT, 600 N. McClurg Court, Suite 502-A, Chicago, Ill. 60611.

The Declaration of Independence and How It Came About, first of the Americana series by Words and Music Studio, P.O. Box 156, Newtonville, Mass. 01260.

I Love America, audio tape of songs about the Constitution and America by children. Audio cassette available. Contact Young Citizens for America, 310 Constitution Avenue N.E., Washington, D.C. 20002.

The Living Constitution of the United States, a recorded reading of the Constitution, with music. Available on LP record or cassette. Contact Project Constitution, P.O. Box 302, Little Falls, N.J. 07424.

Mr. Adams and Mr. Jefferson: A Dramatization for the Radio. Contact Carleton College, Northfield, Minn. 55057.

News Reports, eighty-eight three-minute programs. Contact America Studies Center, 426 C Street N.E., Washington, D.C. 20003.

Voices of Freedom, three-minute segments by Walter Cronkite on tape, reciting passages about the Constitution by George Washington.

User's guide available. Produced by People for the American Way, 2000 M Street N.W., Washington, D.C. 20036.

We the People, twelve thirty- to sixty-second audio documentaries on the Constitution, the Soldier Signers, and the role of the Army Reserves in the ratification process. Audio cassette available. Contact Office Chief, Army Reserves, Attention: DAAR-PA, Room 434, 2461 Eisenhower Avenue, Alexandria Va. 22331.

Bibliography

Kermit L. Hall

Since its creation, the American Constitution has stimulated a steady stream of literature about both its history and operation. This bibliography is an introduction to that vast literature. It is selective in the truest sense of the word. The numbers of books devoted to the Constitution run into the thousands; writings in history and political science journals and law reviews are even more extensive. This brief bibliography should nonetheless have value for teachers of American history and civics and the general reading public curious about our constitutional history. A fuller listing of the historical literature on the Constitution, especially that available in article form, can be found in Kermit L. Hall, comp., *A Comprehensive Bibliography of American Constitutional and Legal History,* 5 vols. (Millwood, N.Y., Kraus Thomson International, 1984).

Creation of the Constitution and the Founding

Bailyn, Bernard. *The Ideological Origins of the American Revolution* (Cambridge, Mass.: Belknap Press of Harvard University Press, 1967).

A penetrating analysis of the ideas that shaped both the revolutionary era's politics and the development of a distinctive form of American constitutionalism. Bailyn identifies English republican writers as the chief source of American constitutional thought.

Becker, Carl L. *The Declaration of Independence: A Study in the History of Political Ideas* (New York: Alfred A. Knopf, 1956 [1st ed., 1922].)

An indispensable introduction to the text of the Declaration of Independence. Becker believed that the ideas of John Locke shaped not only the Declaration but the American Constitution, a position hotly disputed in Garry Wills, *Inventing America: Jefferson's Declaration of Independence* (Garden City, N.Y.: Doubleday, 1978).

Wills contends that Locke counted for little and that the ideas of the Scottish Moral Enlightenment better explain the Declaration.

Bowen, Catherine Drinker. *Miracle at Philadelphia: The Story of the Constitutional Convention, May to September 1787* (Boston: Little, Brown & Co., 1966).

293

A highly readable and reliable account of the day-to-day events in the Constitutional Convention.

Brant, Irving. *The Bill of Rights: Its Origin and Meaning* (New York: New American Library, 1967 (paperback); Indianapolis: Bobbs-Merrill, 1965 (hardback)).

A history of the Bill of Rights from its beginnings to the recent past. Brant, who was also the biographer of James Madison, offers valuable insights into the intellectual background of the founding era. On the politics of the Bill of Rights, a fascinating subject in its own right, see Robert A. Rutland, *The Birth of the Bill of Rights, 1776-1791* (Chapel Hill: University of North Carolina Press, 1955).

Corwin, Edward D. *The "Higher Law" Background of American Constitutional Law* (Ithaca, N.Y.: Cornell University Press, 1955).

An eloquent introduction to the idea of the Constitution as "Higher Law." From the time of its first publication in the *Harvard Law Review* in 1929 this exploration of the remote sources of the American Constitution has been one of the most universally admired and heavily used essays in the history of constitutional law and political thought.

Levy, Leonard W., ed. *Essays on the Making of the Constitution* (New York: Oxford University Press, 1969).

A fascinating collection of some of the best writing on the political and social forces, as well as the philosophical notions, that shaped the Constitution. The essays range from Charles Beard's famous "economic" interpretation of the Convention to Stanley M. Elkins and Eric McKitrick's provocative analysis of the relationship of the framers' youth to their continental vision.

McDonald, Forest. *We the People: The Economic Origins of the Constitution* (Chicago: University of Chicago Press, Midway Reprint Series, 1976 [1st ed., 1958]).

The most convincing attack on the Beard thesis. McDonald shows that the framers operated under a complex set of motives and that the factions in the Constitutional Convention were a good deal more fluid than Beard had believed.

Morris, Richard B. *Seven Who Shaped Our Destiny* (New York: Harper & Row, 1973).

A lively account of the most important figures in the revolutionary era and the creation of the Constitution. Biographical in nature, but filled with insights about the development of American attitudes toward liberty and authority.

Rakove, Jack N. *The Beginnings of National Politics: An Interpretive History of the Continental Congress* (New York: Alfred A. Knopf, 1979).

A clearly written and forcefully argued account of why the

Articles of Confederation eventually gave way to the Constitution. Certainly the best account of political activity leading to the calling of the Constitutional Convention.

Wood, Gordon S. *The Creation of the American Republic, 1776-1787* (New York: W. W. Norton, 1972 [1st ed., 1969]).

One of the most important books ever written about the Constitution. Wood stresses the inherent conservatism of the Federalists in writing the Constitution, and he also shows that they made a distinctive contribution to western political thought through republican ideology.

The Nineteenth Century

Beth, Loren P. *The American Constitution, 1877-1917* (New York: Harper & Row, 1971).

A volume in the New American Nation Series, this book provides the single best synthesis of constitutional developments during these years. Beth, a political scientist, does particularly well at relating institutional developments to broad changes in constitutional policy making by the Supreme Court.

Fehrenbacher, Don E. *The Dred Scott Case: Its Significance in American Law and Politics* (New York: Oxford University Press, 1978).

A brilliant examination of one of this nation's most famous constitutional law cases. This Pulitzer Prize-winning study probes the issues of slavery, the coming of the Civil War, and the meaning of judicial power in our constitutional order.

Hyman, Harold, and William Wiecek. *Equal Justice under Law: Constitutional Development 1835-1875* (New York: Harper & Row, 1982).

A scholarly study filled with insights based on the most recent historical writing. The authors analyze extensively the Thirteenth, Fourteenth, and Fifteenth Amendments, and they argue provocatively that the significance of each must be understood in relationship to the others.

Levy, Leonard W. *Legacy of Suppression: Freedom of Speech and Press in Early American History* (Cambridge, Mass.: Belknap Press of Harvard University Press, 1960).

A critical assessment of the early struggles over freedom of speech and press, particularly the attitudes that fueled the famous Alien and Sedition Acts. Levy gives low marks to the Jeffersonians as well as the Federalists on matters of civil liberties.

Newmyer, R. Kent. *The Supreme Court under Marshall and Taney* (New York: Crowell, 1968).

A readable synthesis of the work of the Marshall and Taney Courts that stresses their fundamental nationalism. It is also a good introduction to the basic workings of the Supreme Court.

Stites, Francis N. *John Marshall: Defender of the Constitution* (Boston: Little, Brown & Co., 1981).

A brief, highly readable account of the nation's greatest Supreme Court justice. It also provides an excellent sense of the interaction of law and politics in the early Republic.

The Twentieth Century

Carter, Dan T. *Scottsboro: A Tragedy of the American South* (Baton Rouge: Louisiana State University Press, 1979 [1st ed., 1969]).

A fascinating analysis of the famous Scottsboro, Ala., rape case and the problem of Southern racism during the 1930s. The book is especially important in relating the constitutional commitment to fair trial and the right to counsel in the context of super-heated social tensions.

Cortner, Richard C. *The Supreme Court and the Second Bill of Rights* (Madison, Wis.: The University of Wisconsin Press, 1981).

A systematic description of the nationalization of the Bill of Rights through decisions of the Supreme Court. Cortner explains how the Supreme Court interpreted the "due process" clause of the Fourteenth Amendment to mean that the Bill of Rights, originally a limitation only on the federal government, also protected individuals against state government action.

Kluger, Richard. *Simple Justice: The History of* Brown v. Board of Education *and Black America's Struggle for Equality* (New York: Vintage, 1977).

A fascinating account of the battle against segregated schools. Kluger starts with Reconstruction and ends with the civil rights turbulence of the 1960s. Particularly good in explaining the litigation strategy pursued by the National Association for the Advancement of Colored People's Legal Defense Fund in *Brown* and other civil rights cases.

Kutler, Stanley I. *The American Inquisition: Justice and Injustice in the Cold War* (New York: Hill and Wang, 1982).

A provocative yet balanced analysis of the interaction of anticommunism and constitutional values during the cold war. Kutler draws expertly on case studies to drive home the personal and institutional consequences of political persecution.

Lewis, Anthony. *Gideon's Trumpet* (New York: Random House, 1964).

A highly readable account of the Supreme Court's 1962 landmark decision in *Gideon v. Wainwright*. The Court extended the right to counsel to the poor, and Lewis shows forcefully how human actors in the constitutional process contributed to the development of this important right.

Murphy, Paul L. *The Constitution in Crisis Times, 1918-1969* (New York: Harper & Row, 1972).

A historical overview of constitutional developments with emphasis given to their social and cultural roots. Murphy gives heavy, but not exclusive, attention to the emergence of civil liberties and civil rights.

General

Berger, Raoul. *Government by Judiciary: The Transformation of the Fourteenth Amendment* (Cambridge, Mass.: Harvard University Press, 1977).

A trenchant attack on the Supreme Court's development of the Fourteenth Amendment. Berger throws darts at all of the twentieth-century liberal proponents of an activist judiciary. He hits the target often enough to make the book important, although flawed.

Bickel, Alexander M. *The Least Dangerous Branch: The Supreme Court at the Bar of Politics* (Indianapolis: Bobbs-Merrill Co., 1962).

A brief, forceful meditation on the relationship of the Supreme Court to the two other branches. Bickel carefully defines the limited role of judicial review in the American system while simultaneously arguing that the principled nature of American constitutionalism depends upon judicial power.

Burns, James MacGregor. *The Deadlock of Democracy: Four Party Politics in America* (Englewood Cliffs, N.J.: Prentice-Hall, 1963).

A penetrating discussion of the divisions within American political parties between their executive and legislative wings. Burns, one of the nation's foremost political scientists, brings a sharp analytical sense to the practical operation of parties in the American constitutional system.

Kelly, Alfred H., Winifred A. Harbison, and Herman Belz. *The American Constitution: Its Origins and Development,* 6th ed. (New York: W. W. Norton & Co., 1983 [1st ed., 1948]).

The 6th edition is newly revised and rewritten. It provides a sweeping and detailed examination of the development of American constitutionalism from its English origins to the present. It also contains an excellent annotated bibliography.

McCloskey, Robert G. *The American Supreme Court* (Chicago: University of Chicago Press, 1960).

A lucid account of the development of the Supreme Court and its power of judicial review. Although the book covers only the period through the 1950s, it remains perhaps the single best introduction to the history of the Court.

McLaughlin, Andrew C. *The Foundations of American Constitutionalism* (New York: New York University Press, 1932).

A brief, lively analysis of the historical origins of the principle of constitutionalism. McLaughlin emphasizes the role of New Englanders in transforming seventeenth- and eighteenth-century ideas into workable frames of government.

Schlesinger, Arthur M., Jr. *The Imperial Presidency* (Boston: Houghton Mifflin, 1973).

A shrewd analysis of the growth of presidential power written from the perspective of Richard Nixon and the Watergate disaster. Schlesinger deftly blends the development of constitutional law with political drama and international relations.

White, G. Edward. *The American Judicial Tradition: Profiles of Leading American Judges* (New York: Oxford University Press, 1976).

White skillfully puts biography into the service of constitutional and legal history through an examination of the lives of the nation's most prominent judges. Its panoramic coverage provides a sense of change within unity in the American judicial tradition.

Suggested Additional Bibliographical Sources

Earlean M. McCarrick, ed. *U.S. Constitution: A Guide to Information Sources.* Gale Research Company, 1980.

Stephen M. Millett, ed. *A Selected Bibliography of American Constitutional History.* ABC/Clio Press, 1975.

Kermit L. Hall is professor of history and law at the University of Florida. He has held grants from the National Science Foundation and the National Endowment for the Humanities, and he is the author of *The Role of Law in American History*. He is currently engaged in a study of the impact of popular election on state judicial decision making.

Illustration Acknowledgments

Part I

Fort Oswego on Lake Ontario, p. 5, engraving for *London Magazine*, 1760, American Antiquarian Society; George Washington, p. 12, Massachusetts Historical Society; John Adams, p. 16, Library of Congress; Judith Sargent Murray, p. 22, portrait by J. S. Copley, Courtesy of the Frick Art Reference Library; Black soldiers at the Battle of New Orleans, p. 25, engraving by O. Pelton for *Abbotts' Lives of the Presidents,* Library of Congress; *The Residence of David Twining* by Edward Hicks, p. 29, Abby Aldrich Rockefeller Folk Art Center, Williamsburg, Va.; James Madison, p. 33, Library of Congress; Benjamin Franklin, p. 34, engraving from the original painting by Chappel, Library of Congress; Edmund Randolph, p. 36, Library of Congress; George Washington, p. 38, *George Washington on a White Charger;* AMERICAN; National Gallery of Art, Washington; Gift of Edgar William and Bernice Chrysler Garbisch; William Jackson, p. 41, from a miniature by Charles Willson Peale, Library of Congress; Elbridge Gerry, p. 47, Library of Congress; George Washington, p. 55, portrait by Rembrandt Peale, Independence National Historical Park Collection; Edmund Randolph, p. 56, portrait by Flavius J. Fisher, Virginia State Library and Archives; John Rutledge, p. 56, portrait by John Trumbull, copyright Yale University Art Gallery; Roger Sherman, p. 57, portrait by Thomas Hicks after Ralph Earl, Independence National Historical Park Collection; James Wilson, p. 58, The Historical Society of Pennsylvania; Gouverneur Morris, p. 59, portrait by Thomas Sully, The Historical Society of Pennsylvania; George Mason, p. 60, portrait by D. W. Boudet after John Hesselius, Virginia Museum of Fine Arts; William Paterson, p. 61, portrait by unknown artist, Midlantic National Bank/North; Luther Martin, p. 62, portrait by unlisted artist, Museum and Library of Maryland History; William Samuel Johnson, p. 62, portrait by Albert Rosenthal after Gilbert Stuart, Independence National Historical Park Collection; James Madison, p. 63, portrait by Charles Willson Peale, The Thomas Gilcrease Institute of American History and Art, Tulsa, Okla.; Thomas Jefferson, p. 66, statue by Charles Grafley, Library of Congress; draft copy of the Declaration of Independence, p. 69, Library of Congress; Monticello, p. 73, Library of Congress.

Part II

John Locke, p. 80, Library of Congress; the first seal of the United States, 1782, p. 81, Library of Congress; Alexander Hamilton, p. 83, portrait by John Trumbull, Library of Congress; James Madison, p. 86, Library of Congress; John Jay, p. 88, Library of Congress; advertisement for *The Federalist* in book form, p. 91, *The Virginia Independent Chronicle,* February 13, 1788, Library of Congress; cartoon ridiculing the Anti-Federalists, 1793, p. 95, The Library Company of Philadelphia; Patrick Henry, p. 98, Library of Congress; Richard Henry Lee, p. 101, Independence National Historical Park Collection; p. 107, *Liberty*; AMERICAN; National Gallery of Art, Washington; gift of Edgar William and Bernice Chrysler Garbisch; illustration in celebration of New York's ratification on July 26, 1788, p. 110, *New York Packet*, July 29, 1788, American Antiquarian Society; emblematic eagle appearing with two odes to the Constitution, p. 113, *New York Packet,* July 25, 1788, American Antiquarian Society; Daniel Webster replying to Robert Hayne, p. 117, Library of Congress.

Part III

Fisher Ames, p. 123, portrait by Stuart, National Portrait Gallery, Smithsonian Institution, Washington, D.C.; Robert Morris, p. 124, Independence National Historical Park Collection; Rufus King, p. 125, engraving by T. Kelly from original by Stuart, Library of Congress; Frederick Muhlenberg, p. 128, Library of Congress; interior of the House chamber in Federal Hall, New York City, p. 133, Library of Congress; Oliver Ellsworth, p. 138, Library of Congress; Richard Henry Lee, p. 141, engraving by P. Maverick from a drawing by Longacre, Library of Congress; William Few, p. 143, engraving by H. B. Hall & Sons, Library of Congress; Charles Carroll, p. 146, engraving by A. B. Durand from a painting by Harding, Library of Congress; the first cabinet, p. 150, engraving from the original painting by Chappel, Library of Congress; Alexander Hamilton, p. 152, Independence National Historical Park Collection; site of the first American Foreign Office, Philadelphia, Pa., p. 155, Library of Congress; Henry Knox, p. 158, Library of Congress; Samuel Osgood, p. 160, Library of Congress.

Part IV

James Madison, p. 175, engraving by T. B. Welch from a drawing by J. B. Longacre, Library of Congress; restored chamber of the Supreme Court, p. 181, Supreme Court Historical Society; Benjamin Gitlow, p. 183, Library of Congress; Charles Evans Hughes, p. 184, Library of Congress; John Marshall Harlan, p. 187, Library of Congress; Earl Warren, p. 188, drawing by Miriam Troop, National Portrait Gallery, Smithsonian Institution, Washington, D.C.; Bill

of Rights Sesquicentennial poster by Howard Chandler Christy, p. 193, Library of Congress; Oliver Wendell Holmes and Louis D. Brandeis, p. 195, Supreme Court Historical Society; protest against the Vietnam War outside the Pentagon, 1967, p. 198, Library of Congress; cartoon, p. 200, Sidney Harris; *The First Prayer in Congress* by T. H. Matteson, p. 205, Library of Congress; Baptist Meeting House, Providence, R.I., 1789, p. 208, engraving for the *Massachusetts Magazine*, 1789, Library of Congress; cartoon by Thomas Nast, p. 211, *Harper's Weekly*, February 25, 1871, Library of Congress; Georgetown Convent School, p. 213, Library of Congress; cartoon, p. 214, Sidney Harris; John L. DeWitt, p. 219, Library of Congress; evacuees at the Santa Fe train station, April 1942, p. 221, Library of Congress; Santa Anita reception center, Los Angeles, Calif., April 1942, p. 225, Library of Congress; examination of baggage of Japanese-Americans as they arrived at Santa Anita reception center, April 1942, p. 228, Library of Congress; woman suffrage in Wyoming territory, p. 235, Library of Congress; Carrie Chapman Catt, p. 237, National Portrait Gallery, Smithsonian Institution, Washington, D.C.; laundry of Curt Muller, p. 240, Supreme Court Historical Society; Elizabeth Cady Stanton and Susan B. Anthony, p. 245, Smithsonian Institution Photo No. 74-847, Division of Political History.

Index